a difference in addressing complex societal problems . . . [by gaining] the 'outside-the-building, silo-busting' skills needed to take on 'messy, complex systems problems' ranging from income inequality to human trafficking. In this striking book . . . Kanter tells riveting stories of bold, imaginative leadership. . . . In each case, the societal issue is rife with ambiguity and conflict, with no single organization in charge, and the challenge is to find fresh, convention-defying approaches engaging many stakeholders."

—*Kirkus Reviews* (starred review)

"*Think Outside the Building* is an excellent and inspiring guide for anybody who is trying to make change in the world. Drawing on the stories of dozens of effective efforts, Rosabeth Moss Kanter has created a guidebook that, with wisdom and optimism, extracts the essential techniques for success—especially for new initiatives with a mission to improve society."

—Nicholas Lemann, Joseph Pulitzer II and Edith Pulitzer
Moore Professor of Journalism and dean emeritus,
Columbia University School of Journalism

"As our world moves from complicated to complex, those who strive to be great leaders cannot limit themselves to 'thinking inside the building.' We must instead become advanced leaders who can think outside the building—stepping outside, knocking on other doors, creating new teams who can deliver the innovative solutions the world needs, and providing promising entryways for the people of tomorrow to enter."

—General (Ret.) Stanley McChrystal, author
of *Leaders: Myth and Reality*

"I feel so strongly about this book and its message that I want everyone who aspires to make a difference to read it. It is the quintessential guide for answering the question we all eventually ask: Have I accomplished my purpose in life? As a graduate of West Point and an airborne ranger infantry officer, I learned to ask, 'If not me, who?' Here are the personal tools for getting it done, showing us how small pebbles can make big waves."

—Robert A. McDonald, eighth US secretary of veterans affairs; retired chairman, president, and CEO, Procter & Gamble

"Kanter's book lays out the next big step in innovation: the bold leadership to imagine new solutions to big problems of communities and the world. Her brilliant new book is a compelling read, full of fascinating stories and breakthrough ideas."

—Indra Nooyi, former chairman and CEO, Pepsico

"In this season of public appetite for big solutions to big problems, Kanter's *Think Outside the Building* is both a clarion call and a map for new leaders to step up."

—Deval Patrick, former governor of Massachusetts

"Buoyed by strong writing and an encouraging tone, Kanter's thorough and thought-provoking guide will be a boon for veteran leaders who want to put their well-tested skills to new—and socially constructive—use."

—*Publisher's Weekly*

"Brimming with compelling stories of action focused on measurable impact and transformation, this book by distinguished scholar and practitioner Rosabeth Moss Kanter lays out the argument for a new kind of leadership—'advanced leadership.' In this moment where vivid instances of failed leadership around the world are evident in every sector, and when the complexity of problems and the frequency of crises are growing at an accelerated pace, adopting the strategies and methods presented in this terrific book has never seemed more urgent."

—Judith Rodin, president emerita, University of Pennsylvania, and former president, Rockefeller Foundation

"Rosabeth Moss Kanter has done it again! This is the best book on leadership written in this century. It may change the world—or at the least make it better."

—Congresswoman Donna Shalala, former
US secretary of health and human services

"Kanter provides leaders with new ways to innovate in a future where technology is advancing at a speed never seen before and is poised to solve some of our most vexing problems. She expertly outlines how leaders can harness the power to achieve beyond what's expected."

—Hans Vestberg, chair and CEO, Verizon

THINK
OUTSIDE THE
BUILDING

THINK
OUTSIDE THE
BUILDING

How Advanced
Leaders Can
Change the World
One Smart Innovation
at a Time

ROSABETH
MOSS
KANTER

PUBLICAFFAIRS

NEW YORK

PublicAffairs
Hachette Book Group
1290 Avenue of the Americas, New York, NY 10104
www.publicaffairsbooks.com
@Public_Affairs

Printed in the United States of America

First Edition: January 2020

Published by PublicAffairs, an imprint of Perseus Books, LLC, a subsidiary of Hachette Book Group, Inc. The PublicAffairs name and logo is a trademark of the Hachette Book Group.

The Hachette Speakers Bureau provides a wide range of authors for speaking events. To find out more, go to www.hachettespeakersbureau.com or call (866) 376-6591.

The publisher is not responsible for websites (or their content) that are not owned by the publisher.

Print book interior design by Amnet Systems.

Library of Congress Cataloging-in-Publication Data

Names: Kanter, Rosabeth Moss, author.
Title: Think outside the building : how advanced leaders can change the
    world one smart innovation at a time / Rosabeth Moss Kanter.
Description: First edition. | New York : PublicAffairs, 2020. | Includes
    bibliographical references and index.
Identifiers: LCCN 2019037439 | ISBN 9781541742710 (hardcover) | ISBN
    9781541742727 (ebook)
Subjects: LCSH: Leadership. | Organizational change. | Social change. |
    Diffusion of innovations.
Classification: LCC HD57.7 .K3625 2020 | DDC 658.4/092—dc23
LC record available at https://lccn.loc.gov/2019037439

ISBNs: 978-1-5417-4271-0 (hardcover), 978-1-5417-4272-7 (ebook)

10   9   8   7   6   5   4

To Alison, Natalie, and Jacob,
who love to dance and draw and would rather be outside,
and to Boswell, because every pontificator needs a best friend

CONTENTS

HOW TO ATTACK
A CASTLE

D on't try to attack a "castle"—the established order, the dominant way of dealing with issues—head on. A direct attack provokes defensive actions. Fortifications get deployed. Every window shows a weapon. Iron grates drop, and drawbridges rise to make it impossible to cross the moat. Legions of protectors are mobilized. Occupants become even more defiant, not wanting to be displaced. They hunker down for a long siege, secure in the knowledge that they are superior to the peasants and barbarians outside. They think they have the resources to outlast attackers, sometimes smugly ignoring them. They fail to see that there might be a new way of life taking place beyond their walls.

The world is littered with literal and figurative castles. In Europe, they are museums to a medieval past. In America, castles take a more modern physical form as suburban corporate headquarter campuses, heavily guarded office towers, gated communities with hidden delivery entrances, or massive government buildings with intimidating security lines. These edifices are designed to protect executives and functionaries from unwelcome intrusions—or the need to change. In some places, it is possible to get from home to work and back without ever feeling the weather outdoors: moving from an elevator to the underground garage to the car to the next garage to the next elevator.

Castles are representations of institutions. Health is equated with hospitals, education with schoolhouses, news with newspapers, spirituality with the church, a city with city hall. Headquarters become the impersonal embodiment of the established structure ("the Pentagon says").

Castles are pernicious because of what they leave out. The social order seems cast in concrete even when it becomes less than optimal. Health isn't the hospital or even the doctor's office. Health might be a function of nutritious food, clean air, or stress-free work. But behemoth establishments dominate health care, including rival fiefdoms such as providers and insurance companies, full of fortification and defenses, sometimes shutting out alternatives for treatment or blocking routes to wellness. Similarly, education isn't the classroom. Beginning in the nineteenth century, education professionals wrested control from families, making education equivalent to the school building. Teachers are vitally important, but so are parents and after-school enrichment, which not all students get. And the city isn't only city hall or even the avenues of fixed buildings with fixed activities. It is also the life and culture of the people as seen in pop-up stores, food trucks, events, festivals, sidewalk chalk artists, and outdoor mural painters.

Castles are any set of institutional structures that loom large and feel permanent. Castles are monuments to the past and to past thinking, museums of preservation. They are establishments harboring the establishment, the elites of business and society.

Knowing the nature of castles helps challengers develop a plan of attack or a mode of change. The best way to attack a castle is not head on. (Unless you command a mighty army and are willing to risk mutually assured destruction.) The best way is to go around it or underneath it. Instead of rushing the front door, look below. Sneak around the back, and befriend disaffected but talented occupants on lower floors or underground who might leave to join you. Hold private meetings downstairs to strategize, invisible to the upstairs occupants. Find the secret backstairs passageways. Burrow underneath, expand the tunnels, and exploit weaknesses until eventually the foundations crumble. Then pry open the windows to let in fresh air and fresh thinking.

Or stay outside. Erect tents, and start camps on the outskirts of the castle grounds. Instead of fighting, try dancing to new music. Create small villages with new activities sufficiently enticing that some castle occupants will wander out and join the festivities, emptying the castle of defenders. The flexible campground becomes the hot new place for attracting the best talent so that moving to the top of the castle is no longer the pinnacle of a career. The castle's power weakens as it becomes less relevant. Attention goes to the new opportunities to improve the wider world.

As every change-seeking leader and entrepreneur knows, innovation rarely comes from deep inside the establishment. Incumbents tend to defend past decisions and won't give up power easily. Or sometimes they simply feel bewildered by what's happening, fearful of the uncertainties of change. Or they stay ignorant of the positive possibilities that change might bring. So they stay inside the castle and fortify the walls of its many chambers that confine occupants.

Given such strong defenses against change, fresh ideas come from those who do more than think outside the box. They think outside the building.

TAKING LEADERSHIP TO A NEW PLACE

Irritation and impatience were a constant background noise as I wrote this book. I had spent too much time at dinner table conversations accompanied by fine whines—the complaining cry, not the chardonnay. On both social media and in face-to-face conversations, I heard people whining about an almost endless number of complex, divisive, and seemingly unsolvable problems and then grumbling about an absence of bold, imaginative leadership to fix them.

Only ostriches could fail to notice that the world is full of scandals, crises, disasters, and warnings of more catastrophes to come—not to mention hurt feelings, real losses, greater stress, and a diminished sense of opportunity. I sometimes poured the whines myself. But as a generally upbeat and optimistic person, I wanted less whining and more doing. If there are big problems, I thought, then we shouldn't just sit around and complain about them. We should mobilize more people to think bigger and differently about how to engage in positive action.

That is why I wrote this book. It reflects a search for new possibilities for positive change. I want to show more people how to innovate and drive change that can reshape current institutions and stimulate the creation of new ones. It is a manual for moving leadership to a whole new level.

Turning Whines into Works:
The Basis for Advanced Leadership

Too many people get set in their ways. They prefer routine tasks and the comfort of the status quo to the risk of innovation. But passivity is depressing, and grumbling without a goal for change turns people into victims. In contrast, doing something, almost anything, is energizing. Taking actions to address big challenges, however small the steps seem at first, can whittle the seemingly impossible down to manageable size. Positive actions can generate a sense of purpose that provides meaning to life—and improves health too. Positive actions can start changing the culture by showing people new possibilities. Grab people with exciting demonstrations, and their hearts and minds will follow.

Over many years of focusing on leadership and change, I've seen outstanding examples of people with courage and imagination. These innovators and entrepreneurs are motivated to break convention and think outside their professional buildings to take on big problems with new approaches. As the late, great management theorist Peter Drucker liked to say, every problem is an opportunity for an entrepreneurial solution. I tell the stories of many of these role model leaders in this book. But the issue is that there just aren't enough of them. Time and time again, I have also observed that the skills for changing culture and social institutions are woefully underdeveloped. Even people at the top of their game in businesses and professions who thought they could take their expertise and apply it to a big problem such as climate change, racial justice, gender equity, or health disparities often fell on their faces, despite all the good intentions in the world.

To open new pathways and light the way, I'm offering this book as a source of inspiration and a guide to action. I want it to awaken a sense of purpose for an augmented kind of leadership that can make a difference in the world.

I distill the best lessons from my years of researching, consulting, teaching, and walking the talk by not just observing others but by doing it myself. My work included cofounding a bold social innovation aimed at deploying a new leadership force for the world. In late 2004, Rakesh Khurana, Nitin Nohria, and I wanted to take a shot at filling the leadership gap and identifying underutilized leadership skills. We started envisioning a new stage of higher education, one that would target experienced leaders transitioning from primary careers to their next years of service. Imagine that: we thought we could get accomplished people off golf courses and into college courses.

It was an audacious goal in other ways too. We felt that all the big problems, whether in health, education, communities, or the environment, couldn't be solved by any one profession or discipline alone. So we had to get all of Harvard involved—every single field and school—a daunting outside-the-building, silo-busting goal.

In this book, I describe the natural history of innovation and change through the eyes of dozens of other leaders, accomplished or aspiring, including challenges, effective practices, obstacles, setbacks, and celebrations. This is not just theory. We lived through every one of them ourselves.

The Harvard Advanced Leadership Initiative (ALI) was in operation by December 2008 with our first cohort of courageous pioneers (including a former astronaut who became head of NASA). This 2009 group would devote a calendar year to the program, as did others since. On my watch as chair and director for fourteen years, over ninety top faculty members, over twenty staff, and over three hundred other experts contributed to this new education for new leadership. By December 2018, ALI had proven its concept, accumulating nearly five hundred ALI fellows and partners in ten cohorts, moving from pilot project to permanent entity, and is still growing.

The critical test was what the renewed leaders did afterward. Many fellows took on big, important problems and opened new pathways for improved lives worldwide—the estimate from surveys was that perhaps one hundred million lives were touched by fellows' innovative social purpose projects in the first ten years. ALI fellows started over one hundred new entities, products, or services, some of them making a profit. Others joined existing social change organizations to help transform or grow them, and a few ran for public office.

What Is "Advanced" About Advanced Leadership?

The name *advanced leadership* started out as a bit of wordplay to entice experienced, distinguished people to join a still-embryonic movement. But the intent had never been about age; the name refers to the additional skills necessary to address messy, complex systems problems. In fact, we never used the *R* word (*retirement*), even for people who are transitioning from their primary income-earning years to their next years of service; they are merely shifting their main focus, which can happen at any time in life. In today's multicareer economy, with lower job security and more gig-economy opportunities to use spare time and a car to drive for Lyft or to rent spare space through Airbnb, people can have a portfolio of activities at any one point. Only in a shrinking number of large corporations or bureaucracies do people have long-term employment, linear careers, and a fixed date to leave completely—but even then, they might stay on as part-time consultants. And professionals—lawyers, physicians, headhunters, consultants, investors—can maintain some clients while turning their attention to projects with a social mission. They are in transition rather than gone.

But that is not the most important point. Advanced leadership refers less to a life stage than to a mode of action. It is a step beyond the kind of leadership, great or otherwise, that is exercised primarily within a single organization or field single-mindedly focused on furthering its own goals. Advanced leadership broadens the scope of leadership. It involves working beyond boundaries, across silos, and outside established structures. It stems from a sense of purpose oriented toward changing the system, whether a particular ecosystem or a broader array of institutions and expectations. It touches on skills and insights useful for entrepreneurs and innovators of any profile who are trying to solve significant problems that cut across sectors. Those are exactly the kinds of problems plaguing the world that produce barrels of whines.

A quirky analogy can help explain this difference. Advanced leadership is to leadership as Ginger Rogers is to Fred Astaire. Those famous movie dancers of another era covered a lot of territory to wide acclaim. But although Fred Astaire was a great leader, guiding the dance, Ginger Rogers was the advanced leader. As the old joke goes, she had to do everything he did but backward and in high heels. Like Astaire, great leaders can operate on well-mapped territory where they can see where they're going because goals are clear. But advanced leaders see and tackle problems that are intractable precisely because no one really knows exactly what to do or what the direction is. There is a Ginger Rogers–like aspect in feeling extra encumbrances from tottering on the high heels of controversy and always worrying about stumbling.

When a male partner from a private equity firm said that the challenges of his project on college affordability for low-income students made him "feel like Ginger Rogers," I knew that a new set of leaders was ready to start dancing with the stars.

* * *

This book tells the story of many imaginative, energetic men and women who create smart innovations by using advanced leadership skills. They include people whom I came to know in depth; some stories were captured in nearly fifty detailed case studies and hundreds of interviews. I observed and advised numerous others around the world exercising advanced leadership at all ages and in formal jobs, and some of their stories are told here too. I saw that CEOs and top executives in established organizations wanted to take their companies in new directions and needed advanced leadership to stimulate innovation, maximize impact beyond financial success, or address institutional problems that get in the way of business, such as a reliable food supply, the impact of climate change, the introduction of new technology, or an education system failing to produce enough skilled workers. My observations included civic leaders and social entrepreneurs working tirelessly to build coalitions to address societal and community problems that others had neglected or abandoned, such as removing the vestiges of racially insulting statues from a city or developing a new kind of high school. I worked with rising younger leaders who brought the entrepreneurial spirit to find new solutions to old problems, such as founding a service corps or helping Israeli and Palestinian youth create ventures together that could build both peace and broader prosperity.

What all of them have in common is the desire to move beyond established structures to chart new pathways where ambiguity, complexity, and conflict reign. They find new ideas and engage in new modes of action. They must think outside the building.

Exercising Advanced Leadership: Themes and Skills

Advanced leadership rests on persuasion, not the power of position. It involves hustle, not hierarchy. Innovators use advanced leadership skills to create smart innovations for societal impact—savvy, creative, and well-informed projects. These ventures take many forms and use many financial models. Sometimes they are also "smart" in their use of the latest digital tools and technology.

The chapters ahead tell the stories of numerous men and women with diverse backgrounds tackling projects to make a difference in the world. Seeing them in action illuminates essential ingredients of advanced leadership. Key lessons include the following:

- Why there's a need for advanced leadership. The prevalence and nature of big, intractable social, environmental, and institutional problems. How established structures impede change, but how small steps outside the building, sector, or industry can transcend negativity and find new possibilities.
- How to find a new supply of leaders motivated to tackle big problems. How the three Cs of capabilities, connections, and cash can be used in new ways.
- How to see and break out of the seven perverse traps of career success. Erecting the scaffolding that supports moving outside the building to take on new work with a new identity.
- How to read the mood and needs of the times, awaken a passion for social change, and tune in to opportunities. Understanding the role of purpose and meaning in defining an area for attention. Why it's worth it to dream big and think bigger than you are.
- How to find gaps that can be filled by creative new approaches. Using contextual intelligence, taking random walks and far afield trips, and shaking kaleidoscopes.
- How to create a new narrative and tell an inspiring story that galvanizes audiences. Why reframing the past helps to create the future. How to pitch a big, inclusive tent. The virtues of showing more than telling.
- How to identify the right allies and supporters. Applying the Change Agent Rule of Three: engaging allies, neutralizing opponents, and converting undecideds. Why advanced leadership takes more than a village—it takes a cross-sector, multistakeholder coalition.
- How to exercise influence without formal authority. How to persuade, cajole, and even beg in order to assemble the resources to move forward. Preselling, trading favors, and becoming an expert and connector.

- How to master the messy, muddled, miserable middles of change. Why innovation always takes longer and costs more. What can go wrong, and how to be prepared for overcoming obstacles. Who gives up, and who keeps going. Knowing when to pivot and persist instead of pulling out.
- How to move along the road to impact. Finding paths to scaling innovative ventures: growth in size or growth by idea diffusion. The principles for being ready for growth from the beginning. Joining forces to create wider ecosystem change.

Innovation and change can't follow a fixed script. The work is more like improvisational theater, which takes shape in response to observer feedback. The leaders who define the action can stumble, fumble, hit dead ends, and even fail; the work can be improved upon at many points. Over time, ventures that once were innovations that changed institutional pathways can stagnate and get stuck inside the building. That's the nature of institutions. But when the mission is strong and coalitions of support have been built, advanced leaders can find new ways to renew and continue the effort. Along the road to impact, projects gain power from connections across many initiatives, ventures, innovations, and campaigns, which merge to create movements and change the world. This takes leadership to a whole new place.

The Past and Future of Leadership

Advanced leadership rests on reading the zeitgeist, but I propose that it is also part of forming the mood of the times. It involves a way of working on complex, messy problems begging for innovative, outside-the-building thinking. It is an emerging worldview of direct positive action, of a creative entrepreneurial mind-set, of taking on leadership without anyone asking you to do it. This mode is critically important for addressing the problems that people care about.

The pace of change might seem impossibly fast now, generating confusion and anxieties, but it seemed that way to our recent ancestors too. For a century or more, observers have said that change is speeding up. As a result, in the decades after World War II, planned change became a discipline intended to manage transitions and upheavals. In 1969, leadership guru Warren Bennis wrote that change was the biggest story in the world he saw then.[1] Fifty years ago, he delineated just about all the issues the world still faced in 2019. His list is like old whines in new bottles: the environment, racial and gender disparities, impoverished communities, fears of technology, and dysfunctional politics. Leadership emerged as a key factor in whether change could be tamed.

An interesting thing happened along the way from then to now: the study of leadership tracked the times. It started as "great man" (yes, overwhelmingly male) histories of monarchs, generals, tyrants, presidents, and prime ministers. Governing or its overthrow were at the forefront for audiences relishing tales of wars, battlefields, and huge historical events. Another wave was added as leadership became something that chiefs of any kind were supposed to exercise, and business CEOs became the heroes, some of whom wrote their own books about how they transformed this or that company. Riding that wave, leadership was soon said to be a career asset for anyone, with a burgeoning advice genre for aspiring corporate ladder climbers or start-up founders. Leadership theory moved from the art of war to the art of business-building.

What's next? I think it is the positive and democratizing force of advanced leadership, which looks beyond single organizations and heroic commanders to wider systems. This approach is sorely needed in my home country. Many analysts have decried the loss of social capital in America since the 1950s, as Robert Putnam did in his famous book *Bowling Alone*. Technology appears to have increased that social isolation, enabling people to retreat to their screens rather than talk with the people around them, as Sherry Turkle showed in her book *Alone Together*.[2]

But the situation is perhaps not so grim. I think that a swelling force of advanced leaders could create new versions of engagement and new clubs of people united in a quest for a better world. Although people might bowl alone rather than in leagues, they start projects and raise money together, and not just in fancy homes and hotel ballrooms. I'm struck by a story I was told about how cattle ranchers in rural Montana, who lived far apart, drove long distances to host or attend spaghetti dinners to raise funds to help any member of their community who was in trouble. Whatever their political views or ethnic differences, the ranchers took responsibility for improving their corner of the world.

In the nineteenth century, French aristocrat Alexis de Tocqueville wrote about a self-organizing America. That's the same spirit that *New York Times* columnist Thomas Friedman said makes politics still work, even in troubled times. It's what award-winning social entrepreneur Alan Khazei called "big citizenship." It's the activism that Report for America journalists are finding in small communities that don't usually make the national news.[3]

For every trend we whine about, there's often a countertrend that can provide the basis for new kinds of action. As many Americans appear to retreat into homogeneous enclaves full of xenophobia and tribal "my group first" sentiments, some so-called left-behind communities illustrate the opposite of the hostility and divisiveness they are assumed to foster. The fading, mostly white town of Lewiston, Maine, for example, found its economy revived and community renewed by an influx of black Somali immigrants. That was not without problems, to be sure, but it is an example that says that racial tensions and fear of strangers are not inevitable. Rewriting the past to emphasize those American values, which encourage leadership from anywhere, would be a good basis for creating the future.

Major established organizations are showing their ages—not to mention their roles in numerous scandals and abuses that were covered up in once-revered buildings, including universities and churches. Institutions cry out for rejuvenation through innovation. New starts can come from the actions of advanced leaders who take responsibility for finding a better path. As more castles crumble, establishments will have to share power, and buildings will have to open to the streets. In some cases, this is literal; the streets are sites for protests and rallies. Those modes can sometimes help start movements for change but can also fizzle (consider Occupy Wall Street or Arab Spring), and they can turn into angry crowds that emphasize destruction rather than showing new models. The way to avoid letting chaotic mobs seize control is to pitch inclusive tents and build purpose-fueled villages outside the castles of our era.

When more people flex their leadership muscles and find the courage to take on big problems, they exude the optimism of activism. That positive energy can be contagious and can unite us in new ways. By undertaking the daunting yet meaningful task of making a difference in the world, advanced leaders can transform the lives of many people—including their own.

Mobilizing for positive institutional change should be the responsibility of aspiring and accomplished leaders everywhere. If we think of ourselves as spectators or consumers, imbibing fine whines without doing anything about the problems, then we abdicate leadership to possible demagogues. But if legions of people get involved, I'm hopeful that outside-in or bottom-up renewal can overwhelm top-down toxicity. When the national gets ugly, the local can be beautiful.

This book offers a wake-up call, numerous inspiring stories, and a field guide for the journey toward leadership with significant positive impact. It's high time that the journey begins.

PART I
Demand and Supply

UP FROM THE DEPTHS

*Big Problems and the Need for
Advanced Leadership*

For anyone who wishes that the world could be a better place, there is no shortage of pressing problems to consider. A starter list might include chronic homelessness, health disparities, education access and quality, natural disasters attributed to climate change, threats and displacement from new technology, gun violence, opioid abuse, sexual harassment, racial discrimination, and refugee crises. Not everyone agrees on the nature of causes and solutions. Yet the problems seem to hit closer to home all the time. Diseases once contained in obscure, distant nations now fly to other countries on an airplane. Droughts give rise to ruinous rural wildfires, and coastal cities experience destructive flooding. Refugees cross borders into settled middle-class neighborhoods. Drug overdoses and teen suicides can hit any family.

Many of these are intertwined and show up on a next-generation priority list. The world's top three urgent problems, according to a survey of 31,500 rising leaders from 186 countries, are climate change; large-scale conflict and wars; and inequality, including income inequality and discrimination.[1] It's one thing to name the problems; it's quite another to do something about them. Big issues like these are hard to put in one container. They flow across communities and nations; they spill over the walls dividing organizations, industries, sectors, and professional disciplines.

Behind every big problem are hardened institutional pathways reinforced by taken-for-granted norms and an array of established organizations and groups that think they have the answers (but often don't). The public has low trust in elites, experts, and establishments because some problems have worsened on their watch. Societal problems are messy and complex; addressing them takes multiple efforts on multiple fronts, not just one. We are constantly urged to think outside the box, but that is no longer enough. We need a bigger and bolder frame of reference that can create more and better leaders along with a new theory of leadership to guide them.

Some intractable institutional problems are so enormous that it might not seem possible to do anything about them. That's where a broader array of leaders, armed with advanced leadership skills, come into play. When problems can't be solved using conventional approaches, motivated leaders can use innovative thinking to find new routes to change. Consider one problem almost as big as the planet itself: the health of the oceans.

Boiling the Ocean

A piece of folk wisdom—"you can't boil the ocean"—is often used as a warning about taking on an impossibly gigantic task. Are we right to be cautious, or is it just an excuse for accepting the status quo? If someone did want to boil the ocean—or stop it from boiling under climate change—she would first need to know why it is an important problem, understand the institutions that constrain change, and then find a way to dive in.

Torsten Thiele, for example, was determined to find new approaches to keep the ocean from boiling. He grew up on the coast of the North Sea and in his youth helped create a sanctuary for dolphins, the first one for the type of dolphin that lived in those waters. Years later, Thiele reached a stage in life when he could have relaxed on the beach. Instead, he plunged into the ocean.

A multilingual German working in London, Thiele had been a top financial executive with the European Bank for Reconstruction and Development and later with Investec Bank. Thiele had seen big challenges before. At Investec, he had worked in telecom finance including projects to bring the internet to Africa and undersea cables across the Pacific Ocean. That's when he was struck by the simple economics of deep-sea sensors on subsea cables: the ability to get advanced warning of a tsunami appeared to be worth so much more than the cost of installing these sensors. He wondered why there was so little investment of this sort. "What a difference this could have made at Fukushima!" he exclaimed later about the earthquake that caused devastating damage to a nuclear reactor in Japan.

Out on the water, he saw other Pacific Ocean problems firsthand. "In Indonesia I sailed along the Wallace line to commemorate the centenary of this great naturalist," he recalled, referring to the British explorer Alfred Russel Wallace, who marked the change of ecosystems between Asia and Australia. "I was shocked to see the conditions of the sea in which local children were swimming and playing, full of plastic and other debris." He flashed back to the playful dolphins of his childhood. His close-up focus on the Pacific began to raise his concerns about the health of the oceans in general. He zoomed out to see the big picture.

An avid environmentalist, Thiele began learning everything he could about the problems, the existing groups, and the approaches.

Ocean Health as Human Health

Oceans are fundamental to life, producing more than half of the oxygen in the atmosphere, encompassing 97 percent of all the water on

Earth, and playing a fundamental role in weather patterns.[2] This is just one reason that people in Columbus and Chattanooga should care about oceans as much as people in coastal Portland, Maine, or Portland, Oregon. As if that weren't enough, oceans provide a major source of food, either directly through fishing or indirectly through shipping. Oceans are vital platforms for getting food and other goods from one place to another, via about $4 trillion worth of shipping annually.[3]

Damage to oceans creates surges of harm. In vitally important ways, ocean health is human health. But the condition of the oceans is deteriorating. Over 90 percent of global fish stocks are overexploited or fully exploited.[4] And coral reefs—home to over a million species that provide food and resources for hundreds of millions of people—are projected to disappear by 2050 if current trends continue.[5] That's why Rachel Silverstein's first action as the Miami Waterkeeper, leading a small nonprofit affiliate of a global alliance, was to sue the US Army Corps of Engineers for further damage to the reefs while it was dredging the Miami harbor.

Who's in Charge?

Who should care about the fate of the oceans? Nearly everyone: businesses, governments, ocean farmers, consumers, coastal homeowners, scientists, activists. Who has responsibility for solutions? No one.

An ocean has no sovereignty. The high seas, which cover half of the planet's surface, are beyond national jurisdictions and fall into the cracks between existing international institutions. There is no authoritative body with rules, monitoring, and enforcement of ocean-related activities or impact, leaving all parties—whether shippers, fishers, or trash dumpers—free to pursue their own interests without regard to the welfare of the whole. This is a classic tragedy of the commons in which users take what they want while depleting resources for the future.

Torsten Thiele wanted to break through structural impasses and fundamentally rethink what is to be done about the oceans. He gradually came to see gaps in the conventional solutions. He saw that even environmental coalitions tended to operate in disciplinary silos. He felt that one of the keys to protecting the oceans, and combatting climate change in general, was seeing the many elements as an interconnected mosaic. Thiele's vision was to connect the politics of ocean governance with the science, technology, and economics that could bring new resources and actions.

After leaving his bank position and attending every relevant international meeting he could, Thiele began to envision a structure for ocean governance that could be supported in a new way: through technology and finance, linking public and private sectors, civil societies, and politics to push a healthy oceans agenda. He wanted to add connectivity where little existed and to create a clear message where there was only a set of vague platitudes. He wanted to pin the goal to specific, achievable projects and add economic actors to the usual, somewhat ineffective nongovernmental organizations (NGOs) and global organizations. After a year of putting his thoughts together and joining with leaders of a multinational Arctic Oceans initiative, he formed a new, overarching umbrella organization in January 2015, called the Global Ocean Trust. It was a vehicle to link disparate efforts and groups and demonstrate achievable results.

Thiele started "boiling the ocean"—undertaking what to many would seem like the near-impossible task of doing something about the fate of the oceans. He traveled extensively to speak on panels and build relationships. He created a brand and online presence for the Global Ocean Trust, and on its behalf, he joined two major existing coalitions: the Ocean and Climate Platform and the High Seas Alliance. His travels and work with conservation initiatives took him around the world—from the Galapagos in Ecuador to Halong Bay in Vietnam, and from Myanmar to the Maldives. Along the way, his idea for innovative financing for ocean renewal came into clearer focus.

"Blue Bonds" to Save the Oceans

A few months later, Thiele helped orchestrate the publishing of an open letter in the *Times of London*. It appeared on June 8, 2015, World Oceans Day, and was signed by nineteen representatives of marine organizations. The letter highlighted the potential of expanded marine protected areas as a way to build up ecosystem resilience; it also urged governments, businesses, and communities to collaborate in an attempt to build the financing structures required to do so. The letter stated that we "need to look beyond existing structures and think of an ocean sustainability bank. There are development banks around the world, but no bank for 70 percent of the planet's surface."

Thiele's affiliation with the Ocean and Climate Platform helped him present the concepts at UNESCO's World Ocean Day conference in Paris, and by mid-July 2015, he had completed the first draft for a proposed Global Ocean Bank for Sustainability and Development (OBSD). Cooperating with the Green Climate Fund, a large-scale financing source operating through a multiparty coalition of backers and others, the OBSD could offer its own "blue bonds" alongside other debt, equity, or grant financing.

In essence, the concept was a kind of World Bank for oceans that could tap private as well as public funds for innovations, especially using new technologies. OBSD would build ventures that could produce economic returns as well as long-term ecological benefits. One was potentially conserving marine protected areas (MPAs) with important ecosystem and biodiversity implications estimated in a recent study to exceed a trillion US dollars of economic value. One venture example: a sensor-based infrastructure for ocean data aggregation (combined with next-generation satellites) could help inform global conservation through better analysis and understanding of the oceans as an integrated system and could potentially deliver real-time information on climate processes and monitor overfishing and pollution. This would have significant predictive capabilities for big industries such as insurance and agriculture, industries that would pay for the service.

Thiele's Global Ocean Trust was a way to enter the conversation and shape it, to get the attention of existing entities and focus them on moving toward clearer goals with new methods for problem-solving. It was a start at adding economics, finance, and the private sector to the mix. Thiele was not alone in seeking to push beyond establishment thinking to save the oceans. A growing number of other business leaders awakened to the need and what a new sector might add. Luminaries included Salesforce founder Marc Benioff and private equity investor David Shaw, a founder of Maine ocean conservation group the Sargasso Sea Alliance, think tank trustee, and former spouse of actress Glenn Close, who brought celebrity power to the cause.

The more leaders who tackle big problems, the better. The predicaments are too big for any one entity to handle alone, however well endowed and well intentioned. But as Torsten Thiele's case illustrates, it is possible for one determined leader to make something as big as the oceans the focus of change efforts, when he is willing to think outside of conventional channels. We'll meet Torsten Thiele again in chapter 5 and see how he uses advanced leadership skills to move from thought to action. But for now, this story shows what makes some problems so hard to address.

The Nature of Big Institutional Challenges: Why Change Is Difficult

The human temptation is to reify—to take a broad idea and associate it with one concrete form, like a building that looms over everything. That structure comes to stand for an entire set of people and activities. Occupants—incumbents—act as though they alone own the issue and set up barriers to other approaches. That's how problems get stuck in silos and thinking gets stuck inside already-established structures.

Institutions are bigger than the buildings that represent them. As I've said, health is not the hospital. Education is not the classroom. News is not the newspaper. A city is not city hall. Religion is not the church, synagogue, or mosque. A state is not the state house. If we want to ensure good health, education, information, community, religion, or government, then we must think beyond those established structures. That's why a world of institutional problems and disruptive change needs more and better leaders who can find and fill gaps, moving beyond conventional wisdom. How to do this constitutes the new perspective on leadership I offer in this book.

It is, of course, possible to fix a building from the inside. Operations of single organizations can be upgraded without looking at the broader institutional context. If a hospital, for example, has problems with the way people are admitted to the emergency room, executives with authority can simply order change. But there are differences between running a good hospital and pursuing better health outcomes that prevent getting sick in the first place, between improving a school and changing how much children learn, or between adding a digital offering to an existing media company and rethinking the entire way content is created and distributed.

Such issues differ greatly in their particulars, and yet they share five characteristics with big challenges like boiling the ocean. These features are exactly why such systemic issues are so daunting, so overwhelming to contemplate, and require the extra boost of advanced leadership.

1. *Big scope and significance, with many layers*: Whatever the issue is, it is of great importance to many parties. For some, it provides direct livelihoods and benefits (e.g., fishing fleets or cargo ships); for many more, it affects their ability to carry out their own activities. But as long as the ocean appears healthy on the surface, for example, it's hard to get attention to the underlying systems dysfunctions;

institutions are often taken for granted as long as everything is working. Similarly, education did not become a major American issue as long as public schools appeared to serve children (at least privileged white children); then disturbing trends were reported in the landmark 1983 report commissioned by President Ronald Reagan, and attention turned to urban school reform. Of course, public education was a source of contention in the 1950s because of school segregation, and schools remain segregated sixty years after a landmark US Supreme Court decision requiring desegregation. So here's the challenge. Parsing the problem enlarged its scope. As continuing inequities surfaced, a range of other contextual factors were identified—family situations, hunger and malnutrition, health challenges for the less advantaged, transportation problems, and more—which required much broader action well beyond the classroom. The more one tries to peel the onion, the more layers of connected problems are revealed.

Thus, sometimes the significance of a major systems problem is unrecognized until problems mount—traffic, for example, can seem like merely a daily annoyance of a rush hour commute for people without awareness of the larger system context surrounding transportation availability and policy choices. Attempts to put the issue into an existing container or to isolate it in a silo are doomed to fail. For example, the implications of e-commerce and social media for traditional brick-and-mortar retailers were brushed off and put into a separate department that didn't affect the mainstream company until e-sales climbed high enough to threaten the core business. Lesson learned by retail survivors: the change problem is much bigger than they thought.

Left unaddressed, without effective intervention, the problem can get worse, and that increases its significance. Negative consequences can't be suppressed and appear to be on a path toward proliferating. Previous attempts to address the problem fell short, or they became less effective over time. Signs of decline are increasingly apparent, piling up like the plastic debris forming islands of trash in the Pacific Ocean.

2. *Ambiguity—vague or unspecific goals and pathways.* The problem is defined at a high level of abstraction. That can be a good thing, because it means the wider context is included, but it obscures the path to problem-solving, and it makes consensus difficult. What exactly does it mean to tackle climate change or racial justice? Torsten Thiele and other ocean saviors have lofty goals. Unlike the problems of daily life, big problems are hard to pin down. Saving dolphins is easier to comprehend than saving oceans. But even this simpler goal has a great deal of uncertainty associated with it, and there is no clear path to action.

   Intractable institutional problems are inherently ambiguous as well as complex. There is no single clear goal to be pursued, let alone a consensus about its meaning. Statements of the problem can't easily be translated into action implications. Stating the problem is not enough, as the issue connotes many different things, pointing in different directions for solutions. This means that the route to change is not well mapped. Where to launch and how to navigate is as unclear as the ocean exploration must have seemed to the first hardy voyagers.

3. *Limited mandates and lack of authority.* No one is clearly in charge of the big problems plaguing the world. Who has the sole charter to cure cancer, end racism, close the gender pay gap, or clean up the oceans? The big scope means that no single entity or person, however powerful—monarch, president, prime minister, CEO, or designated executive—can wave his or her executive order, and bingo, it's fixed—assuming that elites would want to fix the matter anyway. For intractable systems problems, no one entity has a monopoly on

legitimate control or governance rights over all aspects of the problem. That's certainly true of environmental challenges such as the
oceans, over which no nation has sovereignty. This is also true of
practically every other major societal predicament, which can face
multiple jurisdictions and multiple claimants to "owning" the problem. As contagious, infectious diseases cross borders, a complex of
NGOs and UN agencies try to deal with them, but there is a tangle
of organizations that have to work it out rather than a single responsible party or a clear chain of command.

Sometimes this is the result of a longstanding system design—
such as the American federal system, with "shared" responsibility for such major public concerns as education and health care,
lending confusion to who can do what when. Multiple potential
sources of authority mean that current approaches and structures
can't handle the problem alone, and the problem seems even more
intractable. The continuing existence of the problem undermines
the authority of existing entities because it exposes their inability to
create effective change and thus threatens their power. Other concerned parties who attempt to act might lack legitimate authority
or even a formal organizational position. There are no unequivocal
mandates to take care of the issue.

4. *Multiple conflicting stakeholders.* Stakeholders can be like different
   species swimming the ocean as predators and prey. The complexity of big systems problems means that there are many dimensions
   to the problem and many groups involved. Each group might view
   it differently (who is aggrieved? who deserves help?). Stakeholders
   might bring a different disciplinary lens to it (law? medicine? education? finance?). Some might want to see the problem addressed their
   way to bring benefits to their specific group—or perhaps they don't
   want to see it solved at all, because they benefit from the status quo.
   Each group has its own priorities and would benefit differentially

from particular solutions. Degrees of concern vary; some care more than others, and those who care a lot are likely to get very active or very agitated and make a disproportionate amount of noise. Moreover, as stakeholders work to advance their own interests, they might advocate without regard to the welfare of the whole, sometimes intentionally and sometimes because they can't see the whole.

In addition, because no one discipline or approach can solve the problem alone, stakeholders might compete for action rights. Claims by one set of professionals (e.g., physicians over patient health care) are contested by other groups (e.g., insurance companies making health decisions for the same patients). It can be hard to find a common cause, let alone unite people behind it. Intractable institutional problems remain that way because there is no agreement about what should be done. Finger-pointing and squabbling among stakeholders deflect time and energy away from problem-solving action. Stakeholder conflict is more debilitating when there is a status gap among groups that means that elite voices, for example, might receive more attention than those of people at the grass roots. And incumbents—those who have power today—can dominate the narrative at the expense of others.

5. *A mismatch between resources and needs.* Sometimes it seems like it shouldn't be so difficult. In some cases, assets or resources exist to solve the problem, but because of structural barriers and institutional shortfalls, they are misapplied, unapplied, or unable to reach the target. For example, food or medicine sent to disaster areas can decay at ports of entry because there are no ways to identify supplies or move them to places where people are hungry or ill. Here's a sobering statistic. The UN World Food Programme estimated that 1.3 billion tons or 30 percent of all food in the world is wasted, yet 821 million people worldwide and 40 million people in the United States, including 12 million children, are regularly hungry.[6] Wasted

but safe and edible foods might be there in affluent suburbs but nowhere near the people who need it. Imagine if there were a distribution system and retail outlets to bring nutrition to food deserts.

There are other problems with resource mismatches. The United States has numerous open jobs requiring new skills and a shortage of trained workers to fill them because of a range of educational shortfalls, requirements of unnecessary credentials, or bias and discrimination. Or resources exist that could be usable if applied in different ways. Waste and underutilized assets present opportunities. Unutilized private cars could be deployed for ride-sharing, alleviating community space problems; or trash could be turned into art, such as graffiti on city streets; or damaged tires could become part of the material for roadbeds. These innovations point the way.

It's almost a truism that the people who are harmed the most from big institutional problems don't have the resources they need to end their suffering or get to the underlying causes. Climate change, which deniers see as a cause embraced by well-off liberals, actually hurts the poor more than the affluent. Poor people in low-lying urban areas are often the flood victims—like those hurt by Hurricane Katrina in New Orleans, who lacked transportation to get themselves out or health care facilities close enough to serve them.

Mismatches and disconnects mean that the system functions for advantaged groups but not for others. The possible silver lining is that it's often not resources that are in short supply; what's missing are human imagination and leadership to find new pathways that make better matches.

* * *

This high-level view from fifty thousand feet reveals just what makes big, intractable societal problems so tough to tackle. Things stay as they are because institutions breed many forces of resistance to change. Structural inertia holds things in place as they are. The same leadership that built them can't easily change them. That's one reason we can't count on established institutions to fix them—at least not unless they, too, think outside the building.

Crossing Sector Divides

Expectations for who should act evolve over time. In 1969, governmental resources put men on the moon; fifty years later, outer space has become the commercial cause of tech billionaires such as Elon Musk. At one point, and in many places, the government was expected to take care of major social problems, while nongovernmental organizations helped dispense comfort and charity. Then attention turned to the business community for its deep pockets and supposed efficiency. I recall an earlier era when US companies were preoccupied with a focus on their own competitiveness, with allegiance only to shareholders and profits; any attention to the institutional environment surrounding the firm was a matter of dealing with regulations and finding the right resource inputs. Everything else was called externalities—side effects that were to be handled by other parties, regardless of the costs of schooling or pollution. But pressure from the public urged businesses to take responsibility for the effect of their outputs (product safety or workplace health) as well as inputs (where supplies came from); to embrace multiple stakeholders, not just investors; and even to get involved in making the wider world a better place. This is obviously much harder than tweaking manufacturing operations or streamlining accounting practices.

Big systems problems spill across sectors, and they land in different places depending on the setting. In some countries, early childhood health and education belongs to government; in other places, it is left to parental discretion. There are no rules defining who can solve problems and the sector from which they emanate. For-profit, not-for-profit, or public sector actors and solutions can be involved.

But this can also be a contentious issue, as ideologies serve to maintain activities within only some sectors. The idea of "business solutions to global poverty" as an alternative to charitable giveaways is a challenge to conventional thinking, yet microlending and finding "the fortune at the bottom of the pyramid" potentially open new possibilities for the poor.[7] A "World Bank for Oceans" including private investment funds and profit motives can potentially join government and nonprofit efforts to accelerate solution-producing innovations.

At the same time, problems formerly "owned" by NGOs and governments can benefit from private sector thinking and involvement. For-profit entities can take actions that nonprofits might be expected to lead, and they can form cross-sector partnerships. For example, a major profit-making corporation, Procter & Gamble (P&G), established a not-for-profit organization to distribute water purification tablets for safe drinking water in partnership with UN agencies, NGOs, and the US government Centers for Disease Control. P&G won a social innovation contest sponsored by American Express for this work. I was one of the judges, and I confess to being uneasy at first with a big consumer-products company winning an award in the social realm, but then I rethought my sector biases and realized that the important thing was the imagination and the impact, not the source of the idea. It certainly required outside-the-building thinking to envision and enact the coalition that brought the possibility of clean water to places without it.

Corporate giving, however, too rarely brings about real change. Too often, it takes the form of spare change, providing leftovers to charities trying to ameliorate suffering without doing much about the underlying system that produced the problem. But if big business has its skeptics, so does big charity and big philanthropy. Charles Mac-Cormack, who spent eighteen years as CEO of the global giant Save the Children, merged forty-five thousand people from one hundred countries into a more unified federation. But he saw the many ways that internal turf battles, the desire for sovereignty over budgets, and change-averse donors made it hard to break out of traditional modes to better address childhood poverty. He felt he didn't have tomorrow's skills on the staff and had to wait for an entire generation to leave the organization before anything meaningful could be done.

A senior official of another NGO giant expressed similar frustration at the difficulty of adding digital modes with a staff brought up in an analog world. These officials felt that what was, in essence, building maintenance—constant repairs, the search for funds for ongoing operations—prevented fresh thinking about mission. Other critics complain of the power of entrenched interests even in the realm of doing good.[8]

Money, technocratic expertise, and high-level backing might not be enough to solve big problems. The well-endowed, well-respected Gates Foundation has been on both sides of the problem of adequate leadership, stumbling in one initiative while serving as rescuer in another effort.

In 2009, the foundation invested nearly a billion dollars in the Intensive Partnerships for Effective Teaching Initiative to improve student achievement among low-income and minority students across seven sites in five US cities: San Francisco, Los Angeles, Memphis, Tampa, and Pittsburgh. Alas, a six-year evaluation by the RAND Corporation concluded that the initiative failed to meet its goals for student achievement or graduation rates.[9] The lack of success was attributed to incomplete implementation due to a lack of capacity and insufficient attention to changing local and state contexts. The large sums of money involved were sure to focus educators only on some solutions, which might not be the best ones. Of course, education is one of those institutional problems with contested terrain and sometimes conflicting stakeholders.

Almost simultaneously, the Gates Foundation was on the other side, as the rescuer of a health initiative that was floundering and perhaps even making matters worse. The Roll Back Malaria Partnership, initiated in 1998, was a blue-ribbon coalition of the World Health Organization, the World Bank, and several UN agencies, with an explicit goal of cutting the number of malaria cases in half in ten years. To augment global support, fifty-three African heads of state endorsed the goal in the year 2000.[10] Yet, five years into the effort and several failed executive directors later, malaria deaths had actually increased.[11] The high-level coalition was said to have stalled decision making and limited accountability. The Gates Foundation stepped in, took on the effort, installed more skillful administrators, and redirected it effectively to more promising paths.

Don't get me wrong. There's a lot to do, and big institutions—companies, governments, foundations, and charities—are essential players mostly to be applauded, but they are not enough. Too often their good motives are trapped within castles and fortresses that can prevent innovation. Big societal challenges are complex and daunting, especially at first glance. System problems are not fixed by cosmetics or bandages, or even by a new flow of money. They can't be isolated in silos, confined to a single sector, or contained within buildings. Although single groups or organizations can contribute—the domain of traditional leaders—significant change requires understanding the connections among organizations and filling the gaps between them. The best of established organizations understand this, but they need to find enough leaders to help them. That's the job of advanced leaders who define new norms and pathways for action.

Before Problems Get Worse: The Urgent Need for New Approaches

A growing set of problems and the inability to rely solely on mainstream established organizations to handle them with yesterday's ideas translates into greater demand for a supply of leaders with the skills to tackle them.

Some big institutional challenges are getting decidedly worse, such as the increasing damage to the oceans. Regardless of one's view of the causes of climate change, scientists have shown that average global temperatures are rising. There were five times as many climate-related natural disasters in 2014 as in the 1970s—floods, temperature extremes, and wildfires.[12] Warmer temperatures have increased the destructive force of hurricanes, which has devastated communities and caused 5.5 times the economic damage in the 2010s than in the entire decade of the '70s.[13]

"Worse" might stem from better data and more accurate reporting. The growing awareness of problems might propel many professions to act. Human trafficking is that kind of problem. In 2017, an International Labor Organization report estimated that 40.3 million people have been trafficked, almost double the 21 million people in 2014, often crossing borders.[14] Comparable US data from the well-regarded National Human Trafficking Hotline showed 8.524 cases reported in 2017, up from 3.272 in 2012.[15] Transactions are facilitated online, and they heavily involve young girls. Awareness has grown more slowly than the problem, and it is not clear who should act at what point in the activity.

A decade ago, the county prosecutor in Miami, state attorney Katherine Fernandez Rundle, barely knew that the trafficking problem existed. Then she discovered its prevalence and began dedicating her office to prosecuting traffickers and trying to improve conditions for the victims. She found that this was a complicated systems problem with no easy answers. A few years later, when she added the growing opioid addiction crisis to her "to fix" list, she found that, like trafficking, it wasn't so simple. Effective action involved an array of complex stakeholders and institutional change challenges well beyond the legal profession: framing addiction as an illness, not a crime; setting up special drug courts; finding and prosecuting sellers, not users; working with clinics and community groups to prevent sellers from stalking clinics; tackling homelessness; and more.

Other problems show better progress, but not enough. On the positive side, in 2018, a University of Oxford–based data repository reported that virtually all major dimensions of human well-being—poverty, health, freedom, and education—have shown major improvements over the past centuries. Compared to 85 percent of the world's population estimated to live in extreme poverty in 1800, the number dropped to two billion (under one-quarter) in the 1970s and was down to eight hundred million by 2018.[16] Since 1900, the average global life expectancy has more than doubled and was seventy-two years by the year 2016.[17]

But progress in general can mask huge inequities—for example, what's good for dominant groups isn't always good for minorities. Problems lurk underneath general trends, and trends can reverse. Polio and smallpox were eliminated, only to start recurring; measles is also back. Majority-black communities suffer from higher rates of many diseases, such as asthma and hypertension. Left-behind white populations, too, can suffer disproportionately. In Stillwell, Oklahoma, the average life expectancy is 56.2 years, putting this pocket of the United States on par with Somalia and Cameroon, African countries with some of the highest poverty rates in the world.[18]

I was startled to learn of glaring disparities in life expectancy within a few miles of my office and home. A 2012 report on Boston proclaimed that "the tract with the longest life expectancy (91.9 years) is in the Charles River Basin (between Massachusetts Avenue and Arlington Street, north of Commonwealth Avenue). The tract with the shortest life expectancy (58.9 years) is in the Roxbury neighborhood (between Massachusetts Avenue and Dudley Street and Shawmut Avenue and Albany Street)."[19] The first is predominantly white; the second is predominantly black—and these statistics are despite proximity to world-class medical facilities for both populations. Indeed, although America spends the largest amount per capita in the world on health care, thirty-nine countries have longer life expectancies than the United States.[20]

Or consider violence. Psychologist Steven Pinker assembled impressive evidence that the rate of violence has declined in the modern world. Homicide has declined in most nations in the previous fifteen years, a 2015 UN report showed, and gun violence has declined in the United States since the 1990s—down from 15.2 deaths by firearms per 100,000 people to 10.3 per 100,000.[21] But try telling that to the families of victims of mass shootings in Pittsburgh; Parkland, Florida; Las Vegas; Orlando; or Newtown, Connecticut, to name just a few. Most of us don't live inside "trends" or "statistical averages." Most people live with the consequences they see. As people become aware of the danger of such incidents, they fear these could happen to them. The sensational nature of the occasional can arouse deep concern and trauma—which is why some people still fear flying, even though the safety record has been strong (at least until the Boeing 737 Max 8 problem) and the odds of a crash exceedingly low.

Expectations rise faster than problems can be solved. Progress whets appetites for more progress. Awareness of even positive trends reveals gaps and illuminates the distance still to go to solutions. Is it wonderful that 60 percent of girls in low-income countries now finish primary school, or is it appalling that 40 percent do not get even that far?[22] The classic revolution of rising expectations leads to demands for more change, faster, in more places. This is often absolute rather than relative. It doesn't help to tell a suffering person that someone else is worse off.

In a 24/7 social media age, all problems have greater visibility than they did in broadcast TV days, and enormously more than in the print media, radio, and carrier pigeon eras. Big institutional problems once occurred in distant, remote, barely imagined places; now they are in people's faces every day. Greater interdependence and spillovers from one issue to the next add to the complexity and the urgency of the new leadership imperative. Meanwhile, there is a loss of confidence in established institutions, especially big ones.[23] In the United States, only the military enjoys high confidence.[24]

For people who are directly affected by these problems, or those who simply care, the demand for new leadership approaches should rise exponentially.

From the Depths of Despair to the Optimism of Activism

The litany of woes is enough to make some people want to go back into the building, lock the doors, shut the windows, find a mattress, and put their heads under the covers. When overwhelmed with gloom, it's tempting to tighten fortifications to prevent access and to lose hope, clinging to one's own incumbency in whatever position in whatever profession.

It is too easy to be negative and thus have an excuse for doing nothing. Negativity is a familiar part of the human condition; sometimes we seem to crave it. "The end of the world makes a better story," veteran journalists like to say. *No* is always an easier answer than *yes*. A negativity instinct might stem from human psychology, traced to an evolutionary tendency for those more alert to danger to be likelier to survive.[25] Research shows that negative information is retained better than positive information; it takes five positives to cancel out a negative.[26] Thus, the greater reporting of bad news than good news leads people to think that the world is getting worse, even in areas in which it's getting better. It is also intellectually fashionable to be critical and pessimistic. Critics who negatively evaluate a book might be viewed as more competent than those who give it a positive review, according to research by Teresa Amabile.[27]

It is harder to be positive, but "positivity" stems from action. (*Positivity* is an actual word, which the Oxford English Dictionary claims preceded *negativity* in the English language by 145 years.) I've long found that turning passive and believing that nothing will ever change is a self-fulfilling prophecy characteristic of losing streaks; winning streaks involve constantly acting and learning from it. Activity is energizing; passivity is depressing. Those headed for success just go ahead and do; they believe there is time to adjust later. One secret of success at innovation is simply to try more things. More tries produce more failures, but they also can produce more successes. Challenging conventional wisdom by breaking out of the building produces a sense of purpose that is itself a source of energy.

So let a thousand flowers bloom, especially if you have a butter-fly on your shoulder. The term *butterfly effect* comes from climate sci-ence. In complex systems, small, sometimes unpredictable variances can have profound, unexpected impacts. The late MIT meteorologist Edward Lorenz saw this in nature, suggesting that the flap of a butter-fly's wings in Brazil could eventually cause a tornado in Texas.[28] That's a chain of events that could produce dire consequences in weather pat-terns. But in human hands, big, positive change can also emanate from small actions.

No building is so water-tight, no establishment so completely powerful, that a little change can't make its way in. (That's what opti-mistic activists think.) There is a range of small actions that can arise spontaneously in peripheral places outside of the careful watch of building security. In my research on corporate innovation for my book *The Change Masters*, I saw that departures from tradition and modest rule-ignoring went on all the time; in fact, in times of crisis, those vio-lations of norms were relabeled as innovations and elevated to become part of new strategies.[29] I've also been struck by how many big policy matters, such as mergers and acquisitions, came about because of a chance meeting between two CEOs who immediately hit it off; only later did history get rewritten to make this seem like the deliberate result of careful strategic analysis by inside-the-building experts. And sometimes outright mistakes can open the door (or the wall) to bigger change with truly world-changing consequences.

The Berlin Wall fell in 1989 because of one person's mistake.[30] It wasn't intentional, and it wasn't leadership—advanced or otherwise—but it is a striking illustration of the opportunities for leaks, cracks, and crumbling foundations to open the way to change. A former senior East German official, Guenther Schabowski, accidentally announced the opening of the Berlin Wall during an otherwise-dull news confer-ence on the evening of November 9, 1989, when asked by a journalist about the current travel rules. Newly appointed in the role, Schabowski didn't realize that new rules would be implemented the next day, complete with fine print and many stipulations. Instead, Schabowski accidentally announced that East Germans would be allowed to travel wherever they wanted immediately and without delay. This small mistake contributed to the fall of Communism in Eastern Europe, the collapse of the Soviet Union, and the reunification of Germany. Traditional diplomacy was slow and had not yet produced results. "Ask any American who brought down the Berlin Wall, and nine of ten will say Ronald Reagan," former US secretary of state James Baker told a researcher. "The truth is that we had hardly anything to do with it."[31]

Positive deviance, a concept popularized by Tufts nutritionist Jerry Sternin, refers to the ways that promising solutions to challenging problems sometimes pop up when social norms are violated.[32] Sternin observed experts from NGOs looking into the issue of children's stunted growth in Ketchua Indian communities in Bolivia. They saw that families fed their children exactly the same food with exactly the same utensils, so they recommended looking into hygiene, only to find that one mother violated community norms by ladling the soup in such a way that her children got nutrients from the solids at the bottom just as adults did, and they thrived. Thank goodness for simple mistakes.

When experts rely on entrenched institutional thinking to implement a standard model in a top-down hierarchical fashion, they can spend gazillions of dollars but miss simple solutions, such as using mosquito nets to prevent malaria. Stanford educator Debra Meyerson coined the term "tempered radicals" to describe people whose small deviations started organizations on the path to change.[33] Similarly, Francesca Gino found "rebel talent" to be an asset in producing innovation that could break the mold and change institutions.[34]

Today's taken-for-granted social structures were often yesterday's big, intractable institutional challenges that were reinvented by positive deviants, tempered radicals, and innovators departing from tradition.

While managing nursing care at a primitive military hospital during the Crimean War of 1853–1856, Florence Nightingale saw unsanitary conditions contributing to a high death toll; she wanted to do some cleaning. It wasn't easy. British army officers didn't like her meddling, and they undoubtedly didn't like to see a woman seize leadership. But Nightingale took her ideas to a wider audience. In 1859, she published *Notes on Hospitals*, which furnished a revolutionary guide to hospital construction, just in time for the American Civil War, with that war's unprecedented casualties and need to create the modern hospital. In 1860, she established the Nightingale Training School for Nurses, which led to the transformation of informal nursing into a respectable profession.[35] That's two new social institutions initiated by one imaginative lady.

Or consider the saga of Rowland Hill, whose small innovation in England in 1840 helped establish the modern postal service, complete with norms adopted by snail-mail systems worldwide. Hill wasn't even a postal employee; he was a schoolmaster. He noticed that postal revenues in England did not increase from 1815 to 1835 despite the country's significant economic growth. He attributed this to high handling and administrative costs compared to much lower transportation costs. His small innovation was the postage stamp.[36] The stamp was, in effect, a prepayment system at a uniform price that vastly simplified the system. Naturally, the postal bureaucracy didn't much like this idea from an outsider. But it worked. It still does.

Of course, these lone hero stories are not the whole picture; many other people and many other institutional changes had to occur before the world saw the modern hospital or the modern postal service— themselves now aging forms of buildings disrupted by digital technology and in need of major reinvention. But still, these cases are examples of the power of butterflies. The point is that big problems remain intractable when they are viewed only as the responsibility of incumbents trying to operate within established and hardened structures.

Tackling climate change, health, violence, inequality, education, or other big problems requires more leaders going outside the building to find—create or stumble upon—new ideas that become the flapping wings of bigger change.

It Takes a Street

This chapter has focused on big problems and the case for more and better leaders operating under a new theory of leadership. When leaders see the wider scope of problems, are aware of the multiple dimensions and complexity, and challenge existing structures and constraints, they can also propel existing organizations to reach greater heights. Institutional change that reinvents organizations also takes advanced leadership skills to wrestle with ambiguous problems, deal with contending stakeholders, and take positive actions across sectors.

Let's end with a visit to one of the happiest places on the planet (other than the Asian mountain nation of Bhutan): *Sesame Street*. *Sesame Street* itself began outside education buildings, using the power of a recently ubiquitous medium, television, to beam directly into homes to provide early learning as an alternative to formal preschools, which weren't available to everyone anyway. *Sesame Street* was home to appealing characters such as Big Bird, a big yellow Muppet, and his friends, both other Muppets and human companions. Together, they taught toddlers their numbers and letters. This was a huge advance on an important problem: early childhood education for every child regardless of family income.

But by 2014, Big Bird was really sick. The big yellow guy kept up a good front, but all around him, *Sesame Street* was full of potholes. Its parent, Sesame Workshop, was a failing icon; once a pioneer, it was running out of money and losing audience share. Sesame Workshop (which began life as the Children's Television Workshop) had always played an outsized role in early childhood education, attracting enormous audiences worldwide. The problem it addressed was even more vital, as evidence piled up that preschool learning was vital to later achievement. But it was in jeopardy and might fail. Technology had changed; free broadcast television began to shrink; and Big Bird faced commercial competitors such as *Dora the Explorer* (which was animated only and had shorter episodes). That was a tough situation for Big Bird's parent, a small nonprofit organization working through the Public Broadcasting System (PBS), as a public service. PBS could reach the most deprived children because it was free, but broadcast television was losing audiences. For years, Sesame was stuck inside its building, in a losing streak that included stale thinking and internal turf battles. Resuscitating Big Bird and his friends and making the mission relevant to changing circumstances required a new type of leadership willing to bust walls, challenge conventions, and climb across sectors, even if that meant risking stakeholder ire.

Enter Jeffrey Dunn, an outsider with a commercial TV background but who was inexperienced in nonprofit and public sector organizations.[37] As the new CEO, he brought in some newcomers but also relied on Sesame veteran Sherrie Westin and her philanthropic focus. Still, to save Big Bird and accelerate action on the grand mission, he saw that he had to look beyond Sesame's traditional practices and not just throw around the weight of his executive authority. Better internal communication was easy, but the world outside was messy and complex. Early childhood learning was one of those big systems issues with the characteristics discussed earlier: big scope and significance to many people, vague or unspecific goals and pathways, diffused authority and responsibility, multiple stakeholders, and a mismatch between resources and needs.

Fresh ideas, a new way of telling the story, unusual coalitions, the willingness to take risks, and bold new initiatives could reinvent the street. With his new team, Dunn led outside-the-building thinking of several kinds:

- *Think outside the framework.* Sesame Workshop adopted a new, simpler mission statement that emphasized impact, not input: Make children smarter, stronger, kinder. Nowhere did it mention television. Moving away from a single main emphasis was liberating. It suggested numerous new possibilities using any method or device.
- *Think outside the sector.* To stop the bleeding and find resources for the mission, Sesame made a tradition-shattering deal with commercial cable channel HBO to license *Sesame Street* for showing on paid TV. There were immediate outcries from stakeholders and the press at the idea that Big Bird was for sale. PBS didn't like it much either. But Dunn also embraced the nonprofit and public mission and felt that Sesame could reside in several sectors simultaneously. HBO paid for new programming; PBS could broadcast it for free nine months later.
- *Think outside the studio.* And think way outside the industry. Sesame Workshop always had licensing revenue from toys, books, and merchandizing, as was typical in the entertainment industry. The new partners, however, came from industries that had been disrupting Sesame, including both big and small tech companies: IBM, whose Watson machine learning capability could be joined with Sesame to accelerate early childhood learning; and digital start-ups in which Sesame invested—in essence, befriending their enemies.
- *Think outside the characters.* Get to today's issues, not just the ones present since the founding. Turning Cookie Monster into Veggie Monster didn't work (as any parent could have told them), but the arrival of Elmo's friend Julie, an autistic Muppet, was radical and won a Smithsonian innovation award. Two Muslim Muppets, Zari and Zeerak (a special friend of Ernie's), came to visit. The ideas had been there but had stalled due to the internal silos and squabbling associated with losing streaks.
- *Think outside borders and boundaries.* Think big and high impact. Dunn elevated Westin to president of global impact and philanthropy.

This enabled Sesame Workshop—now connected to the private sector via HBO—to enlarge its impact on the lives of children in impoverished countries and refugee camps. A partnership with the International Refugee Committee (IRC) came about in part because Dunn had recently developed a close connection with IRC board member Gillian Sorensen, former assistant secretary-general of the United Nations. Together, Sesame Workshop and IRC planned to bring early childhood learning tools (and Zari and Zeerak) to refugee children in some of the world's most troubled places. This partnership won the MacArthur Foundation's 100&Change competition in 2017, garnering $100 million for this work.

Breaking out of the TV box vastly enhanced the potential for impact on the children who need *Sesame Street* the most. Without new leadership, the organization wouldn't be on this path. Now, the only question is whether a troop of little Muppets from America can continue to help improve some of the most troubled places in the world. Stay tuned.

* * *

Big institutional challenges come in many shapes and sizes, whether boiling the ocean or giving preschoolers a leg up in life. But they all have this in common: conventional approaches through established organizations can't do enough to address them, and those establishments might themselves be part of the problem. The world is not getting better by itself. Making the world a better place demands more and better leaders.

WHO WILL LEAD?

Hierarchy to Hustle, Careers to Causes

A burly executive seated behind a massive desk in a *New Yorker* cartoon tells a startled subordinate, "I'm counting on you to do my part to make the world a better place."

That's funny and sad at the same time. Hierarchy and delegation might fit cut-and-dried business situations, but complex, messy, ambiguous, contentious institutional problems require more of leaders than exercising the authority inherent in their roles; they take entrepreneurial hustle. That also requires a larger pool of leaders willing and able to tackle them.

Who will embrace today's grand institutional challenges? Cash-strained governments can do only so much, and often they are mired in politics and stuck in institutional structures that limit their actions or effectiveness. Corporations with power and resources are stepping up, but their top executives, too, are limited in how much they can do within a for-profit, quarterly earnings framework. Those that find the sweet spot where business values and social values grow together are noteworthy in their rarity. How many CEOs like Jamie Dimon can lead a big bank like JP Morgan Chase to invest $150 million in repairing a broken city like Detroit (e.g., health clinics, grocery stores, and affordable housing) and hope to make money at it? Former General Electric (GE) CEO Jeffrey Immelt tried refocusing GE around "eco-imagination," making money on greener businesses and practices, such as reducing carbon emissions, but that was not enough to save GE from shrinking and imploding or to make a major dent in climate change problems.

Established organizations, whether government, business, or traditional NGOs, can be stuck in sector silos that make change difficult. Innovation requires fresh ideas that challenge conventional pathways and establishment preferences. It requires a pool of people with the motivation and energy to chip away at otherwise intractable problems, who are willing to use their own human, social, and financial capital—their capabilities, connections, and cash—to make a difference in the world. Where can a supply of potential advanced leaders be found, and what is required to unlock their potential?

Finding Advanced Leaders:
The Wendy-Kopp-to-Michael-Bloomberg Continuum

Let's hear it for youthful idealism! In their youth, innovators have created remarkable enterprises that shake up institutions and open new pathways, even if they didn't seem possible at first. Fred Smith, founder of Federal Express, sketched his idea for a national, private overnight package-delivery service in a college paper at Yale.[1] His professor found it wildly implausible and gave him a C. That idea became Federal Express, a multibillion-dollar global enterprise that challenged the US Postal Service and changed the way goods reached households and businesses. Michael Dell started his computer company in his dorm room at the University of Texas and didn't even bother to make an academic paper out of it; he dropped out of the premed program and made a fortune instead. Like Smith, Wendy Kopp also used a college paper to propose her idea, this one a nonprofit that would create a national teacher corps. Presumably, her senior thesis at Princeton got a better grade than Smith's proposal did at Yale. After graduation, Kopp started the well-known Teach for America, and, later, its international equivalent, Teach for All, as a force for improving the delivery of public education by tapping a new pool of college graduates and signing them up for two years of service as teachers. Although not without controversy, this met an urgent need for teachers while challenging long traditions of the education establishment because they didn't get "normal" education credentials.

Legions of young for-profit entrepreneurs and social entrepreneurs form ventures that challenge institutions, whether through online lending, organic beverages, ride-hailing apps, green apparel, instantly accessible educational videos, or coding classes for low-income communities. Bring them on! Values-carrying millennials are one source of talent for solving big institutional problems. Are they enough? No, they're not, but they're a start. Some substitute new ventures for existing ones without getting to an underlying problem (e.g., Uber and Lyft are highly capitalized new forms of competition for taxicab companies and mass transit, but traffic congestion and the social ills associated with it continue to grow).

The question about social enterprises, in particular, is about whether they can scale to great impact or whether they will remain niches. And for all new ventures: Are they sustainable just on founder energy? Wendy Kopp, along with a handful of others, such as New Profit founder Vanessa Kirsch and City Year cofounders Michael Brown and Alan Khazei, stand out because they built successful growth organizations over many decades. But sometimes youthful exuberance isn't enough to grow an enterprise, social or otherwise, to transformative impact. Larry Page and Sergey Brin at the original Google found that, to grow the company, they needed "adult supervision," as Silicon Valley denizens say, so they hired the experienced tech leader Eric Schmidt to serve as CEO and later as executive chairman while he taught Larry Page how to run a giant company.

Well then, let's hear it for experience and wisdom! When Bill Gates, cofounder and longtime CEO of Microsoft, was young and the geekiest of tech geeks, he left social causes to his parents, who were active in numerous Seattle nonprofits and civic associations. When Microsoft matured and Gates saw the world from the helm of a giant corporation, he used his wealth to found the gigantic, influential Gates Foundation with his wife, Melinda—and his father as chairman—and the grand, noble goal of solving global health and education problems.

Michael Bloomberg first made his fortune as an entrepreneur, creating and leading Bloomberg enterprises, which had a powerful effect on the delivery of financial information. He then turned his talents to a big institutional problem: the transformation of cities. He leaped from the private sector to run for office and serve three terms as mayor of New York City. After his time in public office, his foundation, Bloomberg Philanthropies, not only supported urban improvement causes and campaigns; it was also a mobilizer of grand new schemes to improve management and use technology to improve infrastructure and quality of life for people in cities. Gates and Bloomberg succeeded as youthful entrepreneurs and then succeeded as experienced advanced leaders, with Bloomberg a trisector change agent.

Tapping Values, Creating Value: Seeking Capabilities, Connections, and Cash

On the continuum between Kopp and Bloomberg are vast numbers of people with the remnants of youthful idealism and successful careers who are eager to do something to make a big difference in the world. There is a growing pool of accomplished professionals, executives, and entrepreneurs who found success in a traditional career and who are motivated to do something even bigger. They're not household names like Kopp and Bloomberg, but they are emblematic of the new army of talent that can be mobilized to tackle pressing problems in communities, nations, and the world.

Consider two of them and their distinctive paths from Kopp-like youthful activism to later-life Bloomberg-like aspirations. John Dubinsky enlarged his focus on St. Louis; Richard Fahey went back to Africa with fresh ideas. Starting from different places and pursuing different careers, both had accumulated the three Cs of capabilities, connections, and cash. Each was willing to use those assets to seed the work of addressing a problem he had long cared about.

Race and Economic Opportunity in St. Louis: A Banker's Quest

John Dubinsky, a third-generation St. Louis native, headed seven different banks before he decided to shift the racial composition of the construction industry in the region dramatically.[2] Big, burly, and occasionally brusque, he had a big heart and swelled with pride for his artist wife and songstress daughter.

As a young student, he was driven to care about injustice. In college at Washington University during the Vietnam War, he was influenced by the activist currents flowing around late-night dorm sessions and the crafting of protests and also by the inequities and racial disparities he observed in the neighborhoods around him. He saw injustices in who fought the war—the poor, who lacked the means to avoid the draft. He witnessed the formation of radical movements, but he said to himself that he could make a bigger difference working from within the power structure to promote more enlightened views. That might be self-serving, but that's what he did. He chose banking, which he felt was the most conservative, discriminatory, noninnovative field he could find, and thus held the most potential for a former student rebel to provoke change. (And it paid well.) He was highly capable, and he rose. He claimed that he did his best from his bank CEO perches to promote community responsibility and equitable workplaces. He was feisty rather than fusty, speaking out about the responsibilities of financial institutions.

Over the years, Dubinsky grew in prominence, and his relationships also grew, which made him rich in social capital. He was invited to serve on a sweeping range of boards for important companies, arts groups, universities, medical centers, and others. Now he was in position to use his financial capabilities, deep community connections, and even some personal cash to focus on racial disparities in a much bigger way. In the region that contained Ferguson, Missouri, where the fatal shooting of eighteen-year-old Michael Brown Jr. brought increased attention to the Black Lives Matter movement, Dubinsky was ready to found the Contractors Loan Fund to ensure that minority contractors could get the capital to bid on big construction projects so they could build economic opportunity along with buildings.

Clean Energy and Education in Liberia:
Lawyers Ready to Serve

Richard Fahey is also on the front lines of that new leadership force, working globally rather than locally. Fahey, who exuded seriousness of purpose, was a successful corporate lawyer in Columbus, Ohio, who served on the school board and was also interested in environmental problems. His mind kept returning to the time before law school when he served as a Peace Corps teacher and rural development volunteer in Liberia, where he met his future wife. After working in Liberia, he graduated law school and worked for the Navaho Nation reservation in the American West. Afterward, he entered public service as an assistant attorney general in the Ohio attorney general's office, working on environmental law. But like many public service–minded young professionals with families to raise, he was drawn into a typical large corporate law firm.

He kept one pro bono toe in public service by being elected to the Columbus school board and thinking about education, as he had done in the Peace Corps. When he was eligible for an exit package from his law firm, he wanted to find a way to do more for Liberia than small-group teaching, and perhaps create a model for Africa. This was partly stimulated by returning with his wife, forty years post–Peace Corps, and attending ceremonies with Liberia's first democratically elected president, Ellen Johnson Sirleaf. She urged him to do something big for the country.

Fahey took the time to gain additional knowledge to identify opportunities, learn about new green technology, and shake off a lawyer's mind-set to understand relationship-building. He hit upon a gap in the educational system: that the lack of lighting in village homes prevented kids living in developing countries from studying for school or learning on their own. Suddenly, Fahey's environmental concerns matched his passion for education. He created the Liberia Energy Network (LEN) to bring alternative affordable energy to rural areas. Solar cells were not only green and sustainable; they enabled children to read at night. Soon after, he found a soulmate and partner in another lawyer, Robert Saudek from Atlanta, whose operational skills were a good complement to Fahey's grand vision.

Two different interests were married—the environment and education—and the idea for an institution-challenging project was born. LEN, which we'll revisit later, was on its way to bringing electric power to previously unserved people while creating jobs for an all-Liberian team. Fahey and Saudek came from outside the building to bring a fresh and innovative energy pathway to Africa. Starting with their own money, they attracted other funders; the World Bank was among those investing in their model for sustainable development for left-behind regions.

And Millions More . . .

There are millions more people like John Dubinsky and Rich Fahey in America alone. They are men and women who have achieved career success and now seek to turn their skills into significant impact. In the United States and most other developed nations, there is a surging population of baby boomers with a longer life expectancy and better general health—over a quarter of the American population.[3] Advances in health and longevity (living one hundred years is increasingly common) give boomers twenty to thirty more years of potential productivity after they reach the time when societal expectations had defined finishing their primary jobs.[4] About a quarter of those engage in some sort of volunteer service.[5] And many of them continue to work, whether out of desire or financial need. Some analysts call this "bridge employment" in a "second middle age" and point to the number who use time in an "encore career," as Marc Freedman termed it, to follow interests that fell by the wayside during their primary careers, as we saw in John Dubinsky's and Richard Fahey's stories.[6]

There's another thing this growing pool has in common: their espoused values. On a recent survey, a majority of them said they are concerned about "helping and caring for others, caring for nature and the environment, endorsing equal treatment for all, and seeking to understand people who are different from them" and that they "actively pursue goals that are both personally meaningful and contribute to the greater good."[7] Furthermore, this sense of purpose and commitment to meaningful goals were universal across social divides; the expressed values were roughly similar regardless of age, income, health status, or geography.[8]

Those values bring the generations together. The large US population of millennials, born roughly between 1981 and 1997, appears just as concerned with improving society, according to research by Sylvia Ann Hewlett and the Center for Work-Life Policy (CWLP).[9] I don't want to leave out the many people who are busy raising families, building careers, or barely employed and struggling to make ends meet. They might also want to help others and care for communities, and they might do so within the confines of their life circumstances. But younger millennials have the relative freedom that college students Michael Dell and Wendy Kopp once did to envision ventures and social innovations to change the world before needing to change diapers. The other enormous group with that luxury of time is the one that has already raised children, achieved success, and now can shift its focus to make leading with values, not paychecks, its central goal.

This large pool of purpose-oriented people contains numerous accomplished leaders at or close to the top of their game in every field or profession, whether bankers like Dubinsky, lawyers like Fahey, or legions of executives from the worlds of business, medicine, education, or the military. Their years of experience have netted them the three Cs that we will see throughout this book are central to leadership for innovation and social change: capabilities, connections, and cash. They can bring to a cause abundant skills and experience, many relationships with other potentially influential people, and the money to invest (either their own or capital they can tap into). The more fortunate enjoy an unprecedented accumulation of wealth, providing disposable assets that could be put to work in making change, not just making more money. This embarrassment of riches could be part of a new "Gilded Age," as some authors have noted.[10] Although many of the top one-percenters don't seem to be too embarrassed, it's not hard to imagine that they would rather be celebrated for positive impact than pilloried for plunder.

But here's a big paradox and a barrier to be overcome: the very people most interested and most qualified to take on institutional change challenges are often constrained by their positions and handicapped by their successes. Demographics alone can't produce change.

Limits to Advanced Leadership:
Seven Perverse Traps of Career Success

Ironically, big careers can be narrowing. The very professional focus and specialization that bring significant career accomplishments can make it harder to translate that capability outside of the company, profession, or field. Some would-be institutional change agents are trapped in the very systems they might wish to change. Some are imprisoned in what pioneering sociologist Max Weber called the iron cage of bureaucracy.[11]

A top leader can accumulate accolades as an effective executive while also accumulating habits complicating the leap from great to advanced. It's not so much a difference in difficulty as a difference in kind. Big companies, for example, often tie executive compensation to the amount of assets under control, thus undervaluing the difficulty of growing a new venture compared to the relative ease of managing an already-established line of business. Being in the executive suite can make it harder to understand life on the street outside.

As president of Trader Joe's, Doug Rauch had large teams and model formulas for opening new stores and territories. But to create an entirely new retail concept that he called the Daily Table, addressing problems of wasted food and nutrition for low-income people, he was pretty much on his own and in uncharted territory with new kinds of alliances to forge. Furthermore, a portion of what he took away from his success at Trader Joe's was diametrically opposed to what he needed to create the Daily Table innovation (which will be described in detail in later chapters). In Rauch's case, the relative creativity and flexibility of Trader Joe's culture and his own wide-ranging curiosity made it easier for him to shed corporate habits and become a social innovator. For other people, this transition can be much harder. Another top executive recounted how the authoritarian, assertive, technocratic leadership style that worked for most of his career failed him when he tried to open a facility in a multiethnic community in another region. He said later that he had lost the ability to appreciate the richness of culture, build relationships, and act as an advisor, not a commander micromanaging technical fixes.

Trained incapacity is a sociological term often attributed to early twentieth-century chronicler of the rich Thorstein Veblen.[12] It refers to blind spots or inadequacies that come with focused experience—people getting better and better at something that limits their ability to do other things or makes it challenging to change once they succeed. Executive coach Marshall Goldsmith's book title, *What Got You Here Won't Get You There*, hints at a similar phenomenon.[13] Habits of mind engrained by past successes can prevent change and, in fact, can make people want to repeat the pleasurable past rather than question themselves and do new things in new ways.

The perks of success are numerous, including the capabilities, connections, and cash that can be applied to problems outside the building. Yet, many highly successful people struggle when they try to tackle a discipline-crossing institutional challenge. The distance from suite to street seems unbridgeable. Occupations and professions differ in their grip on people, but all must beware of seven common traps.

1. *Already know it all.* One perk of success is to put the lessons and exams away. The higher one rises in a hierarchy of any kind, the more that person begins to believe that he or she already has the necessary knowledge and should be imparting it to others. Despite common talk of continuous learning or lifelong learning in a disruptive era of new knowledge development, people who reach high enough statuses can finally put studying behind them. When they get to the top of the heap or earn handsomely enough, some people start thinking that they never have to learn anything again. Aren't they asked to be mentors? Now they tell others the right answers and show them how to do everything the right way, and they become

unaccustomed to saying the three little words leaders have the most difficulty with (hint: they're not "I love you"). The three hard-to-say words are "I don't know."

Rather than admitting to not knowing (even to oneself, as a lot of not knowing is not knowing that you don't know), they make pronouncements. I've found this syndrome among a wide swath of successful people: very wealthy financiers, large company CEOs, entrepreneurs, corporate lawyers, private equity partners from big firms, and, infuriatingly, some top surgeons who think that their medical training and ability to "play God" with patients' lives makes them experts on everything. In medicine and other sciences, the top people get their names first on publications even when more junior people generate the ideas and do the work. It might be even worse at the pinnacle of financial occupations. Investment bankers and financiers who rescue troubled companies feel they can improve on anything based on their successes; they assume that their incomes prove their superior knowledge.

There are exceptions. In the corporate world, Verizon's former CEOs Lowell McAdam and Ivan Seidenberg stood out for their humility and willingness to listen (which is useful in an industry upended by technological upheavals); Seidenberg waited in line at public ceremonies, and McAdam sat in the back of a room anonymously (at first) to listen to employee presentations.[14] I've seen military leaders who've attained the status of multistarred generals be among the humblest about what they don't know. And there are CEOs who believe in reverse mentoring, using interns and newly minted graduates to informally teach them about new technologies. The ALI experience shows that very accomplished people at later life stages can absorb new knowledge quickly, sometimes learning faster than younger people, if they are motivated to do so. But some top leaders have lost these habits. I've heard complaints from other C-suite occupants that their CEOs don't listen. Along with that goes a lack of interest in learning. These CEOs make declarations rather than ask questions. They agree to speak on panels but rarely stay to hear the other speakers. They don't go to executive education programs after a certain level of attainment.

All that makes it hard to take on ambiguous problems fraught with uncertainty, and it certainly makes it harder to bring new tools or knowledge to them. When we started ALI, a colleague confessed her nightmare: that former Goldman Sachs investment bankers, as she put it, would start trampling over African villages trying to tell them what to do. What people think they know in the suite might not translate to the street.

2. *Bubble wrap—insulation from disagreement.* A related perk of success is the ability to join a circle of people who agree with one another and who never have to talk to anyone who disagrees with them. If their positions make them visible and controversial, a lot of criticism might swirl around them, but they can enter their bubbles of supporters and never have to confront it directly. That is certainly the strategy of powerful politicians who shun press conferences but speak at pep rallies of carefully screened supporters, or of powerful CEOs who live and work behind gates or security guards and get filtered versions of the media from aides and go to social events with like-minded peers.

They are surrounded by people who flatter them, because the others want to court favor from those with power and resources. Coming to believe the praise can lead to self-delusion—even more so when one never hears different points of view. In the aftermath critiquing of the global financial crisis, I titled a column, "What If Lehman Brothers Had Been Lehman Sisters?"[15] The point wasn't that women necessarily take fewer risks (although they might) but that a homogeneous group of top people reinforce a crony culture in which people of one kind think alike and might not see troubles brewing on the outside.

That's why diversity is currently a hot quest in companies—to get many kinds of people and, supposedly, perspectives around the table. I've worked with companies now bringing millennials into top executive meetings to challenge them. However useful this step, much of this dissent is still inside the building; the rest of life often remains in the bubble wrap, because affluent people go home to places that are cut off from the turmoil outside. They might tour a disaster zone, for example, then board their private planes to return to suburban utopia. They can live among those who profess to love them, never really seeing those who might resent or hate them, or, if not that extreme, at least those who see the world differently.

3. *Assumed rights and privileges.* Some arrogant people who've reached their career pinnacle act as though there's a quasi–Bill of Rights written just for them: the right to exercise power and get their own way; the right to bully others to get them what they want; the right to interrupt and dominate the airtime; the right to go straight to the front of the line. There is no waiting to be called upon or to take turns in a discussion group and no need to read the rules manuals; the rules don't apply to people like them.

Some occupations and professions make it likelier that would-be advanced leaders could flash their supposed behavioral privileges on nearly every occasion. Corporate law firms are still notorious for being hard-driving hierarchies where partners can demand what they want, sometimes in a bullying tone, and subordinates just take it. I recall a few top people from those settings who felt they carried those rights with them into other settings where discussions were expected to have a different tone and where they were just one in the group rather than top gun. One lawyer invariably ignored others waiting to speak, expressed contrarian positions rather impolitely, and then tried to buttonhole people with waving fingers, chasing them at breaks between meetings.

The financial world is a close second in allowing aggressive cultures and take-no-prisoners approaches at the top. I observed a few former financial executives approaching staff members in an organization where they were guests as though those people were there to do the executives' bidding—even when the request was out of line and a clear exception to any stated policy—becoming insistent and trying to bully them into compliance. A few successful entrepreneurs and financiers who tried to monopolize airtime had to be reminded to take turns. Such domineering behaviors alienated their peers, who eventually got them to tone it down. But it's interesting that these were often people who struggled the most with the transition to advanced leadership. In contrast is the military again. Countering the assumption that command-and-control dominance is the main behavior mode for top military leaders, the generals were polite, informal (e.g., they used no titles), and kind to everyone.

4. *An army of helpers. Trained incapacity* is a felicitous term. It signifies that the more training and experience one has to get better at a professional area of focus, the less capable the person is at performing other tasks. Add the division of labor, another great sociological concept, and it's a perfect description for why successful people become highly dependent on many other people to perform tasks that they can't do for themselves.

   In fact, one of the privileges of power is to be surrounded by a large organization of people who help the top people get things done by picking up the other pieces. This is positive dependency, but it's still dependency. In some cases, the direct help is so good that the top person himself or herself doesn't even bother mastering an issue or activity personally; he or she can rely on others to handle the other pieces. It's well known in hospitals that physicians sometimes count on nurses and pharmacists to interpret or improve upon instructions or to steer them toward appropriate actions.

Some top executives count on assistants to help them define messages or master new technologies. The absence of the set of helpers is disconcerting to some people who leave the top ranks. General Claudia Kennedy and General Colin Powell reported discomfort at realizing, after retiring from the US Army, that they no longer had an army.[16] Powell had been accustomed to having a staff of ninety to do everything for him. The day after retirement, he had to fix a kitchen sink by himself.

In addition to the direct help that key aides and assistants provide, they also learn how to interpret the moods and desires of top people, anticipating preferences or requests and fulfilling them before being asked. Occasionally this has disastrous ends, as T. S. Eliot illuminated in his famous play *Murder in the Cathedral*, about King Henry IV, who was at odds with Thomas Becket, the archbishop of Canterbury.[17] After the king muses out loud, "I wish someone would get rid of that pesky priest," supporters killed Becket, causing Henry to spend many years in penance. That's fairly extreme, but research and theory on dominants and subordinates, including Simone de Beauvoir's classic *The Second Sex* and my own work on tokenism, show that people who are among the dominants—in social type, and especially in power—become accustomed to being "read" by others who have to court or please them but don't learn how to read other people themselves.[18]

That kind of unconscious dependency handicaps many successful people when they venture beyond the structures in which they've operated. I've seen successful people try to turn those around them in a new setting (e.g., business to university) into the assistants they had been familiar with; helpful staff members (especially young females) might be asked to do personal errands of a very inappropriate kind. (Not to mention the other risks that occur when senior people fail to respect the people below them.) People who have been in top positions in a hierarchy who think they want to help a community might not understand how to communicate effectively with community members living very different lives. They have been "trained" into incapacity in terms of taking on the perspective of someone who doesn't have their own privileges or life experiences.

5. *Narrowing mental frames.* Call this the price paid for the benefits of expertise. Every field has its specialized knowledge, specific vocabulary, and ways of communicating in shorthand, whether by abbreviations or cryptic remarks. This permits efficiency for those in the same discipline, and it limits entry, thereby privileging its insiders because the field remains mysterious to those outside—like secret societies with secret handshakes. In fact, one of the ways that professions maintain their near monopoly on certain activities (e.g., only physicians can prescribe medications and only lawyers can argue in court) is by claiming specialized knowledge that has been acquired after years of training and that certifies them as experts (and subject to licenses, peer reviews, and codes of conduct). Licensing extends widely. Investment professionals must be licensed and are subject to regulation. There have been attempts to turn management into a profession; but even without that, management is replete with jargon and theories.

In sociology speak, *socialization* is the process by which people learn a set of attitudes and behaviors and adopt a special vocabulary that will be recognized by others in that field. Mechanisms for socialization are both formal and informal; they include education and training, peer group values and pressures, and work norms and processes. Approaches to problems and decisions reflect this socialization, which is further reinforced by previous successes using those mental frames. If a boy with a hammer sees everything as a nail, then a person with a law degree might see every conflict as a potential lawsuit, or one with an MBA might see financial disciplines as the solution to every problem. To become successful, people must learn the habits demanded by their occupations, and even more so for elite professions.

That very success at becoming a master of a discipline can be limiting when a person tries to venture outside established structures or tries to work on a problem that proves intractable from the lens of only one discipline. I've seen entrepreneurs think start-ups are a solution for lower-income communities without first seeing all the barriers faced by disadvantaged people, including the likelihood of interruption for family medical emergencies or a lack of safety nets to catch them if they fail. Successful entrepreneurs and venture capitalists can be socially motivated people who want more than anything to help poor people gain incomes and self-respect by having their own businesses, but they can fall into this trap, assuming that other people from different ethnic communities are just like them.

Sometimes the narrow mental frames gained through years of success can be applied in ludicrous ways. In a discussion of how to bring digital tools to improve health outcomes in impoverished, remote rural villages in India, a former hospital system CEO became impatient with the discussion about persuading villagers to stop using traditional quasi doctors and declared that the villages should "adopt a capitation model." Huh? Apart from the fact that participants from other fields and countries had no idea what he was talking about, this was an inappropriate hammer with no nails in sight. Villages were just a few thousand people operating in neighborhoods of perhaps 150 people, without hospitals or health systems guiding anyone's behaviors.

6. *Gratification rhythms: impatience for outcomes.* We expect impatience in the young, including aspiring millennial social entrepreneurs, but not necessarily those of older generations who have lived long lives. Yet when success means getting better and better at doing

something, some accomplished people become accustomed to the gratification of doing it fast, getting it over with, checking it off a list, and moving on quickly. I imagine the adrenaline rush experienced by dealmakers and others who must act quickly and decisively in the thrust and parry of their work lives. Calendars are filled, items are checked off, and empty spaces or times are discomfiting.

People become accustomed to being rewarded at particular points in the process and become impatient if rewards are not forthcoming. I think of veteran members of a technology company sales force who found it difficult to deal with new business models as the company sold cloud-based subscriptions that were payable over time rather than the traditional, large lump-sum contracts payable in big sums at and just after signing; the former, which was considered the model for the future, offered fewer immediate rewards. One private equity firm head who wanted to invest in green agriculture pushed farmers and other landowners too fast and too hard for their commitments and alienated many of them; he simply couldn't slow down.

Impatience is a trap that keeps people from exploration. After accumulating decades of success, some people who want to move from single organizations to institutional innovations find it hard to remember how long it took to get to where they were in their main careers. They want to know the end point now. They want to begin at the end. Every year, the ALI program contains people who are impatient to be at the end before they've even started the work. When told that they will get detailed instructions for something in two weeks, some jump the gun and try to get the guidelines immediately. Others see empty spaces on their calendars and panic, pressing to create events and activities—ironically, some of the same people who had previously craved time off. Where would they find time for self-guided activities, exploration, and reflection if every moment is filled? This time trap limits innovation, which needs free-form, open-ended development of ideas.

Of course, impatient professionals can come into conflict with those whose fields taught them to think in decades, such as faith leaders or scientists. I've seen this kind of clash play out for some leaders with financial backgrounds who want to improve health outcomes by speeding up drug development. In some cases, their time horizons make it difficult to join forces for a worthwhile cause that both camps care about. This trap also manifests itself in the start-at-the-ending phenomenon: wanting projects to bring instant results and losing faith when the path to a social change is longer and bumpier than they wish. This, in fact, is a problem for all innovation efforts. But for people who don't really know how to start over and don't want to, the slow drip of time when exploring new ideas can feel disturbing.

7. *Identity conformity.* Occupational identities are comforting. They give people a place in the world—a title, an affiliation, a signal of who you are and what you know. One thing that makes transitions difficult for many people is the loss of a clear-cut identity. For many people, going from VIP to FIP (formerly important person) is demoralizing. Not only do they have no army, they have no business cards. Relationships that they thought were solid turn out to have been tied to their roles, not to their charm. But the inner turmoil at this kind of loss is not what I want to highlight. The trap preventing effectiveness at embracing the broader cross-discipline nature of advanced leadership tasks is the conformity that has come with identity and that makes it hard to question established structures.

Social identity is expressed in various kinds of conformity to a set of peer group norms about how to present oneself—what uniform to wear and with whom to associate, like the military's officer clubs. Work tends to be the realm in which people conform. For all the varieties of cultural or religious style and family choice that diverse people might have at home, work tends to offer common occupational expression, including uniforms or uniform styles of dress. Those are perhaps less important in themselves than as signs of membership in an identity group, a kind of club. Such "in-groups" often produce social similarity—commitment to a standard that leads to conformity, whether conscious or not. Do elites begin to look and think alike? Do they become committed, true believers in what their peer groups believe? These are empirical questions. But observations at elite gatherings such as the World Economic Forum in Davos, Switzerland, suggest that a certain kind of conformity comes with success, the basis for the coinage "Davos man" (most, overwhelmingly, are male).

Thus, successful people who have the stature and means to be independent might fall into a conformity trap. Someone who worked hard to get into an exclusive, elite club is slightly less likely to tell the club about its flaws than someone who wasn't included in the first place. That's why certain top executives stand out for their courage; Deloitte chairman Mike Cook resigned from a major New York City club known for its business connections because it discriminated against women—after Deloitte took on the cause of gender equity in its partnership.[19] Still, that courage can be exercised cautiously while in office: Cook resigned from one club in protest but did not become a crusader against all single-gender clubs. And he still knew who he was: the CEO of a major accounting and consulting firm.

The tug of identity gained through a long period of rising to success is strong even when interacting with people from other fields. It remains potent even when people leave that career. It is invoked in anecdotes about experiences or analyses of current issues. Even if people shift their focus from single-organization or single-field leadership to take on broader cross-sector institutional problems, they can still feel the powerful tug of career identity and can find it hard to climb out of all the perverse traps of career success that are keeping them in an iron cage.

* * *

The seven familiar dangers go along with the benefits of rising in a hierarchy of power or prestige, but let's not be discouraged. Although such traps can contribute to inhibiting effectiveness at the innovative thought and actions required for advanced leadership, they are not fatal flaws. There are many ways to help people break out of cages and castles and get some fresh air outside the building.

The Courage to Break Out

What I've described are tendencies, not inevitabilities. They are structural propensities, not character traits. They affect people in some occupations and professions more than others. The more hierarchical the conditions of the career, the harder it is to let go of command mode and start hustling. Yet, just as scientists have found that brains continue to develop well beyond childhood, I've seen that it is possible for even die-hard curmudgeons who are set in their ways to loosen up (although I'm not counting on the curmudgeons to be in the vanguard of advanced leadership).

Under the right circumstances, successful people can find the courage to move from structured careers to ambiguous causes and from hierarchy to hustle—from the security of the building to the messy, chaotic, uncertain, contentious world on the street. I'm reminded of a joke in the how-many-of-what-does-it-take-to-change-a-lightbulb genre. Question: How many psychiatrists does it take to change a lightbulb? Answer: Only one. But the lightbulb must really want to change.

Readiness to change involves the willingness to take risks. As I've indicated, the very people most interested and most qualified to take on institutional change challenges, because they possess the three critical

Cs of capabilities, connections, and cash, are also often the most constrained by their positions and handicapped by their successes. They need a fourth C—courage. They need courage to break out of the building, courage to overcome the constraints, and courage to transform themselves and build a new identity as a social innovator. It takes courage to present oneself in a new way to people they had known and to make new relationships, often with people who are very different.

For former Pitney-Bowes CEO Michael Critelli, for example, Fortune 500 CEOs who knew him as a supplier and peer didn't automatically respond to his overtures when he decided to become an advocate for health care reform; he was no longer one of them.[20] And health advocacy groups and government entities didn't automatically respond to his advocacy efforts, because he was seen as "corporate" and not one of them. Critelli's success at Pitney-Bowes with dramatically reducing health care costs through wellness activities, including aligning incentives among the company, employees, health providers, and health plans, was too easily written off as unique to his particular company. It took courage to move outside a CEO post to play an advocacy role and face the threat of rejection or outright failure.

Leadership courage is often in short supply. For every Kenneth Frazier who spoke up against racism while heading Merck (he resigned from a national business council over the issue, precipitating its closing); Paul Polman, who was an activist on climate change while Unilever CEO; or Howard Schultz, who tried to educate his employees and customers about discrimination while at the helm of Starbucks (through a campaign in the stores), there are hundreds more who don't speak up about controversial causes. It is understandable why public company CEOs steer away from controversial or divisive topics. They are beholden to shareholders and to diverse groups of stakeholders; they must speak for the whole organization, not just for themselves.

Certainly, CEOs have taken on big problems of health (a specialty of Michael Critelli when he was CEO of Pitney-Bowes), nutrition, environmental sustainability (Indra Nooyi as CEO of Pepsico), and public education reinvention (IBM CEOs Lou Gerstner, Sam Palmisano, and Virginia Rometty). All those CEOs needed advanced leadership skills to navigate the cross-sector nature of the problems and use persuasion, rather than direct authority, to build coalitions to work with them. Of course, as incumbents in the establishment themselves, like Mike Cook, they also took care not to venture too far outside.

Doug Rauch ran an equally important corporation at the helm of Trader Joe's and knew the courage it took to move outside the establishment to create a new mission-driven organization focused on hunger and nutrition for people in food deserts, which he eventually called the Daily Table. He recalled: "[Trader Joe's] is a phenomenal retail success story and I could have continued on there as president for the rest of my career. There would be nothing wrong with that, but it would be more of the same. At fifty-six years old, I asked myself, 'There's enough gas in the tank, what if I step off?' I took some time to step back and reflect on what else I could do with my life. I decided, 'I don't know what it is, but let's take that road less traveled." It took courage for him to break out and courage to quiet the skeptical voices all around him, some of whom felt he was betraying them. He reported, "A number of people said, 'Hey, Rauch, why are you doing this? You got this great pedigree at Trader Joe's, this history. Trader Joe's is one of the great retail name brands in America. You helped build that? You did the private label program, the expansion program, you were president all those years? Sit back and enjoy that. You go out and do this hunger thing and if this thing falls flat on its face, that's what you're going to be known for. Why do that?"

Rauch recalled his response: "Because it isn't about me." First get over yourself, then you can get out of the building.

Courage is the mental or moral strength to confront difficulty despite potential for personal harm and to be brave or confident enough to do what you believe in. Sometimes the battlefield requiring courage is inside the person. Gilberto Dimenstein, a much-honored journalist in Brazil, described the "war in my soul" as he wanted to move outside the newspaper world to create projects developing more prosperous, accessible, and just communities.[21] Courage to win those internal wars and break out of the iron cage benefits from external support.

Structures for Courage: Scaffolding for Identity Change

The journey to advanced leadership often begins with identity change. Leaders must think of themselves as agents to make a difference in the world, not merely as presiding over whatever their organization makes. Former IBM executive Hansueli Maerki is a prime example. Maerki had spent his entire career scaling the heights at IBM up to the chairmanship of a gigantic region: Europe, the Middle East, and Africa. The affable Maerki was a consummate insider. His job took him to many places, but it stayed within a familiar structure of high-level meetings and diplomatic negotiations, whether at posh palaces, aboard private jets, or in company boardrooms, all with a relentless focus on technology. He "bled blue," as it was said about longtime executives of the company dubbed Big Blue.

Then he left IBM. Gone were the title, most of the privileges, and the always-full calendar. Maerki still had the three Cs that came with his success—technology experience and diplomatic capabilities, an enormous database of personal connections, and cash accumulated from a well-paying job and a generous pension plan. But what would he do with them?

IBM prided itself on its values and corporate social innovation work, so a group of top executives became intrigued with the idea that people who exited should continue to reflect social improvement values. They decided to send Maerki to ALI to increase his engagement now that he was in the outside world, a bigger world that bled many colors besides blue. Maerki was Swiss and lived in Zurich; over the course of the year, he flew the Zurich–Boston route across the Atlantic many times. Each time he entered the United States with his Swiss passport, an immigration officer in Boston asked him what he was doing in America. He replied to one of them, "I'm a student at Harvard." Looking at Maerki's white hair as he stood across the counter, the official asked, "What could you possibly be studying?" Maerki replied, "I'm learning to be a social entrepreneur." The officer paused, then said, "Is that a fancy name for gigolo?"

Maerki retold this as an edgy joke that social entrepreneurship was not yet widely known to the public. But my point in telling it is about Maerki himself. He was slowly and subtly changing his identity. There were many things he could have said that day, but he was beginning to identify with a new quest and a new role. He presented himself not as Hansueli the IBMer but as Hansueli the social entrepreneur, someone who could think outside the corporate building. For him, the scaffolding he was now standing on nudged the transformation.

Scaffolding is a temporary structure put up outside a building to enable workers to stand and reach its higher parts. That's exactly the right metaphor for what it takes to give potential advanced leaders the courage to take on big institutional challenges and to think outside the building. The motivation to change can be stymied by a lack of support for change. The interplay of structure and motivation is clear, as I found years ago in my work for my book *Men and Women of the Corporation*: without opportunity, it is hard to develop aspirations. Structures help individuals reinforce latent motivation to reach their higher goals.[22] Although the iron cages of careers can hem people in, three kinds of scaffolding can help them break out: bridges, clubs, and ashrams.

Bridges and Boards

Bridges are structures that carry us across the gap, from one place or position to another. For potential advanced leaders, bridges help them cross the divide between their work identities and a broader view of the problems they might use their skills and resources to address. Many kinds of experiences can move people across the divide between the acceptance of established pathways and a new identity as a change leader. Volunteering can take them into places they'd never see inside the building, meeting people they'd never otherwise meet in the course of their daily activities, and if it's more than episodic, it can change mental frames, teach new vocabularies, and stimulate ideas for innovation. This is why I've long urged companies to develop future leaders by giving them opportunities to do service projects in communities far away from their normal or familiar routines. I helped conceive of IBM's successful Corporate Service Corps, which took rising leaders in diverse teams far outside the building for six-week assignments to bring tools and solutions to places and organizations (with no commercial motive).

A hidden truth about change lurks in the classic Simon & Garfunkel song, "Bridge Over Troubled Water." The song is about helping someone you care about get over the turmoil in their lives; the bonus is the gain to the helpers who begin to see the impact they can have on others and thus view their own identities differently. Richard Fahey long had a piece of his identity tied to his Peace Corps service in Liberia, alongside being a corporate lawyer in Columbus, Ohio.[23] Vivian Derryck attributed her founding of an organization actually called Bridges, which was used to support better governance, civil society, and economic development in Africa, to a summer she spent as a student on the ground in Côte d'Ivoire.[24] These are like footbridges, the small, short kind.

For potential advanced leaders, one mega-bridge looms large: service on boards. Especially when outside the daily grind, boards can function as bridges to readiness for taking on big institutional challenges. As careers progress from inclusion or getting in the door, boards are critical to the influence stage of having a seat at the table.

In theory, people are selected for board seats because of their expertise and because of what they have already accomplished and can bring to the decision-making process. In practice, of course, some boards can be crony enclaves in which like-minded people make decisions that favor incumbents, resist change, and benefit people like them, which is one reason for pressure to diversify public company boards and major government-related boards. Successful people consider the tradeoffs in board choices. On corporate boards, they can earn a lot of money; on nonprofit boards, they're expected to give a lot of money. Still, regardless of type, sitting on some kinds of boards can serve as a bridge from one career identity to another.

Boards are certainly useful sources of connections. A seat at the table brings influence and enlarges networks. In St. Louis, John Dubinsky, described earlier as the founder of the Contractors' Loan Fund, grew his social capital by serving on numerous for-profit, nonprofit, and civic boards.[25] He sat on bank boards, chairing one, and on the boards of the largest and most impactful institutions in the region, including Washington University and its medical center, and commissions addressing community problems. These helped him walk the bridge from banker to community change agent and tap into the people he needed. Boards were the scaffolding for this network of potential coalition members for his advanced leadership institution-changing work. The range of topics and diversity of people also opened his eyes to a world outside banking.

It's common for boards to be ways to apply one's capabilities and make new connections, but it is less common to see them as environments supporting personal transformation in the board members themselves, as bridges from one identity to another. Though board seats are offered for what the director will give, sometimes people join for what they might learn. CEOs, for example, join boards of other companies to gain perspective, hear perspectives, and enrich their thinking. It is also nearly obligatory, in some communities, for those at the top to serve on boards of major, prestigious, not-for-profit community institutions, such as museums and hospitals, or to represent their organizations on government or civic boards and commissions. Some of these kinds of establishment boards contain enough diversity of people, issues, and experiences to stretch people's thinking, even jar them and provoke new aspirations.

Garrett Moran moved from his successful financial career to leadership of a major social change organization by way of a direct board bridge.[26] He had been an investment banker, eventually joining The Blackstone Group as senior managing partner and chief operating officer of its private equity group, a sure route to riches. Moran exercised his concern for social justice by designing Blackstone's social impact strategy. He had turned to Year Up to offer internships to inner-city youth that nonprofit Year Up trained in technology and social skills. One thing led to another, and soon Moran joined the Year Up board. This was an eye-opening experience that reinforced his determination to address the opportunity gap in American cities. Year Up was itself a bridge to carry youths out of poverty through training and internships, which led to job offers or college. For Moran, the board was the bridge to a new life. He became Year Up's president to lead its scaling to many more US cities.

Multiple boards can serve as platforms. Marissa Wesley, who was only the fifth woman made partner at Simpson Thatcher, an enormous global law firm headquartered in New York City, found that serving on boards showed her what was missing and gave her a new mission.[27] While at Simpson Thatcher, she founded an organization for women partners of the eleven largest law firms in New York, and she sat on others, supporting women in a variety of settings, including the less advantaged. Had she stuck just with law firm partners and not joined the other, more diverse and internationally oriented boards, she would have remained inside a small, elite circle. It was the contrast between the two kinds of activity and focus that made her see the divide between elites and people on the ground, a big gap among women that she was determined to fill.

Board service can play an outsized role in transitions. But for aspiring advanced leaders, boards are bridges rather than destinations. For some people, boards can even be boring. In my own experience, I turned away from a board offer after learning that I would have to chair a committee addressed to one of the things that I found least appealing in my day job. Where would be the stimulation and learning in that? Boards are also scattershot rather than focused and are remote from the action rather than hands-on. They can fill time without being fulfilling. After Doug Rauch left Trader Joe's, he joined many boards in fields he cared about supporting: public radio, a new engineering college, and other education and public good organizations. He observed that after a year of sitting on boards, he had "engaged in that work just long enough to realize that I don't want to spend the next fifteen to twenty years of my life sitting on boards. Board work is not very satisfying or, for that matter, a role with much impact. Most nonprofit board work is really about your checkbook." He craved the next career step, one to take him toward impact, so he founded Daily Table and created its board, to which he could invite others—an opportunity that would probably be his board members' bridge to social impact leadership.

New Clubs: The Supportive Power of Peers

Clubs are a second part of the scaffolding. Clubs are merely associations of people with common interests. They don't have to be formal or named, but they serve many social psychological functions. The peer groups people belong to are a factor in confining them to the iron cage and locking them into establishments. To transform identity and venture into institutional change can be a lonely quest, like being the only *O* in a group made up of only *X*s—the outsider phenomenon I identified early in my career, the configuration that makes it hard to defy the majority and hard to break out.[28] Instead, before moving to impact, it can help to join a new club and find a new crowd of people to cheer you on. That helps with the courage to depart from established norms; it can restore a sense of social desirability, which can be lost when people step outside the building.

There is a great deal of knowledge about the power of groups to shape the individual. Social scientists distinguish between reference groups and primary groups. A reference group is one people use as a basis for evaluating themselves. It is a standard of comparison: Am I like bankers, nurses, lawyers, CEOs, teachers, or what? A reference group is a collection of people whose attitudes, behaviors, and/or beliefs we want to emulate and whose values serve as guiding principles, regardless of whether we are actual members of that group. This can be aspirational, affecting who I'd like to be and how I'd act like that kind of person. A primary group is small and close up—the people with whom one interacts on a regular basis. That's an even more intimate club that can shape identity, clash with it, or reinforce a new identity. The Posse Foundation, which helps students from less advantaged backgrounds succeed in college, uses primary groups as its major tool; instead of students sprinkled one by one in an unfamiliar environment, batches of students go together and support one another.[29]

Clubs are a major factor in confining people to iron cages and keeping them inside the building, as I indicated earlier. As they become more successful, people are invited into circles of other people who are socially similar—they might even look, talk, and think alike. Literal clubs, such as social clubs or intellectual clubs (the Council on Foreign Relations is substantive but still an invitation-only club) or some of both (like the World Economic Forum), confer enticing privileges while demanding conformity to certain behavioral norms. More informal invited networks have a world-changing thrust, such as Warren Buffet and Bill Gates's so-called billionaires club of nearly twenty very wealthy people signing the Giving Pledge to dedicate half their assets to charity in their lifetimes. That is one step toward reframing clubs to encourage advanced leaders to take on major societal problems.

As new fields develop, there is a natural desire to convene, whether to compare notes, to advocate for the cause, or to form networks just in case. Underneath the very substantive nature of these networks is the social psychological function of giving a new identity a name and making it feel legitimate—a social entrepreneur is not a gigolo! The rise of social entrepreneurs mobilizing young people for service in the late 1980s led to people thinking about doing similar things to find one another and then proclaim their identities. City Year was started just before Teach for America; they exchanged ideas and became core to new national networks of like-minded organizations. Similarly, corporate social responsibilities and green businesses have their clubs. Start-up founders—who have often been assumed to have the fierce independence attributed to entrepreneurs—flock to work in shared spaces and stay up for late-night networking events. There is certainly a social element, because if it's not fun and if it doesn't build new relationships, it won't work as scaffolding. The power of clubs should not be underestimated.

Having some kind of new "club" to turn to is essential, especially for people who are leaving a primary career in big, single organizations with lots of structure and support and who may not have ever done anything so entrepreneurial in their lives. Even if they carry the three Cs of capabilities, connections, and cash, they still need the fourth C of courage to change. They can benefit from the psychological support provided by kindred spirits who call people by new names and use new vocabularies, share similar motivations, justify stretch aspirations, and make people feel that anything is possible and so they should persevere even through difficulties. A new club, consisting of diverse people, can also provide material support for the work advanced leaders want to do: increase connections to unexpected places and people, share more kinds of expertise of all sorts, and provide maybe even more cash. This is the reason that student ratings of colleges and professional school programs almost invariably rate peer connections above classrooms in assessing the value of their education.

When we dreamed up the ALI, we didn't think we were creating a new club. Yes, we talked about our goal to deploy a new leadership force for the world. Yes, we included an option for people to join with their life partners, from whom they were often separated during the workday in their main careers. Yes, we built in many opportunities for the first wave of people invited to the fellowship to have a core class every week to discuss and learn concepts and frameworks together. But we also thought successful people would want to maintain some initial distance from one another. We made sure that the first case discussion would feature public figures that participants could discuss at arm's length without having to reveal their own stories. We also assumed that high achievers from diverse backgrounds would come with their own goals, want independence in their choices, and prefer ample solo time to pursue their own interests and potential projects.

We were wrong. We missed the sheer magnitude of the over-whelming importance of the peer group—a primary group on its way to being a major reference group. People such as Hansueli Maerki and a highly diverse set of peers bonded almost instantly. And when I say diverse, they truly were. In addition to Maerki and his Swiss wife, there was a black former astronaut who had attained the rank of general in the Marine Corps; an elected official and public servant from California who was a water activist and LGBT advocate; a top executive from the Middle East; and financiers, lawyers, and other professionals and executives. Less than one hour into their time together, in the first case discussion, they went from ostensibly talking about celebrities such as Paul Newman, Michael Bloomberg, Sherry Lansing, and General Claudia Kennedy to disclosing their own anxieties, challenges, and concerns as though they had been lifelong friends. It wasn't hard for Maerki to start adopting a new identity. Welcome to the new club.

Schools and Ashrams

Places for learning and reflection are the third kind of scaffolding for potential advanced leaders. Educational programs are probably the kind of support structure that most people think of first, but not everyone has to enroll in a transition program to make a transition. For entrepreneurs and social entrepreneurs in the Wendy Kopp mode, boot camps and incubators can be more important, and they come with the potential for a new club; millennials flock to network at Venture Café in Miami, for example. In contrast, people at the Michael Bloomberg end of the continuum have their own opportunities to modify their identities and turn their attention to the work of changing institutions. Bill Gates had the wealth to start the Gates Foundation and hire people to fill in holes in his and Melinda's knowledge; there was, undoubtedly, a great deal he didn't know about the complex problems of global health and education, but he could find the experts and learn fast. Michael Bloomberg had gone to school on cities during his time as mayor, when he could get firsthand experience outside the building, travel to other cities, and join new clubs—such as the US Conference of Mayors and the National League of Cities. His success in business and then as mayor meant that others wanted to learn from him, so he didn't have to become a formal learner. His media company, which he continued to head, and his foundation had great convening power, so he could get access to just about any kind of expertise he wanted.

For most other people, the scaffolding involves institutions that offer knowledge and reflection. There are increasing numbers of training and education programs on how to be an entrepreneur or a social entrepreneur. Venture incubators and accelerators with training components are springing up everywhere—in Boston, St. Louis, Tel Aviv, and Paris; in Jordan, South Africa, and Brazil; and on college campuses as well as in stand-alone facilities. Other organizations offer boot camps to help people develop a project. There are fellowships that include a training component, titles, and social recognition, such as Ashoka for young changemakers, Echoing Green for rising change agents, or encore.org for people at later life stages. Universities are also beginning to focus on this quest. Stanford, Notre Dame, and the University of Texas are among those joining Harvard in adding a new stage of higher education for people transitioning from traditional careers into a new phase of serving the world.

To become an advanced leader involves a chance to learn but also the time to reflect. That's where ashrams come in. In India, ashrams are places to meditate and to put one's thoughts in order while being removed from worldly pursuits. For potential advanced leaders, they take the form of retreats—the time and place for reflection, for absorbing new learning, and for shaping it into an idea for action. People take a pause from their previous lives and gain perspective by shedding the pressures and deadlines that have kept them in iron cages. But they are not cut off from society altogether or from the problems they might want to address. They can take the time to let new knowledge sink in. A recombination of thought takes place when people can set aside pressures and deadlines for a time and let ideas float around. Ashram-like settings are places for slow learning, serving as an antidote to the social media world of instant judgments, just as the slow food movement is a counterbalance to fast food. The ideas become more nutritious. As a result, leaders can think bigger thoughts than they did in their earlier careers and develop bigger aspirations for what they are capable of accomplishing.

When an ashram-like experience is an intense, total immersion, it can have an outsized impact on people and their identities. It's not surprising that Harvard ALI fellows often call their experience "transformative," because they are in the ashram for a full year. But it's striking that rising leaders in the short Harvard Business School Young American Leaders program will occasionally use the same word after a mere four days. How can they possibly say that four days changed their lives? Clearly, it's not the amount of time that matters or even the ideas shared; a short time barely scratches the surface. What matters is the intensity, not the actual time—the chance to be supported in forming a new identity, one that helps leaders at any stage look outside the building.

In their book *Geeks and Geezers*, Warren Bennis and Robert Thomas started out with the intention of contrasting Kopp-like millennial geeks with Bloomberg-type geezers.[30] Yet their probing interviews found that generational differences were not particularly important. Significant leadership for any stage requires openness, curiosity, and the desire to keep learning. That's the personal side of becoming an advanced leader: the person's life experiences and emotional attachments to the causes they choose to embrace. Then scaffolding can help in moving people outside the building to higher purpose achievements.

* * *

Demand for a new kind of leadership, dealing with intractable societal problems, can be matched with supply. It's encouraging that there is a large and growing population of people who really want change. In addition to youthful entrepreneurs, an expanding pool of accomplished professionals and executives who oversaw success while working in an established organization can move beyond the constraints of their careers. They can carry key assets—capabilities, connections, and cash—into a quest to make a bigger difference in the world. With the scaffolding to stand on, they can start moving outside the building to begin the innovation process as a new kind of leader, using advanced leadership skills.

PART II
Skills and Sensibilities

3

DREAMING BIG AND SEEING MORE

Random Walks, Kaleidoscopes,
and Other First Steps

Gilberto Dimenstein had a chance to sell a portion of his social change initiative, Catraca Livre, to friends of George Soros and several global tech giants he won't name, presumably for a great deal of money. He didn't do it.

With fifty million users of Catraca's social media feed, the venture's rapid growth, and increasing revenue from carefully curated cause-related advertising, Dimenstein's project attracted investor attention. "A fund linked to George Soros wanted to buy 20 percent of Catraca recently," Dimenstein said, "but we did not want to sell . . . Another group wanted to buy 40 percent. We refused too, because when we sat at the table, they wanted to talk money, while we wanted to talk about dreams."[1]

Game over. End of negotiations. No dreams, no deal. He walked away.

Dreams were the whole point of Catraca Livre—not riches but enrichment. Dimenstein wanted to come ever closer to making a difference in some of his country's biggest problems. Around the turn of the 2010s, he had resolved the war in his soul (which was still raging when we met him in chapter 2) about leaving a confined journalism job in São Paulo, Brazil, for more independent social activism that challenged established institutions. He had hit upon a way to act on his desire to level the social divides and inequalities plaguing Brazil by providing free access for everyone to culture, community amenities, and opportunities to improve their lives. With his two grown sons, he founded the multimedia venture Catraca Livre, which means "open turnstile" in English—that is, entry without fee.[2]

With Dimenstein as publisher as well as expert recruiter of young, values-oriented journalists who understood urban communities, Catraca Livre soon grew into one of the top ten websites in Brazil, holding its own against international social media giants. In 2018, Brazil had 111 million internet users; Catraca Livre reached 50 million of them across its various platforms.[3] Catraca also garnered international awards, such as the UK's Nominet Trust 100 list of the most inspiring applications of digital technology for social good in the world, announced in the *Financial Times* in 2013.[4]

The goal was always "communication for empowerment," Dimenstein said. Initially, Catraca Livre promoted free or cheap concerts—"a city of possibilities poor people knew nothing about," Dimenstein continued.[5] But the venture quickly added education, health, job, and career tips to give people in lower income classes the advantages of the affluent: free online courses and information about how to download free books, how to prepare for national exams, and how to find subsidized health care.

Catraca Livre also mobilized people for action—for example, starting social media campaigns against sexual harassment during Brazil's famous free-wheeling Carnaval. Catraca Livre partnered with Instituto SEB with funds from Microsoft to develop a bot to detect fake news; as a result, Facebook removed several pages, a first for Brazil.[6] Some

controversial stands Catraca took led to threats and attacks; Dimenstein's characteristically positive response was to launch a campaign
against hate, asking musicians to perform a song called "Peace."

Tapping Dreams: The First Steps to Advanced Leadership

To exercise advanced leadership and move the needle on big institutional problems, leaders must first dream about what it might mean to
achieve a larger purpose. For Dimenstein, the passion for progress and
the vision of change came early in life, and over time, his dream became
more vivid. He roamed the world and gained new perspectives. He
tried a variety of projects beyond his formal job and gained new allies.

Dimenstein's passion for justice came from his religious upbring-
ing, and it gave power to his communications. As a young journalist,
he saw problems of persistent poverty and abuse; he won an international human rights award for mobilizing other journalists to cover
children's rights and human rights. He progressed to become one of
the nation's most influential media stars, writing columns and doing
a radio broadcast from São Paulo. But for all his time on the street, he
was still caught inside the building, in a traditional journalism model
that equated news with a newspaper and held that objectivity required
arm's-length noninvolvement. Dimenstein felt a growing desire to pursue social justice, not just write about it; he wanted to create change
even more than uncover abuses. A year in New York City in 1995 stuck
in his mind. There he saw growing use of the internet and the community's involvement in efforts to reduce crime. He felt that his São Paulo
of the mid-1990s was like NYC in the mid-1970s: widespread poverty,
uncontrollable and rampant violence, and powerless law enforcement.
He tucked those ideas in the back of his mind until he was ready to
explore how to solve social problems in Brazil.

Dimenstein's big dream began as a sensibility rather than a focused
effort. He wanted to transform his city into a cultural mecca, lifting the

spirits and the economic prospects of the less advantaged. I first met him in June 2009, at the start of Brazilian winter, in a community café in Vila Madelena, an inner-city neighborhood of São Paulo, where he lived in a modest urban house with his education-innovator wife and a bird-filled walled garden. The cooperative café, a short walk away, was one of the initiatives he helped create to fund a variety of education and arts projects for the area, which IBM also helped support through community responsibility funds. Dimenstein knew the heads of big companies and some of the most powerful people in Brazil, and he helped them experience Vila Madelena. He brought elites to the streets.

One small project at a time, Dimenstein opened a sense of possibilities in others while continually enlarging his own dreams. Those whom he taught to think boldly fueled his own passion for change and became enthusiastic allies for his causes. He convinced Fabio Barbosa, then the CEO of a major bank considering big environmental commitments, to start locally by turning a crime-ridden alley next to the bank's downtown headquarters—an alley filled with drug dealers, garbage, and debris—into a clean, bustling, festive, art-filled park for the neighborhood. He urged famous pianist João Carlos Martins, despondent over the loss of three fingers that ended his career as a concert pianist, to get over despair and find a purpose-driven alternative: form a youth orchestra made up of talented but poor children throughout Brazil to bring culture to São Paulo and an opportunity to the children. The orchestra eventually performed at Carnegie Hall and at Lincoln Center in New York City as part of a world tour. A few years later, when I heard the orchestra play European classical music with a samba beat in São Paulo's spiffy new concert hall, Martins exuded happiness; he had even regained some use of his fingers. Dimenstein used his cell phone to stream video of the concert across Catraca platforms.

Dimenstein's Escola Aprendiz (learning neighborhood) project was quintessentially outside the building. Aprendiz began to change education without touching the schools themselves by giving students chances to apprentice and learn from the city itself, such as by placing them in a shop that made furniture from used tires. Dimenstein was a driving force behind transforming Vila Madelena from a down-and-out urban neighborhood that was littered with graffiti into a chic art showplace. Beco do Batman (Batman Alley) had already become a completely art-filled set of three intersecting alleys that were named after their first graffiti, a Batman portrait; this was soon highlighted in tourist guides and considered a must-see for visitors to the city. Dimenstein accelerated the focus on street art and access. Because of his efforts to close the streets to cars to form urban parks every week, as other cities had done, some São Paulo officials proposed a bill mandating this. Urban street art was featured on gigantic billboards in São Paulo's international airport for world travelers to see.

All this contributed to a new sense of the city. Vandals turned into artists, waste became opportunities, digital empowerment became common—that might seem like a great deal of action, but it was just the beginning of Dimenstein's steps toward a bigger dream that stemmed from his memories of New York City. He remembered how New York used the internet too; he used a year at Harvard to connect with the MIT Media Lab, gaining a global digital perspective. Catraca Livre took shape out of the bits and pieces of his experiences, reflecting what his dream could mean in action. And it worked.

Although Dimenstein was not worth much in cash, he was a capable, respected persuader, rich in connections that he could use to attract backing from some of Brazil's most influential business leaders and well-endowed private foundations. Using the three Cs enabled him to dream bigger than his own resources suggested. Adding digital tools amplified the reach of his dreams. But he still turned down the likes of George Soros and perhaps Google. That was not out of proprietary feelings; it was all about the purpose that animated his dream.

Impossible Dreams: Discovering Purpose

You don't start the innovation process by consulting a guidebook, reading a cookbook, or choosing from a menu. First comes the dream. Big problems require big ambitions. That was certainly clear for Gilberto Dimenstein, and that's the kind of thinking he urged on others.

This chapter describes the initial steps in advanced leadership: catching an innovation idea in the first place. There are three main elements. One is tapping a big dream, a deeply felt, and sometimes long-held sense of purpose stemming from a feeling of outrage along with an opportunity for action. A second involves the innovation-finding process of reading the context to sense needs and find gaps that can be filled by new approaches—exploring the roots of imagination and creativity. The third element acknowledges that when in uncharted territory, there can be many paths to the same goal. It is important that the chosen route fits what the aspiring advanced leader brings to the dream. The dream and the search for innovation must culminate in a basis for commitment unique to individual circumstances.

The advanced leadership quest begins with a belief that the world could be better than it is, accompanied by a feeling of deep discontent that it isn't. A kind of restless dissatisfaction channels entrepreneurial energy toward breaching boundaries, challenging established structures, and meeting higher standards. Institutional change agents often manifest an almost utopian sense of perfectibility, that they could do better, and they encourage others to do better.

Dreams about a better world open new possibilities. Dreams provide purpose and meaning. Finding the sense of purpose embodied in a dream takes people outside the buildings in their minds; it helps them begin to envision new forms of action. Dimenstein and other advanced leaders exude a can-do sense of potential, because they are committed to doing something, anything, and improvising their way to a new vision that changes communities, societies, or institutions.

Some of the happiest people I know are dedicated to dealing with the most difficult problems: turning around inner-city schools, finding solutions to homelessness or unsafe drinking water, supporting children with terminal illnesses. Like Dimenstein, these leaders face the seemingly worst of the world with a conviction that they can do something about it and serve others, which puts a smile on their faces. Another journalist, Ellen Goodman, a Pulitzer Prize–winning syndicated columnist, turned grief into social purpose. She was distraught over the treatment of her dying mother. After leaving her job at a leading newspaper, she attracted a team to found The Conversation Project, a campaign to get every family to face the difficult task of talking about death and end-of-life care.[7] The mission dealt with a grim topic, but it soon attracted others, such as former law firm managing partner Harvey Freishtat, who embraced the purpose and added his expertise. That made Goodman happy.

People who have faced a major trauma can find purpose and meaning in helping others facing similar situations.[8] "Dream your worst nightmare, then invest in it," digital innovator John Taysom liked to say—in effect, see the thing that upsets you and use it as an opportunity for change.[9]

The purpose and meaning that come with big social impact dreams contribute to happiness and, as a bonus, promote health. "Good genes are nice, but joy is better," declares the headline for one of the *Harvard Gazette*'s most widely read articles on the science of well-being.[10] Though referring to longevity, the headline could speak directly to people ready to be institutional change agents. Start with the hope that comes from dreaming that you can transcend nightmare conditions. Awaken the optimism of activism.

For potential advanced leaders, the optimism of activism can be contagious. A grand mission imbues the dreamer with a charisma that attracts other people. Ideas that are bigger than resources and bigger than individuals can transcend limitations and perform magic. They can even convert waste into opportunity. Gilberto Dimenstein and other effective innovation leaders prove the adage that it takes as much time and energy to dream small as to dream big, so you might as well dream big. And while you're at it, dream bigger than you are.

In fact, solving grand institutional challenges can start with ideas so audacious that they sound like impossible dreams. Vanessa Kirsch founded a successful nonprofit service organization but knew that she wanted to do something on a larger scale. She left Public Allies and traveled the world for a year with her fiancé, visiting community service organizations. I'll never forget the summer day that she stood in a swimming pool in New England soon after her return and declared, "I'm thinking of inventing a new sector." A new sector? No one there that day knew what she meant or had a clue about whether she could do it. Yes, she said, a new sector in between for-profit and nonprofit. A sector with the tools of the private sector that would create high-impact nonprofits to address public issues. Not for-profit, not nonprofit, but "new profit." She had no details in mind, just a big ambition. It didn't deserve to be called a vision yet, because it wasn't clear what she would do or accomplish. It took a year of weekly brainstorming meetings with people she knew to hit upon the first outlines of a plan—to attract investors to funds whose outputs would be significant social change.

More than twenty years later, the organization she founded, New Profit Inc., is a pace-setting leader in the burgeoning venture philanthropy movement. It behaves much like a venture capital firm, assembling investors such as private equity financiers and tech entrepreneurs to fund a portfolio of cause-oriented organizations with growth potential and to take a board seat to help mentor and guide these organizations. Although subject to its share of criticism for the business language, New Profit has boosted the impact of many organizations, including innovations in education such as Teach for America, the KIPP public charter school network, Year Up, and Management

Leaders for Tomorrow. Kirsch did, in fact, help to start a new sector. Many other impact investment funds sprang up to follow New Profit's lead.

The Origins of Dreams for Change

Behind every big dream is a combination of opposites: outrage and ambition, or pain and purpose. A leader feels that something is wrong, missing, or could be improved, and the leader's work is essential to getting action for change. That's the mix of motivations I found in analyzing more than five hundred essays from successful people from every continent, explaining their interests in working on social causes, and hundreds of other informal conversations with people hoping to learn advanced leadership. I found a dizzying array of compelling stories (and some people unable to explain their interests), illuminating the wide swath of reasons people offer for their desire to begin a new kind of leadership journey. Even with a deep discount for retrospective bias—because people want to offer a narrative that makes everything seem to lead up to their chosen paths—three interrelated dimensions of motivations stand out.

Emotional drivers. Some people trace the origins of their desire to make significant change back to an intense emotional event in their lives. Many faced the traumatic and seemingly unnecessary loss of a close relative or friend—often a sibling, parent, or grandparent— that made them want to find and eliminate the root causes. A corporate lawyer working in an unsentimental field returned to an early trauma, when his younger brother died of a rare disease, impelling him to want to get drug innovations to patients faster. The emotional driver can be outrage, turning sorrow into anger and anger into action, like the young survivors of the Parkland high school shootings who refused to be victims, turning tragedy into action to help others. I heard the voices of people of color who were stung by schoolyard taunts from classmates in majority-white schools, which were never forgotten, despite their later successes. Some people described personal frustrations, such as the trauma of getting somewhere without help—to college, to a new country, to their first jobs. Often, a person was fixing something that had been a problem in his or her earlier life. There was often a tinge of emotion involved even for those with lofty rhetoric about leaving a legacy for future generations; they wanted others not to have to suffer the way they did. They wanted to right a wrong even if they wouldn't personally benefit, perhaps because the emotion still lingered.

Firsthand, close-up observations. Direct experience on the ground—from the street, not from theory or secondhand accounts—is a second impetus for wanting to solve big problems in new ways. A big abstract problem takes on a human face, and the leader empathizes with strangers. A physician became an antitobacco activist after witnessing a patient after surgery to remove a cancerous lobe. The patient survived but resumed smoking almost immediately; the doctor could see the shame in his eyes at the first follow-up appointment. It gave him a new view and new motivation to stop blaming the smoker and start blaming the addictive cigarettes. A lawyer spent summer school vacations visiting poor villages around the world with her father, then chairman of CARE, and witnessed the conditions in which women struggled to raise their children, an awareness she returned to later. The close-up experience could be a chance encounter with an assumption-shattering situation. It could come from something extracurricular, not within the job. Because of an eye-opening opportunity, people begin to see something bigger than what they could deal with in their regular work roles. Or perhaps a person immersed in one context sees another that offers a new appreciation for what could be possible. They were inspired by direct experience of a positive model that could be imported into their own circumstances, as Brazilian Gilberto Dimenstein did during his year in New York.

The propensity for action. A third dimension is confidence in one's expertise to do something about whatever problem is chosen. Interest is matched by resolve. The person is not content to sit back, rest on her laurels, and let someone else take care of the problem. There's ego here too—the feeling that if one doesn't fix the situation, no one else will, or the feeling that the leader with experience under her belt now has the know-how to take on something even bigger than before, perhaps completing a task that she wasn't able to accomplish earlier in her career. A successful company founder remembered the failed Christmas tree–delivery service he started as a teenager; he wanted a better outcome for the low-income entrepreneurs he aspired to help. For high achievers, a competitive spirit kicks in—that they can do it better than all the other social innovators that have tried before. That's how a government official turned water advocate felt when she wrote a book to turn an esoteric public works issue into a public issue and thus mount a public education campaign. They don't want to be armchair pontificators—people who whine about social problems in dinner party conversations but don't take steps to do something about the problems and are too cynical to believe in solutions. Advanced leaders want to find solutions. They are big dreamers, not just big talkers.

These three groupings—an emotional charge, a rational and grounded view of new facts and situations, and confidence in one's abilities—are generalizations hardly doing justice to the range of reasons people give for wanting to embrace and lead social innovation. The specifics can be all over the place. They do not always involve tear-jerking trauma; they can simply reflect longstanding interests to match passion, expertise, and societal needs. As creativity expert Teresa Amabile has found, creativity requires intrinsic motivation and little time pressure, all in an environment of positive support.[11]

* * *

Dimenstein, Goodman, and Kirsch are examples of reaching for big dreams. Of course, the dream might not start quite as big as it becomes over time. I've mentioned retrospective bias—the tendency to recount history in such a way as to make paths seem smoother than they were. When history is written, it can look as though leaders like this had the ideas all along, but that would be misleading if not downright wrong. Leaders who break through institutional constraints to tackle big problems find their ideas through processes common to all innovations: they shake up their thinking by roaming widely into unfamiliar territories and seeing a broad context that enables them to challenge conventional wisdom and make new mental connections. That is the essence of innovation.

How to Envision Innovation: From Dreams to Directions

Dreams, whatever their sizes, must be translated into directions. Dreams must become actionable ideas. But where do ideas for innovation come from?

Identifying a problem and giving it a name is not enough. Innovations don't drop themselves on us in the boxes defined by organization charts, job assignments, or established pathways. Indeed, it is likely that scripted solutions stemming from existing institutions have proven ineffective in solving the big, intractable institutional problems that need advanced leadership. Neither do solutions to problems emerge full-blown from the nature of problems. That would be Marie Antoinette–like: "People are hungry and don't have bread? Let them eat cake." Or "people suffer from opioid addiction? Tell them to stop taking the opioids." Clearly, none of that works (though it might foment revolutions, as Marie Antoinette's cluelessness did in France and as unfeeling treatment of left-behind populations threatens to do in the US heartland). In short, there is more to advanced leadership than problem-naming. Empathy for those affected and a fuller understanding of what changes will be required is necessary, and that, in turn, requires finding an actionable new idea that comes from outside the building.

Idea-finding can involve a long exploratory process. Before history begins at the point of announcement or launch, there is often a long prehistory of dreaming without a clear direction. Conceiving of ALI itself illustrates the process. In our first conversations, Rakesh Khurana, Nitin Nohria, and I speculated about something that could deploy a new leadership force for the world, working across disciplines and institutional silos, but we weren't clear about what that would mean in practice.

I recall attending a holiday brunch more than a dozen years ago at which former Harvard president Derek Bok asked me the perennial party-chat question, "What are you working on these days?" It was a playful occasion, and so was my response. "Making the world a better place," I replied breezily. He said, "Could you pin that down a little?" We laughed. Then I tried to describe the barely formed idea for ALI. "We're inventing a new stage of higher education," I stammered, which was a lot like Kirsch saying she was inventing a new sector and didn't much pin it down. That was a little more specific than improving the world, but not much. His next question implied skepticism. "What makes you think you could do that?" is what I remember hearing, although he might have been more diplomatic. Back then, I could barely articulate the idea, and it was hard to say exactly where it came from. Certainly, it came from numerous conversations with Khurana and Nohria, but what lay behind that? How do you find and catch an idea?

The truth is that idea-finding isn't linear, strategic, or planned. One might plan to look for an idea, but that doesn't guarantee an idea will be found that isn't a carbon copy of an existing idea. It is important to be open to experiences—particularly novel, and perhaps jarring—that push at structures and boundaries. Idea-catching is often improvisational. Our ALI idea was classic improvisation; out of the reactions of audiences and of one another, it took form into half-baked fragments of thoughts attempting to make sense of a changing zeitgeist, a new mood of the times involving societal responsibility but also profound social and demographic change. It also resembled the random walk that is familiar in math and applied to investments—a path defined by random steps, with no structured route that inevitably or predictably leads to a destination.

Relatively unrelated but fortuitous fragments of experience went into the ALI-conceiving mix before the idea took shape. It was born out of dozens of events and encounters, none of them directly on the topic: Harvard committee meetings about new buildings to hold leadership conferences; discussions in Davos at the World Economic Forum annual meeting about the coming social security crisis when baby boomers turned sixty; encounters with CEOs and business leaders about turnarounds and the importance of purpose; work on political campaigns and state economic commissions; teaching classes on change and innovation; selecting luminaries for prizes in Israel and the United States; talking public leadership with colleague and CNN commentator David Gergen; nonprofit board meetings about inner-city health and educational needs; a chance meeting with Harvard Law's civil rights star Charles Ogletree on a plane; advocacy for US national service; networking at retreats and leadership conferences; trips to India and Latin America where urban poverty surrounded luxury hotels; and reading books that were critical of intellectuals like us. Some experiences were familiar, but others were discomfiting. Then there were more conversations with Khurana and Nohria and a growing group of curious colleagues who had been consulted on the embryonic idea and became intrigued by it.

In short, our venture concept was the result of a great deal of wandering—a random walk that contained many diverse experiences, most of them well outside of the building. The idea was seeded by a large mix of only tangentially related but provocative bits and pieces. It was like multiple fragments going into one gigantic kaleidoscope, flying around before settling into a clear, usable pattern. Somehow, the concept fit the zeitgeist—the mood of the times—and we shook the kaleidoscope to find our pattern, trying and rejecting several possibilities along the way until we staggered into the idea for getting started, vague as it was at first.

Kaleidoscope Thinking: From Fragments of Experience to a New Possibility

New ideas are often not entirely new; they often come from recombining old ideas. Creativity is a lot like looking at the world through a kaleidoscope.[12] You view a set of elements, the same ones everyone else sees, but then you shake the kaleidoscope to reassemble those floating bits and pieces into an enticing new possibility.[13] Innovators shake up their thinking as though their brains are a kaleidoscope, permitting an array of different patterns out of the same bits of reality. Leaders who take on big, intractable systems problems must be able to break out of prevailing wisdom in order to move beyond it. They start from the premise that there are many solutions to a problem and that by changing the angle on the kaleidoscope, new possibilities emerge. Where other people would say, "That's impossible. We've always done it this way," they see another approach. Where others see only problems, they see possibilities—like the optimism of activism Gilberto Dimenstein exudes. Kaleidoscope thinking is a way of constructing new patterns from the fragments of data available, patterns that no one else has yet imagined, because they challenge conventional assumptions about how pieces of the organization, the marketplace, or the community can fit together. Kaleidoscope thinking is systems thinking with a new twist.

Innovators reframe the situation and reset the kaleidoscope on a new pattern that can ultimately become the convention for everyone else. You take away a piece, add a piece, reshuffle a piece, or put together a new combination of pieces—and new possibilities appear. Prematurely settle on an idea because of work overload or deadline pressure, and it is likely to resemble what already exists. Take time to let more and more fragments of experience float around, including unexpected events and disturbing encounters, and it's likelier that an advanced leader will find a new model that cuts across sectors, structures, silos, and institutional expectations.

Making Every Fragment Fit

Doug Rauch (whom we met in chapter 2) left the presidency of Trader Joe's without a coherent plan. He just had a lot of idea fragments and a strong conviction that he could make a meaningful contribution. Rauch's big dream was that no one should go hungry in America. His first idea, to pin down the dream, was a social venture that would collect unsold bread from grocers and deliver it to food banks all over America. But food banks were already doing something like that, and they weren't always very effective. The idea seemed stale, and it didn't seem big enough. It was only one aspect of food waste, a problem that had also started to bother him as climate change reached the news and he talked with environmentalists. And what would that idea do about nutrition? Giving them their daily bread (paraphrasing a prayer) would add carbohydrates—an increasing villain to nutritionists with whom he spoke and not much better than the cheap fast food the poor often consumed, as he found when he visited food banks and spoke with community members. Furthermore, the surplus bread idea wouldn't alleviate much hunger either.

Rauch's wanderings through adjacent issues gave him much food for thought but also left him frustrated about what to do. I recall a conversation with him in my office in mid-2010; he scribbled his three big interests—climate change, hunger, and health—on a piece of paper and wondered which to choose. We tossed around the fragments, and then he wondered whether he could make a dent in all three. Two months later, his mental kaleidoscope connected them. He saw a need to reach those who were food insecure with healthy, affordable meals rather than empty calories, and he saw that perfectly healthy but about-to-be-wasted food could be a solution for the poor and for the environment at the same time. Many redefinitions later, Rauch determined that nutrition was the issue, not hunger. Nutritious food must be available at affordable prices that would foster dignity and respect, not seem like charity. He felt that good food could be found in the surplus that is wasted every day, which has detrimental effects on the climate from the greenhouse gases it releases. With a workable idea in hand, and with his capabilities from his career in mind, he could begin the process of lining up suppliers and starting a new idea for retail food service in impoverished areas. He had broken through the existing paradigm and institutional patterns and was on the verge of inventing a promising new approach.

Becoming fixated on an idea prematurely and discarding the other possibilities can be a trap, another kind of box that prevents broader creative thinking. Stale bread delivery was where Doug Rauch's thinking started but not where he ended up. Instead, his story illustrates the value of taking the time to struggle with connecting the previously unconnected to find a big innovation that could address big problems in novel ways. Openness to a wide variety of experiences before deciding on an idea helps stimulate advanced leadership. Rather than settling for obvious first ideas that fit neatly into existing structures, advanced leaders see ways to combine elements that were previously separated or relegated to the periphery.

Making Multiple Experiences Count

Collecting fragments to be tossed into a mental kaleidoscope can be a process of accumulation over time. Vivian Derryck took a long, random walk to catch the idea for social innovation that would fulfill her dream of a prosperous Africa with gender equity.[14] Loosely related experiences and frustrations had accumulated over many years. Derryck was a prominent African American international development expert living and working in Washington, DC. She had first set foot in Africa as a college student when she spent a summer in Côte d'Ivoire; she observed that girls, such as her neighbor Fatamou's daughter, worked in the fields while boys went to school. This image stuck in her mind during a successful career in Washington in top Africa-focused positions at the US State Department, USAID, and a major international NGO. She fit comfortably into the established bureaucracies for foreign aid, which was full of impressive buildings where she was subject to being stuck in what is popularly called "inside the Beltway" thinking, including the belief that big government was essential to getting anything done.

When she returned to Côte d'Ivoire many years later, she was dismayed that the government had made little progress in addressing educational disparities between boys and girls, and agriculture was stuck in premodern modes. She saw gaps in institutions, which included a weak civil society of nonprofit, voluntary, and community associations with weak business leadership. She started talking about this wherever she could and was disappointed, she reported later, by how little educated professionals from other walks of life knew about Africa and how little importance was given to Africa in US foreign policy. She felt that she would have to make the case for why Americans should care about Africa, which meant business interests. She drew on conversations with Chevron Africa executives. She attended Washington meetings focused on other regions, such as the Asia Society and the Inter-American Dialogue, which showed the benefits of gathering experts to discuss events in a specific region. At the same time, she recalled her observations of senior-level government and NGO officials, who had to be very careful about what they said and could not speak out about corruption or abuses of power. Political leaders in Africa would meet in closed spaces constrained by protocols and a narrow range of attendees.

These experiences, which included awareness of what was missing, whirled around in her mental kaleidoscope and led her to challenge assumptions about working with Africa. What was missing, she thought, was business and civil society. Also missing was a format to enable frank conversation and inclusive dialogue that was far-reaching enough to include citizens and civil society organizations that could push for change. She thought she could bring her unique experience and skills to engage civil society, business interests, and policy makers in dialogue to expand democracy in Africa through attention to specific shared interests such as agriculture. That led to Bridges Institute and its expert forum in DC. Her idea for Bridges, a social innovation to bolster civil society in Africa through global business partnerships, soon won an award as a promising idea, which bolstered her motivation to pursue it.

Deliberate Search

In a different context, Tom Santel took a shorter walk closer to home, visiting parts of his home city he had never seen deeply during his affluent executive life.[15] But he also made sure to do his homework and give himself time to reflect before leaping in any direction.

Santel had risen to the top of Anheuser-Busch, becoming CEO of its international operations. When the company was acquired, he benefited financially from its sale and was determined to do something about the educational disparities plaguing St. Louis. Santel wanted to work on the dropout crisis; reports had exposed low high school graduation rates in parts of the city largely populated by minorities. Exploratory conversations helped him recognize that he had to start earlier than high school to give children a strong foundation for education. He learned from research studies that early childhood health affected later outcomes.

To find a base to explore what to do, Santel joined a hospital system, where he could get a wide view of community issues, although he was still in search mode. The effort had a catchy name, Raising St. Louis, but Santel had to work with colleagues to find the content. He could have just started a hospital-based program, sitting comfortably in an office. That would have been easier because it was familiar and wouldn't raise St. Louis eyebrows. Instead, he started to wander farther afield. He traveled to other major US cities to see what worked best in early childhood to get children ready for education.

Repeated experiences made clear that home-based interventions were the most effective. He also saw what didn't work. Often, mistakes were made, and programs failed when experts pushed their favorite ideas from inside their buildings without gaining the trust of the community. Back in St. Louis, he continued multiple conversations. He found established nonprofit education-focused groups with similar goals but that were operating in isolation. He toured departments and made relationships within the hospital. Perhaps most importantly, he reached out to community members, informally and through formal discussion with thirty residents from teens to senior citizens. Community members expressed strong desires for greater involvement of fathers and stronger networks among parents. They wanted reliable information about health, parenting, and available community resources. All this gave shape to Raising St. Louis as a home-based parenting education program connecting health, education, and families. Santel wasn't an expert, but he was a leader. He brought advanced leadership skills to offer an expansive view of institutional change and the ability to connect ideas and people.

One bonus from all this prework to pin down the idea for Santel, Rauch, Derryck, and other advanced leaders: the expansive view of the territory gives them a new set of relationships with people and organizations that can later be allies as the fledgling social venture develops. This underscores sociologist Mark Granovetter's theory about the strength of weak ties; the people close to us can keep us inside the building, but people we barely know can take us to unfamiliar but helpful places.

Wandering: The Value of Far-Afield Trips

Field trips—moving outside classrooms, offices, or industries—are good for learning, but "far-afield trips" are even better.[16] The encounter with the truly different can shake mental kaleidoscopes into seeing new possibilities. I call these trips *expeditions to Labrador* in honor of frozen food innovator Clarence Birdseye, a grocery store proprietor in upstate New York from a century ago, who got his idea for preserving produce while on vacation fur-trapping in Labrador and observing frozen fish caught in the ice; the natives ate them later with no ill effect. His idea for frozen food opened an entirely new industry and ushered in a staple of modern consumption that also improved health through year-round availability of seasonal foods.[17]

At the dawn of the digital era decades later, when Reuters Greenhouse founder John Taysom took Reuters's CEO and top executives from London to California for two days of meetings with Silicon Valley entrepreneurs—complete with fast electric car rides in one company's parking lot to jar minds (as well as bodies)—that was probably as strange as Labrador to many of them.[18] But it opened minds to how the greenhouse could trigger innovation. Consulting firms caught on to a market for bringing executives from one country to another to visit exemplary companies outside their own industries. IBM added a Corporate Service Corps to its leadership development, which took diverse groups of high-potential employees to unfamiliar countries to solve a business problem in a month. There are other benefits to such close-up encounters. A study of Teach for America applicants and teachers found that participants from more affluent backgrounds, who were placed in schools with low-income students, changed their views to align more closely with those of less advantaged Americans regarding the fairness of economic, social, and political systems, an opening of minds that bridged racial and class distinctions.[19]

You don't have to go to Labrador to catch a promising idea. Finding the idea is not always a matter of dramatic brainstorms or gargantuan breakthroughs that move as fast as Uber or Lyft to challenge the status quo. Sometimes leaders find something unexpected that causes them to think differently. Other times, they find an element to add to experiences that have been accumulating and see a missing piece that will help realize their dream of a better world.

Sometimes going far afield can be systematic. For example, Laura Dambier, a top executive at an insurance company in Hartford, Connecticut, had a lifelong interest in American history and political institutions; early in her career, she had served on Capitol Hill for Connecticut's US senator Abraham Ribicoff. Later, during her corporate days, she used vacation time over six years to visit twenty-eight US presidential libraries, museums, and homes, a mere dent in the more than two hundred sites that told the story of America's leaders.

Dambier was also looking at news about shifting American political sentiments. Her reading of the zeitgeist made her concerned about declining civics education, which, she felt, lay behind low voter turnout among young people, mistrust of government, and weakening of the fabric of democracy. If civics education wasn't happening inside school buildings, there had to be another way to revive it. She couldn't do much about it from a corporate post (except whine), but she started imagining how she might eventually use her management skills to address a need that also reflected a personal interest. She left the corporation and began to envision the organization she soon started, a new nonpartisan education organization called With Liberty and Leadership for All, which would use digital tools and the hundreds of presidential homes and libraries for common civics and history lessons. Dambier had found a gap she could fill. A hobby became a calling. She was translating a tourist experience into a way to actualize a grand dream of helping save American democracy.

Noticing Needs, Seeing Gaps: Contextual Intelligence

A combination of needs and gaps constitutes an opportunity for innovation. But you can't notice what that is if you don't first look. Many people of good will and strong values might want to see a problem addressed; they might feel outrage and wish that things would get better. What differentiates advanced leaders from noninnovators is that they can see further because of their quality of preparation and attention. They zoom out to see the big picture; they tune in to the context and read the zeitgeist.[20] Often, everything you need to see trends is already there. Maybe it's a small sign of change or backlash relegated to the periphery while conventional wisdom, or the view from the building, focuses only on what seems to be the central trend du jour.

A personal case in point: Many sophisticated business executives and political pundits were so wildly euphoric about global trade and the rise of the internet in the 1990s that they prematurely declared that global capitalism had won. The 1999 protests against the World Trade Organization in Seattle appeared to take them by surprise. The Aspen Institute interviewed me for a podcast about how my 1995 book *World Class* was able to highlight local tensions and backlash against the global economy during all that elite excitement. But it wasn't hard to see signs of coming discontent in my talks in dying mill towns, a Buy American movement, and Ross Perot's populism in the 1992 presidential election. It was a matter of focusing on countertrends.

Reading the zeitgeist isn't like reading the daily newsfeed (although that might be a good start). Innovation begins with someone being aware enough to see a new need, focusing time and attention on things going on in the environment around you that send signals that it's time for a change. Advanced leaders sense new ideas or appetites emerging on the horizon—sometimes because they feel hungry themselves. They notice problems and weaknesses even before they represent full-blown threats. They see the opportunities when external forces change—new technological capabilities, industry upheavals, regulatory shifts, or voter preferences. And then they identify gaps between what is and what could be. The truly visionary function as idea scouts, attentive to early signs of discontinuity, disruption, threat, or opportunity.

Seeing the context is considered a form of intelligence possessed by the most successful leaders. Numerous scholars have tried to define contextual intelligence and link it to effectiveness. The idea that intelligence takes many forms sprang up in the mid-1980s, based on work by psychologists such as Howard Gardner and Robert Sternberg. Gardner named nine forms of intelligence; Sternberg's model involved three kinds—creative, analytical, and practical, which involve being attuned to the environment.[21] Anthony Mayo and Nitin Nohria picked up on the practical side of Sternberg's triarchy in their study of the most successful business leaders of the twentieth century, finding that contextual intelligence was vital to their success.[22] They concluded that those highly successful top leaders' most defining characteristic was a profound sensitivity to macrolevel contextual factors and an ability to make sense of their time and seize those opportunities.

By appreciating history, staying abreast of news about geopolitics and technology, traveling widely, and thinking strategically, leaders with contextual intelligence could read the zeitgeist or the mood of the times. They could adjust their behaviors to circumstances and take advantage of them. In contrast, those who couldn't see differences and couldn't adjust often failed when they tried to move from one context to another, as Tarun Khanna showed in his studies of the difficulties Western companies have had in entering emerging markets.[23]

Numerous experts on innovation and change have attempted to deconstruct the qualities contributing to contextual intelligence. One calls it thinking in 3D, using hindsight, insight, and foresight to integrate the past, present, and future to see possibilities.[24] Many analysts point to curiosity, effort, and sheer serendipity—being in the right place at the time.[25] Others present variations on preparation and thoughtful concentration, which can provide fodder for eureka moments of sudden discovery—as in the saying that fortune favors the prepared mind, or, in a more recent variation I coined after studying innovation: instant success takes time.

Noticing What Others Miss

Of course, potential advanced leaders must be ready to receive the idea. Readiness means that they are already looking. Their antennae are up. They are attentive and prepared because experience helps them understand the significance of what they are seeing—or not seeing— and they are not overly constrained by the demands of their jobs. Sometimes they look at the same thing repeatedly, not really paying attention until a discordant note strikes, and it clicks. Eric Schwartz got the idea for Citizen Schools, which became a nationwide after-school program, after working inside public schools but not thinking much about what happened after the school day ended, until he started to notice ever-larger groups of students milling around on street corners after school with nothing to do.[26]

It's even likelier that someone from outside the field will see what others miss. David Weinstein, a lawyer for thirty-three years who became the chief administrative officer for Fidelity Investments, wanted to do something to help improve education and was told that literacy education was the rage. After he explored the field with a stranger's perspective, he found something missing: writing skills. Funding was going into teaching children to read, but not to write. He began to hatch the idea for Write the World, web-based peer-reviewed writing contests for middle school students.[27]

Finding ideas for social innovation resembles the process used to produce scientific breakthroughs. Astronomer Abraham Loeb declared in *Scientific American* that scientific innovation is nurtured by informal dialogues in environments where mistakes are tolerated and critical thinking is encouraged.[28] He confirmed the advanced leadership principle that a fertile mind bears fruit when there is the freedom to roam without being bound by traditional thinking or distracted by practical concerns.

The lens through which leaders view the world can help or hinder their abilities to see new possibilities that can address intractable problems or break institutional impasses. Let's add the zoom function on digital devices to the mental kaleidoscope to help with idea-catching.[29] Zoom in and get a close look at select details and put an individual face on data and statistics, feeling the emotional power of individual stories—but perhaps end up too close to the particulars to make sense of them or to see possibilities for change. Zoom out and see the big picture, the whole territory, with all facets of a big, intractable institutional problem displayed like one enlarged Google map. Leaders can see which roads are already well traveled. There's no point in choosing those. They're crowded and not working anyway; that's why there are continuing problems. It is better to focus on what seems to be missing—what the map doesn't show.

As important as it is to know what's there, it's often more important to notice what isn't there. When you map the territory, you can see it broadly and then zoom in on the gaps. Perhaps the network has structural holes—that's sociologist Ronald Burt's important idea about gaps where networks don't connect everyone.[30] Social innovators might see many holes that become potholes for progress (e.g., minority schoolchildren in excellent but mostly minority charter schools or first-generation college students from rural areas who lack connections outside their groups to meet employers who might offer jobs). There are also gaps to be found in so-called institutional voids, where there is no smooth path from one kind of activity to another, whether literally in the absence of transportation or the absence of markets for goods, or figuratively in the absence of intermediaries such as bankers or job recruiters who can make introductions to resources. Troubled social systems in the developing world have institutional voids—areas that are missing a critical aspect taken for granted in the developed world; poor communities face institutional voids.

Holes and voids are exactly the issues that create opportunities for advanced leaders to do something new to fill them. Gilberto Dimenstein's idea for Catraca Livre was to fill a hole by providing information and access to services for people living on the fringes of the city who were disconnected from the social networks enjoyed by the more privileged. Vivian Derryck saw the void between business, civil society, and governments in Africa and pledged to fill it. Doug Rauch found inner-city food deserts were full of institutional voids into which the poor could easily fall, and he envisioned reconfiguring social patterns across the food chain.

* * *

People aspiring to advanced leadership want to make the biggest differences they can. But their range of action is guided and limited by the nature of the three Cs they bring: the nature of their own experience and capabilities; the resources, capital, or cash to which they have access; and their networks of connections. It's not surprising that aspiring advanced leaders who roam far and wide in their journey of discovery end up close to home in the institutional innovations they choose to pursue.

A Basis for Commitment: The Personal Angle

Reading the zeitgeist, or simply the daily news, doesn't tell you what to do. The same sense of outrage, the same big dream, can point people in very different directions depending on their backgrounds, interests, and resources. Even the same process of kaleidoscope thinking, zooming out and in, and taking far-afield trips can produce diverse solutions given individual situations. Random walks might take people to diverse places. And that's a good thing. Big, intractable institutional challenges remain unsolved because establishment castles are well fortified; a thousand flowers must be seeded to provide opening wedges in the quest for solutions. That's a classic lesson about innovation: to get more innovation, one must try more things.

How three different leaders decided to pursue the same big, intractable challenge makes the point that there is no single best target for innovation or perfect path to begin. The form that social innovation takes depends on the commitment that an aspiring advanced leader is willing and able to make. We can see that in the stories of three people who defined different kinds of projects to reduce gun violence.

Gun violence certainly qualifies as a big institutional challenge. In the United States, gun violence has been a problem without a solution for many decades. The right to bear arms is enshrined in the US Constitution. Yet portions of the public are vulnerable to accidental or malicious use of guns. Even though data show that overall rates of gun violence and gun homicides have been declining, large swaths of the public remain concerned about deaths from mass shootings, particularly in schools. Many groups have tried unsuccessfully to pass new gun laws at the federal level, with some limited successes at the state level, but any hint of gun control has been fiercely opposed by gun rights supporters and their powerful lobby, the National Rifle Association (NRA). And there is a private sector ecosystem of manufacturers, distributors, and dealers.

This cross-sector multistakeholder mix makes the gun issue a prime target (so to speak) for advanced leadership and an illuminating illustration of the variations in how potential innovators seek an approach that can cut through the impasse to create significant change. Consider the stories of three aspiring institutional change agents who worked independently to find an approach that fit their capabilities.

Gareth Glaser, Russell Sternlicht, and Christianna Wood were not well acquainted; only two of them even knew each other. They didn't have much in common in their backgrounds or interests, except that their reading of the zeitgeist took them to a similar big institutional goal. They each wanted to do something about lives lost to firearms in America by promoting gun safety. Each had been upset by mass murders and gun suicides. Each had concluded that it was futile to take on the gun rights lobby; they wanted to find a way to at least make guns safer. But they pinned down the goal in different ways, setting out on three different paths. For Wood, it was financial pressure through industry investment principles; for Sternlicht, it was a mass advocacy membership organization; and for Glaser, it was a for-profit new technology manufacturing operation. They brought unique, personal lenses as they zoomed out and in, and they discovered different gaps in established structures depending on what they saw.[31]

Investor financial pressure. Christy Wood made a beeline from her capabilities and connections straight to a practical project. A no-nonsense financial industry leader, she had years of experience as CEO or top executive of investment management companies in the private sector (Capital Z Asset Management and Denver Investment Advisors) and public sectors (hundred-billion-dollar public funds). While working as a senior investment officer of CalPERS, the California State pension fund, she had resisted calls for divestiture from publicly scorned companies, arguing, she recalled, that "it is by virtue of owning shares that we have a say in what companies do," preferring shareholder activism to exit. She took that stance to the NGO boards she chaired, such as the International Corporate Governance Network and the Global Reporting Initiative, and her role as a trustee of Vassar College helping look after its endowment.

Mass shootings at Marjory Stoneman Douglas High School in Parkland, Florida, on February 14, 2018, aroused national outrage, including Wood's fierce anger. Round-the-clock coverage of the articulate band of student survivors who vowed activism for change coincided with Wood's post–Capital Z musings about what kind of venture to pursue next. She began by zooming in on her familiar territory. Chatting with former corporate governance colleagues, she expressed surprise that there were no corporate responsibility standards for firearms that financial institutions could use to pressure the manufacturers or distributors in their portfolios toward practices that would keep communities safer.

She had no personal ties with Parkland, but she felt she knew what to do. "It was really obvious to me right away that we needed principles, and we needed signatories," she said. By April, positive reactions from Chris Ailman, chief investment officer of the CalSTRS, the enormous teachers' pension fund, gave her an "epiphany, like a light bulb went off," that she was on to something. Together, they led a meeting around a borrowed conference room table with representatives of five funds, including CalSTRS and the State of Florida, and three large wealth-management firms to begin drafting principles and finding collaborators. On November 14, 2018, Wood and CalSTRS issued five principles for making civilian firearms safer, securer, and easier to trace, a goal endorsed by thirteen signatories managing over $4.8 trillion in investments, adding Connecticut,

Maine, Maryland, and San Francisco to the public funds and two private investment managers. Wood presented the principles as a sensible, nonpartisan form of risk reduction for asset managers and asset investors.

The announcement was dramatic enough that it garnered major national press, and the idea was distinctive enough that it immediately won an award for 2018 from a corporate governance association. But the work was just beginning. Wood and colleagues had thrown a few pebbles into the pond to begin the ripples of change. And there was work ahead with manufacturers, distributors, and retailers, as their principle 5 indicated: "Participants in the civilian firearms industry should work collaboratively, communicate, and engage with all the signatories of these Principles to design, adopt, and disclose measures and metrics demonstrating both best practices and their commitment to promoting these Principles."[32]

A new national membership and lobbying organization. For Russell Sternlicht, a different approach to the gun safety target came to mind, one a notch more emotional and much more social, but one that required a great deal of zooming out because he didn't know the territory. The 2012 Aurora, Colorado, and Newtown, Connecticut, school shootings ate away at him, he recalled, especially the similarity between the Sandy Hook Elementary School victims and his own young children. He became a single-issue voter, voting against otherwise-attractive candidates because of their lack of support for doing something about gun violence. This concern remained in the back of his mind as he built on his success in hotel management, working with his older brother, the founder of Starwood Capital; then working on luxury brand-building (Baccarat crystal and Taittinger champagne); and creating financial vehicles in Europe and the United States.

On February 22, 2018, he watched a CNN town hall with the Parkland student survivor-activists debating NRA spokesperson

Dana Loesch on the other side, with Florida's US senator Marco Rubio ostensibly in the middle. When Sternlicht heard Rubio promise to bring gun legislation to the Senate floor, he yelled at his big flat-screen TV, "We'll see!" expressing his skepticism and concern. Sure enough, four days later some leaders in the US House of Representatives told the media that there would be no discussion of gun legislation in this Congress. A heartbroken Sternlicht raged with frustration at government inaction. He vowed to try to find a way to tackle the problem.

This was easier said than done. One barrier was that he didn't own a gun. He had never fired one, and he didn't think he knew anyone who did own a gun. (That later proved to be wrong.) So he zoomed out to learn all he could.

He roamed through research on political attitudes. Polls showed that an overwhelming majority favored some kinds of gun-safety legislation, yet politicians didn't pass those simple, specific solutions. He dug into the power of the NRA, finding, to his surprise, that its membership represented only a small fraction of US gun owners. He pondered the successes and failures (mainly the failures) of nonprofits such as Everytown for Gun Safety, which combined Mayors against Illegal Guns founded by Michael Bloomberg in 2006 with Moms Demand Action for Gun Sense in America.[33]

He spoke to a politically diverse set of business associates and friends to get their views. From these random walk conversations, he learned the answers to questions he had never asked before. He was shocked to find that "my closest friend actually owns a gun, and I had no idea about it. One of my other friends carries a gun with him. I had no idea. I literally did a double take and said, 'Excuse me?'" He tapped business contacts in areas such as Texas and Georgia, places where gun ownership is part of the culture, passed down from generation to generation. All told, he spoke with about forty people across the South, about half of whom were NRA members, as well as several more gun-owning friends.

His networking tapped the strength of weak ties, to use Mark Granovetter's felicitous phrase—someone he didn't know particularly well could introduce him to an entirely new set of contacts. A distant acquaintance outside his inner circle introduced him to Casey Woods, a Southerner from the heart of "gun country" and head of Arms with Ethics (AwE), which works at the community level to help stop the illegal movement of guns and raise awareness of proper gun safety storage. In April 2016, AwE had won a Boston Foundation grant to support a partnership with the city of Boston, where Sternlicht lived, announced by the mayor and police commissioner at a New England summit on gun violence. Over an intense dinner on one of Wood's trips to Boston, she gave a thick description of her experience. Sternlicht's mental kaleidoscope shook and produced two big ideas. The first was an old favorite: authenticity. The second was the big brainstorm: beat the NRA at its own game by forming a large organization that people paid to join and, in turn, received membership benefits—an organization that, he believed, could be mobilized as a voting bloc.[34]

Sternlicht began to feel that the debate was framed too narrowly and stuck in silos: gun rights versus gun control. He realized that he needed an organization that was viewed as protecting gun rights while promoting gun safety (a less sensitive term for gun control). He wanted to occupy a nonpartisan middle ground outside the hard-and-fast current institutional structures: NRA and Everytown. Sternlicht's sweet spot was consumers and brands, so he felt that rallying the public and building a brand and a sense of community would be the way to go, especially with the right name.

Sternlicht's kaleidoscope twist gave him a breakthrough idea: the name SAFE—Second Amendment for Everyone. The name had potential power and resonance. Now he had a direction. That was the first step toward an action plan for creating the organization.

Technology for smart guns. Gareth Glaser found a third, very different angle on the gun violence problem. Instead of organizing a small group of powerful stakeholders or a large group of consumers in the general public to put on the pressure, he decided to go directly to the gun itself. It took him a great deal of wandering and many far-afield trips to come to the idea that technology could be used to make smart guns, and smart guns could save lives well beyond mass shootings. For him, this became a moral quest. It used his managerial expertise, but even more than that, it became a consuming passion.

Glaser's background as a lawyer and business executive, and his diverse interests in health and the environment, didn't appear to give him a direct line to smart guns. But a set of personal experiences were rolling around in his kaleidoscope, and he zoomed out widely to get the big picture.

Glaser had been vice president of finance and counsel at an eye-care products company named Alcon in Fort Worth. He had a vivid memory of a call he received from one of the members of his team. "On a Saturday in early 2001," he said, "she called to say that she might not be able to come to work on Monday because her son had accidentally shot himself in the head." Later, when volunteering at the Breckenridge Outdoor Education Center in Colorado, which helped disabled people participate in outdoor activities, he worked with wounded veterans who had served in Iraq. "That brought home to me what gunshots can do to people," he recalled. These and other experiences witnessing the effects of gun-related injuries firsthand made it a moral imperative for him to do something.

He thought about using his legal background to do something about the illegal trafficking of guns. Then he encountered what he considered startling statistics: although mass shootings occupied the lion's share of public consciousness, the majority of gun deaths in the United States were suicides, followed by homicides and accidents, including dramatic ones involving children mishandling guns found in their homes. Deeply troubled by this, he thought about doing something for the population affected by suicides, perhaps organizing communities of survivors. But he saw that he had no expertise and no credibility on this issue, and there were many others with greater knowledge and connections who were already addressing this issue. This realization affected him physically, Glaser said. "I literally couldn't sleep at night. I didn't know how I was going to do it. I didn't know where to start. It didn't feel right."

He had tuned in to a wide context, and one of the items he had run across was advances in technology. He had also reflected about what he had learned about behavior change in public health; for example, deaths and injuries from car accidents were reduced not by exhorting people to change their driving habits but by surrounding them with safety. Air bags and seat belts were more effective than trying to get people to change their habits. He started to realize that "guns were the only product out there that has [sic] not undergone any kind of technological safety improvement in over one hundred years." But there were very few efforts to use technology to reinvent the gun. He became enthralled with the idea of saving at least ten thousand lives a year from gun accidents and suicides using someone else's gun, and perhaps triple that number of injuries.

With that concept in mind, using his finance and business experience, he thought he would start a fund to invest in smart guns. Talking widely about this idea garnered him an invitation to speak at a conference on smart guns in Washington, DC. After his piece of the program, he was approached by Ralph Fascitelli and Ernst Mauch about founding with them a company to manufacture smart guns. That was exactly what he wanted to do. "Instead of relying on other people to do it and funding their effort, why not do it myself?" he recalled. "I'm not an engineer. There's no way I could develop the technology by itself. But when it came to all the rest of it, it seemed to me that, yes, that's something I could do." Glaser became CEO of smart gun start-up LodeStar Firearms. LodeStar's plan was to produce personalized guns that could be fired only by authorized users, vastly reducing the risk of childhood gun accidents, suicides using someone else's gun, and even crimes using stolen guns. Glaser's moral outrage was channeled into the utilitarian practicality of using his skills. Glaser's dream of changing the gun world was underway.

Passion and Commitment

One big problem, three paths to an idea, three noncompeting innovations . . . these distinctive starting points for tackling a big issue reflect different mixes of motivation unique to each individual. For leaders to undertake the hard work of institutional innovation—characterized, as I've said earlier, by unclear or conflicting goals, multiple competing stakeholders, and no clear paths—they must have a passion for the journey, meaning a strong belief. The ultimate part of finding an idea is matching it with what the leader cares about and feels he can do.

Commitment to a cause involves three dimensions of human psychology: cognitive, socioemotional, and moral. Rational thought finds an instrumental purpose that is mainly utilitarian. Emotional feelings stress social bonds; commitment is through membership in a group. Morally driven commitment is values based; it involves a clear sense of a higher purpose, a motivating cause—almost a spiritual quest. This can sound theoretical, except that we all encounter these dimensions every day, and it affects how much time and effort we're willing to put in at work, whether we decide to stay married or to seek new partners, or whether we care about turning our complaints into positive action or just imbibing those "fine whines" without doing anything.

In some of my earliest work, I saw that these dimensions explained the basis for commitment to new or alternative communities that countered norms of the society around them. I later identified similar dimensions of commitment to workplace engagement in technology companies facing strong competition for talent.[35] *Mastery* is the cognitive dimension defining how much the person would learn and grow in the job. *Membership* defines the socioemotional dimension, deriving from the bonds among fellow workers, including the sense that people belonged because they were accepted for who they are. *Meaning* is the moral dimension, the sense of purpose stemming from the feeling that the organization stands for something noble, almost transcendent—a higher purpose that makes a difference for the world.

I found that it takes all three dimensions to bind people to a cause that is sometimes uncomfortable or controversial. Instrumental, emotional, and moral or spiritual motivations sustained communities that were considered strange and different. It also takes all three dimensions to retain talented employees who are in demand and have numerous choices (e.g., Silicon Valley engineers who can easily job-hop). Purely instrumental or utilitarian commitment is easily undone. Just applying one's skills and having opportunities to succeed isn't enough to bind people; there is always a better offer or a more alluring chance to be a social innovator. Even if the person has sacrificed to get started, which sets cognitive dissonance in motion (this must be worth a lot if I get so little for it), it is still possible to cut one's losses and find another mission. Social ties are stronger bases for commitment, because sentiment creates attachments, and peer group pressure can kick in. But it's the third dimension of purpose and meaning that cements the deal for advanced leadership: moral outrage translated into a moral quest.

It's hard to squeeze people and their motivations into categories, and most actions have multiple determinants. But the analysis can be illuminating. Advanced leadership involves aspiring to do great but difficult and complex work. It's not enough to know that you have the skills. It's even more important to find the purpose at the center, the purpose that gives rise to the big dream in the first place. Leaders who create extraordinary new possibilities are passionate about their mission and tenacious in pursuit of it. Many people have good ideas, but fewer are willing to put themselves on the line for them. Passionate commitment separates good intentions but mere opportunism from real accomplishments.

An inner journey of soul-searching can match the outer random walks and far-afield trips to determine the direction and viability of the idea for change. Aspiring advanced leaders can ask themselves a series of questions about whether their passions match their aspirations. These are the kind of questions that Gilberto Dimenstein might have pondered in his urban garden in São Paulo, that Vanessa Kirsch might have mentioned in the New England swimming pool, that Vivian Derryck might have thought about on a plane to Africa, or that Doug Rauch might have asked on his quest to find a way to end hunger:

- Have I dreamed about something like this for a long time?
- Do I feel strongly about the need for this?
- Does the idea fit my long-held beliefs, values, and convictions?
- Do I think that this is vital for the future of people I care about?
- Do I get excited when I think about it and convey excitement when I talk about it?
- Am I convinced that this can be accomplished?
- Am I willing to put my credibility on the line to promise action on it?
- Am I willing to spend time to sell it to others who might not understand or support it?
- Can I make this the major focus of my activities?
- Do I feel strongly enough to ignore negativity and fight for this?
- Am I committed to seeing this through over the long haul?

Passing the passion test doesn't guarantee success, but without it, the journey from idea to impact can't even begin.

* * *

Purpose lies at the intersection of passion, expertise, and the wider world's needs.

Given the time and energy it takes to dream, leaders might as well dream big. Then they exercise curiosity, take random walks and far-afield trips, and shake up their thinking like a kaleidoscope to find new connections. They zoom out to map the territory, zoom in to put a human face on the problem, and identify gaps, holes, or voids that present opportunities for new action. They are open to redefinitions and serendipity. And they find their own unique basis for commitment given their personal motivations and the assets they bring.

The innovation idea is just the starting point for advanced leadership. The concept might change; it might not lead to action; and it might not actually work. But the multiple conversations that give rise to ideas also lay the groundwork for the next steps: absorbing reactions to determine how to tell the right story and get change underway.

4

REVISITING THE PAST TO CREATE THE FUTURE

Telling the Right Story

How many times have you heard the same complaints about the failure to move from an idea to the launch of an innovation? *I thought the facts would speak for themselves. I thought the logic would do it. I forgot I needed buy-in. I thought people knew me and would rush to help. I forgot that they didn't see what I did.* Projects can fail before they even get off the ground unless leaders tell a story that convinces others to support change.

Carol Hallquist could have fallen into that trap. She was taken by surprise by all the ways that her idea did not speak for itself. It was hard to fathom. Her dream was big, her motivation was pure, and her credibility was high. Her reading of the community mood said that there was consensus about the importance of the issue, and she knew she could contribute a valuable innovation. So why was there resistance from the people she was trying to serve?

Hallquist was a well-known civic leader and a former corporate executive at Hallmark in Kansas City, Missouri, where, among other things, she had helped fund many local service organizations.

An energetic leader who made friends easily, she hoped to invest her stash of capabilities, connections, and cash to spark innovation in public school districts, first locally and then throughout the United States. She wanted to make sure that all schools, regardless of their location, funding, or the family circumstances of their student populations, had access to resources that supported learning. After going on the road and visiting a wide range of schools, she uncovered a gap in school improvement efforts—that most initiatives addressed students and teachers, but there seemed to be little or nothing for principals, whose leadership of schools could be unleashed to make giant strides in excellence. She called her idea Principals Connect. She would match principals who were seeking help finding resources or solving problems with accomplished people across sectors who could get them what they needed. The narrative was simple and straightforward, and there were no strings, she thought, only benefits.

Surprise, surprise. Despite the benign intent and potential value of the idea, suspicion and skepticism soon surfaced on many fronts. There were questions about her motives. Was she doing it to have something to talk about at cocktail parties? There was paranoia about her role in going to schools to sign up principals. Was she a spy? (She understood that a recent appointment to the state board of education might hamper her local efforts.) There was passive resistance; some principals didn't return phone calls. There was suspicion by nonprofit leaders with similar-sounding missions. Was she poaching from their territories? Would she siphon off their donors? There was a refusal to budge, even on the part of some school constituencies that could get direct, immediate benefits from Principals Connect; they seemed to feel that something was being imposed on them from outside. Outside? Hallquist was starting in her home community where everyone knew her.

She had to hone her message and tell the right story. Hallquist had to patiently repeat her rationale and goal, saying over and over, "We believe in you." Repetition helped overcome the negativity bias—that it takes five positives to overcome one negative. She reinforced her optimistic message in actions as well as words; showing up face-to-face in a principal's office was one indication (never mind that her phone calls hadn't been returned). It took specific demonstrations of intentions and opportunities to make her story credible: a $1,000 donation for bows for a school's string orchestra. It maybe wasn't the best use of her money, but it showed that Principals Connect was there to do what principals themselves defined as important. The fledgling project took school leaders on a field trip to see innovative schools. Teachers' lounges were renovated to turn them into havens for teachers to refuel.

Accumulating evidence of benefits won support for Hallquist's story. Testimonials and referrals were woven into the Principals Connect narrative, which eased access for her project. Her local pilot program was soon gaining momentum, and she was thinking about ways to take it national, where the story had to reach people she couldn't see face-to-face. To get underway, telling the right story is essential.

Persuasion Rules: The Importance of Stories

The art of leadership is the exercise of influence and persuasion. Former US president Dwight D. Eisenhower called this getting other people to feel that they want to do what you'd like them to do—and he learned the importance of persuasion at the helm of the quintessential command structure, as one of only five army five-star generals in American history, so if anyone could issue orders, he could. But formal command isn't all it's cracked up to be. Leaders within organizations who are supposedly in charge of one element often don't control other elements required to implement their ideas, whether other departments or external entities. They, too, must work through influence rather than authority. Furthermore, organizational practices in the digital age mean that hierarchies have loosened, and flexible project teams are coming to predominate in workplaces and communities. So persuasion rules (so to speak).

The challenge becomes greater the further you move outside the building to envision a big, messy, cross-sector institutional change. Consider how much more essential it is to convince other people when you address a problem for which you have no authority whatsoever. For example, who "owns" the problem of global warming or hunger in a city? How many leaders lay claim to solutions to the opioid epidemic or the gun violence issue? And even if you should be miraculously appointed as the "czar" for such matters on behalf of a government entity or a major corporation, that role would not by itself be enough to change anyone's behavior. Expectations, assumptions, and conventional understandings lurk in the background as reasons to maintain the status quo, sometimes unquestioned and sometimes promoted by current stakeholders to maintain their privileges. The advanced leader's task is not to just have a great idea; it is to convince other people they should support it.

That's why telling the right story is so important. If you don't like how things are going and want to lead change, tell a different story. That's often a first step in breaking out of established structures to tackle big societal issues.

Every significant change involves a campaign to win hearts and minds for new actions, and stories are an essential component. Stories can awaken interest and energy to pursue new ways to address difficult challenges. How problems and potential solutions are framed begins to determine the fate of the idea. It's critical to find the narrative threads that connect actions through time to desirable outcomes—from the past of once upon a time to the imagined future of living happily ever after.

Change is never a certainty; it is always only a possibility. Many possible futures can unfold, depending on human choices. The stories we tell ourselves—our cultural assumptions—are often the limiting factor in whether we act, and they shape the nature of any actions we choose to take. It is too easy to continue on a course set by conventional narratives about how things came to be and why they'll never change. Indeed, in the beginning of the journey to social impact, when leaders first decide to follow their dreams, the major impediment they face is often not outright hostility from other people; it is apathy, indifference, and inertia, which prevent finding allies and building support. Being ignored can sometimes be worse than being resisted.

Narratives are powerful leadership tools for awakening enthusiasm for change. Research has found that people remember stories more readily than they remember numbers, and stories motivate action. For example, when donors are given statistical evidence of a problem, such as the percentage of children living in poverty, levels of charitable donations rise a little. But when donors read a story about one poor child, giving levels rise even higher. Analysts of leadership have shown that organizational stories are more vivid and persuasive than quantitative data and are better at conveying values or other ideas hard to describe in a conventional way. Stanford professor Joanne Martin was among early analysts to point to the shortcomings of communication by data, charts, and graphs in organizations compared to symbolic forms of communication such as stories passed from employee to employee, repeated and embellished until achieving the status of legends. In a series of experiments, she found that Coast Guard recruits and other students remembered stories about policies better than they retained abstract data (though they didn't necessarily understand the policies any better).[1]

In a similar vein, leadership consultants argue that stories are not only memorable, but they can also help people make important decisions, cope with change, learn valuable lessons, and work through history. Although stories don't replace analytical thinking, storytelling enables "us to imagine new perspectives and is ideally suited to communicating change and stimulating innovation," wrote Stephen Deming, a former World Bank manager. In organizational settings, he proposed, storytelling helps leaders learn to listen and forge a deeper bond with employees.[2]

When moving beyond single organizations to tackle big institutional problems, forging bonds and justifying actions through storytelling is even more important. In challenging the status quo, aspiring advanced leaders must craft a compelling narrative to support their visions for change. There are three major pillars of a narrative that can support institutional change: (1) to undo myths from the past and challenge conventional stories, in essence rewriting history; (2) to make the story roomy enough to include diverse stakeholders under a big tent; and (3) to develop demonstrations that prove the concept, in the form of pilot programs or prototypes. These connect the past and present to the future, raising aspirations and making change seem both necessary and plausible.

Confronting the Past: Mitch Landrieu Tells a New Story

First, advanced leaders must contend with the past. Change is constrained by conventional narratives that make the present seem like an inevitable outgrowth of the past and that make the future seem like an unchanging extrapolation. Change is even harder when problems are messy, complex, and contentious, and the conventional story favors dominant groups that maintain their power because the story says that they should. People fear questioning that dominant narrative.

The past is often not one story but many; it is often not fully understood. But its concrete manifestations are found in an array of legacy structures and systems. In Mitch Landrieu's case, the past was literally concrete. The past took the form of four statues that reflected a long-unquestioned power-reinforcing narrative that had to be rewritten in order to change one corner of the world.

Mayor Mitch Landrieu had a dream: to make New Orleans a diverse, inclusive city of the future. To further the cause of racial inclusion and justice, he had to tell the right story. So he crafted a new narrative that reframed the then dominant view of history. That started a significant process of culture change around a seemingly intractable American dilemma.

It's important to know something about Mitch Landrieu's experience and values. I first met him when he was a practicing lawyer and member of the part-time Louisiana state legislature. He was a champion of national service for America, a stance he continued when he was later elected lieutenant governor. In late summer 2005, when the devastating Hurricane Katrina struck New Orleans, he was heavily involved in disaster recovery in his lieutenant governor role, even personally steering boats into water-filled streets to rescue people from rooftops. He also jumped in to show support for Jennifer Eplett Reilly, a Baton Rouge civic leader, as she established new City Year youth corps in New Orleans and Baton Rouge for immediate emergency education efforts.

I saw Landrieu again in the spring of 2009 when I invited him to speak about the aftermath of Katrina; he had left his state position and was preparing to run for mayor of New Orleans. A few months after that, in June 2009, I brought a group to see the situation on the ground. Landrieu joined us in a vegetable-filled school garden, called an *edible schoolyard*, at a New Orleans public charter school, a new model for pushing the reconstructed schools to excellence. The school, which City Year corps members and Teach for America teachers served, was in the Ninth Ward, a racially mixed neighborhood where Landrieu had grown up and still lived at that time. That fall he was elected mayor, taking office in 2010.

He had always been a leader, but as mayor of a city still rebuilding after the destructive hurricane, the scope of issues widened. He had to continue a massive rethinking of public institutions begun by other leaders in the Katrina recovery effort (e.g., innovative charter schools instead of traditional public schools, or localized community health clinics instead of dependence on central hospitals). These were projects definitely outside the buildings. But as New Orleans became a majority-black city, racial justice was the big, intractable issue that moved him further outside the building to exercise advanced leadership.

The city was preparing for its three hundredth anniversary. Landrieu hoped that renowned jazz artist Wynton Marsalis, a New Orleans native and old friend who headed Jazz at Lincoln Center in New York, would return to join the tricentennial commission planning the celebration.[3] They met for coffee in what turned out to be a kaleidoscope-shaking moment for Landrieu. Marsalis pointed out that some Confederate statues in city parks that Landrieu had seen all his life and had barely noticed as a white person were deeply offensive to black residents, who saw them as monuments to slavery and white supremacy. Black luminaries, such as jazz legend Louis Armstrong, moved away because of that culture in the city, symbolized by four statues. So Landrieu started noticing. Seeing and listening, he knew that it was time to break with tradition and change the symbols of the city.

Ideals of fairness and inclusion had been engrained in him from childhood; after all, his father had helped integrate the city while serving as mayor after 1950s Supreme Court rulings ostensibly ended school segregation (but really didn't). In 2016, in his own second term, Mayor Landrieu the son had launched Welcome Table New Orleans, a cross-section of community leaders who met to discuss race and reconciliation with an eye toward developing community projects.

But even so, Landrieu just hadn't understood the significance of those four monuments. It took that coffee conversation with Wynton Marsalis to get Landrieu thinking about whether and how to remove the statues. As he recounted in his book, *In the Shadow of Statues*, he said to Marsalis that it would be a huge political fight. Marsalis replied that it was the right thing to do.[4]

Landrieu also started thinking about the family legacy question that comes up for many advanced leaders: What would he say to his grandchildren? So he looked further. He soon learned about a huge distortion of history in erecting the statues in the first place, and that got under his skin.

When he went to the history books, he found that a dominant narrative had been insidiously crafted that was definitely not the right story when all facets were considered, and, in fact, was not even embraced by most white residents. That dominant narrative, which purported to make the statues worthy of public display, was a myth perpetrated by a radical group well after the South lost the War between the States and well into Reconstruction, an era of de facto segregation, violence, and suppression. The Cult of the Lost Cause, as he learned the movement was called, created a story that made the South somehow noble in a fight for regional autonomy rather than simply fighting to retain slavery as traitors to their country—and losing the fight at that.

It's often said that history is written by the winners, but in this case, it was the losers who had their myth enshrined. The myth was included in an application for a National Registry of Historic Places status for one of the monuments. And Landrieu kept finding more distortions he would have to counter with the right story. He learned from Southern Poverty Law Center data that over seven hundred monuments and statues had been erected well after the Civil War, presumably to keep pushing for racial oppression and injustice with the subtler weapons of symbols and signals. He saw that three statues were of people considered traitors to the United States, two with no real connection to New Orleans anyway; the fourth monument was an obelisk commemorating an attempt to overturn the duly elected government after the war (Landrieu called it the White League Obelisk), a rebellion that virtually ended Reconstruction and led to terrorism against blacks.

Landrieu concluded that the statues were a lie. That lie would prevent New Orleans from becoming the city of the future that he knew it could be. He saw that before he could prepare the city for a better future, he had to rewrite the past. He had to tell the story a different way, using history to make clear the stream of injustices, how they led to the continuing insult to current residents, and why the future could be different.

One would think that position and status as mayor would give Landrieu the power and authority to act on his convictions rather than having to deal with the more ineffable matter of social norms and cultural traditions. That was not at all the case. He carefully researched the legal situation—that the city owned the land and had paid for the statues, that a public nuisance statute could be invoked; but his legal authority was not enough. The fact that Black Lives Matter protests were erupting around the United States, and that southern governors were removing Confederate flags and symbols from state houses, was not enough. Getting a majority vote of the city council was not enough.

Landrieu needed public support, and he also needed to prevent public opposition that could erupt in violence. This was not the usual political controversy. This controversy ranged widely not because of inertia (e.g., people who loved their parks as they are) but because the dominant narrative that was being challenged was the old story of white supremacy. To some people, the very idea of challenging the old narrative was sacrilege, an assault on tradition, and, of course, on their own privilege, but it was the kind of cultural tradition that shields institutions from change and maintains inequities. At the same time, any new narrative had to compete in the political arena with recently elected national conservative officials' views. It was all a big load for a city to deal with. In New Orleans, even a few black officials urged Landrieu to drop the statues issue.

Landrieu persevered. The mechanics were surprisingly challenging because of the controversy. It was nearly impossible to find a crane operator willing to do the work because of threats and intimidation, which also targeted Landrieu's family. And all of that required extra precautions and extra security at the sites. "I was overwhelmed a number of times over the two-year struggle," Landrieu later told me. But he put his fear in perspective when compared to the civil rights movement in the South in the 1960s, when leaders faced beatings and murders. He continued, "Every time I got scared, I thought of John Lewis at the foot of the Edmund Pettis Bridge and all the others who made courageous sacrifices. In that light, what we were doing just looked like a small step."

The controversy over the statues was inflamed because the wrong story had been told, and it was up to Landrieu to exercise leadership by telling the story he felt was the right one—which meant putting the statues in their places (well out of sight). In April and May of 2017, in the dead of night and with tight security, two of the statues, of Jefferson Davis and P. G. T. Beauregard, were removed, one at a time. Workers wore masks to hide their faces, and the names on the trucks carrying the statues were covered to protect identities from threats of retaliation. That got the ball rolling without the world falling apart. The third statue—of Robert E. Lee—and the obelisk were removed in daylight. And the narrative changed.

In a speech in Gallier Hall in New Orleans on May 19, 2017, called "Truth," Landrieu said: "Now is the time to actually make this the city we always should have been, had we gotten it right in the first place . . . We have not erased history: we are becoming part of the city's history by righting the wrong image these monuments represent and crafting a better, more complete future for all our children and for future generations. And unlike when these Confederate monuments were first erected as symbols of white supremacy, we now have a chance to create not only new symbols, but to do it together, as one people." He also said: "Instead of revering a four-year brief historical aberration that we called the Confederacy, we can celebrate all three hundred years of our rich, diverse history as a place named New Orleans and set the tone for the next three hundred years."[5]

In May 2018, Mitch Landrieu received the prestigious Profiles in Courage Award from the John F. Kennedy Library Foundation in

Boston for his work with removing the statues. I was among the audience in a packed banquet room that gave him a prolonged standing ovation for charting a new direction.

Mayors have a broad scope of responsibilities, and they can change the face of a city—streets, building envelopes, public education, police and fire departments, trash pickup, and public parks. But changing hearts and minds—social norms, group cultures, community sentiments, and patterns of who feels welcome and who feels excluded— is much harder. Landrieu could have stayed within the confines of tradition, but he chose to lead people beyond it using the power of a reframed narrative and removing symbols of the obsolete order. The people of New Orleans had a new story to guide them.

Symbols and signals are just the beginning of launching a change effort. There is so much more work to be done to solve big, intractable systems problems. But without tackling beliefs and assumptions, and without telling the right story, a leader can't move very far.

Reframing to Enlarge Possibilities

Change is hard. The right story can become a mantra boosting self-confidence and making it easier to stay the course. Change is also lonely, and even the most advanced of leaders can't do it alone. They need a multitude of allies to get the work done and handle inertia or outright opposition, as we'll see in the next chapter. Sometimes they need catalysts and boosters to rediscover and rewrite the past, as Wynton Marsalis was for Mitch Landrieu, and sometimes they need crane operators and security guards. But they always need to convince their constituents.

Sometimes strategic change is just a matter of reframing. It can involve taking something from the periphery—an anomaly, a demonstration, a small innovation—and redefining it as central. It can be a matter of finding threads in the past that have been neglected and bringing those to the surface, or it can be discovering new facts that point to exciting new possibilities. Shedding new light on the past, not as a set of constraints or excuses, can awaken hope that the current course is not inevitable and that change is possible. Leaders can animate the quest for change by creating a new narrative showing how success will be achieved and why the elements are in place to get there. A different way of viewing the past can suggest a leap into the future. That's one of the things I mean by telling the right story.

Framing is a human cognitive construction, a way to assign meaning and explain where a particular thing fits.[6] There are often several alternative ways to look at the same item, and how it is viewed makes a difference in whether anyone is motivated to act. Consider an example of a systems problem plaguing impoverished communities in developing countries—the kind of problem that well-intentioned first-worlders often wanted to solve: cooking on open fires. Wood fires have been found to have many negative consequences. But is that an environmental problem? A health problem? A labor problem? A nutrition story? An industry market failure problem? This global challenge languished without much attention in US government aid circles because it was historically presented as an environmental matter of air pollution and deforestation. There was little traction until it was presented as a women's health problem (more female deaths are attributed to open fires than infectious diseases) and adopted by the US State Department with that framing.[7] Former Trader Joe's president Doug Rauch had a multifaceted idea for one solution to multiple problems (an environmental dimension of wasted food, an economic problem of poverty, a health dimension involving nutrition), but that was difficult to present to any one audience, each of which tended to be interested in only one part.

Reframing an old problem can point to more promising solutions. It can open possibilities for new partnerships across sectors as common themes are discovered. Hospitals can become hospitable and learn from the hospitality industry (Ritz-Carlton and Disney have hosted many hospital administrators) when physical recovery is reframed in terms of a more holistic issue of healing involving aesthetics and comfort as well as medical treatment. Homelessness can be reduced when reframed as joblessness, suggesting new actions. Reframing the image of women by telling a different history (sometimes itself reframed as *herstory*) is an important tool for gender equality activists such as Webby Awards founder Tiffany Shlain, who produced *50/50: Rethinking the Past, Present, and Future of Women + Power* to change the narrative about women leaders.[8]

A new narrative helped Milwaukee revitalize. Milwaukee's problems as a Rust Belt city were different from New Orleans's issues as a southern city, but change there also required finding new threads in the past to weave into a narrative for the future. Civic leaders changed the city's story from manufacturing decline to growth as a global water hub. A new narrative connected and publicized previously isolated pieces: In the mid-2000s, a few CEOs of pipe and valve manufacturers, who had been considered to be in the plumbing supply industry, got the kaleidoscope brainstorm that they were actually in the water industry, and so were the city's famous breweries—not to mention the Great Lakes fishing on the city's edges. This new narrative reshaped Milwaukeeans' views of their own history and became the foundation for a water council instead of the traditional industry silos, such as manufacturing or not. The council put Milwaukee on the global stage (as one of three UN Global Compact water hubs), helped build America's first graduate school of freshwater sciences, and supported urban agriculture and aquaculture. Entrepreneurs using the latest technologies for energy and water conservation went to work growing local fish and vegetables in abandoned factories.[9] Revisiting the past helped Milwaukee create the future.

Similarly, in the corporate world, CVS Health, which began life as Consumer Value Stores, reframed its mission away from being just a retail pharmacy to innovating to promote better health. CEO Larry Merlo and chief medical officer Troyen Brennan, along with other company leaders, exhibited the courage of a statue-removing Mayor Landrieu by removing tobacco products from CVS stores in 2014. Their new narrative about helping people on the path to better health supported opportunities in new directions: walk-in medical clinics, pharmacy benefit services, and health management, including counseling for people who wanted to stop smoking.

Legacy narratives inherited from the past should be rewritten when they inhibit rather than inspire. Individuals and institutions can get bogged down by narratives that suggest inevitability—"it has always been this way, it was meant to be this way, and it couldn't possibly change." Troubled people mired in despair often tell themselves stories that suggest everything is stacked against them, and so they just give up. At the other end of the continuum, dominant groups tell stories to prevent change that glorify destiny and entitlement—a sure sign of overconfidence that breeds complacency and blinds people to disruptive forces lurking at their doorstep. This might be why national television broadcasters, for example, were notoriously slow to adapt to the digital era.

Pitch a Big Tent: A Story That Enlists and Empowers

A second key element of the right story is that it offers a big enough tent to include those people and organizations with a role to play in a world-changing innovation. The right story is capacious. It expresses a vision that engages and inspires people, one that enlists others in the cause and empowers them to take action that supports innovation and change. The right story has room for a wide swath of people who can make it their story too. By telling the right story, a leader not only persuades people of the value and feasibility of the mission; he or she builds followers, whether those are allies and partners, members of affected communities, or individuals who are enticed to change their minds and undertake new actions. The right story engages, enlists, and empowers.

The late Nelson Mandela, the first democratically elected president of South Africa, was a master of the capacious story. This is one reason that this man, incarcerated for twenty-seven years and called a terrorist by the US government, emerged as one of the world's most highly admired leaders, including in the United States. After South Africa ended decades of apartheid that had excluded and oppressed the black population, Mandela's messages said strongly that he was not going to retaliate by doing the same thing to the former oppressors. In every speech and media appearance, he made it clear that he would be president of all the people, including former apartheid advocates. He famously wore the colors of the all-white rugby team when it played the championship game in Johannesburg. He was steadfast in promoting the narrative that running the nation meant moving forward together, with everyone needed to do their part and ready to display their best selves. Thus, he could lead the first steps in big multi-institutional change while avoiding degeneration into the violence and internecine warfare that has plagued many other African and developing nations.[10]

In a smaller way but on a similarly grand stage, Torsten Thiele had to make clear that his Global Ocean Trust (which I described in chapter 1) was intended to work in concert with every other organization seeking new pathways to enhancing ocean health while Thiele brought a new private sector venture focus. Thiele repeated his big tent vision often in every forum he attended, and he attended many events in every part of the world; indeed, his presence and contributions helped show his interest in the work of many current organizations. He wasn't bypassing them; he wanted to include them. He wasn't replacing them; he was augmenting them.

A big tent builds on five elements of the pitch.

1. *Name and brand.* Conveying roominess can start with giving the project a memorable name, like putting up a shingle to identify

what the leader is trying to do. Calling Thomas Santel's project to improve educational outcomes through healthy early childhoods Raising St. Louis was a well-expressed invitation to join a successful change project because the title suggested that the entire community could be involved and could benefit from a raised-up community. If his narrative had been directed at only some people, with no room for others, then it would have immediately invited backlash. That tinge of controversy, like a whiff of scandal, would then become the story, swamping the noble purpose. It's all too easy for leaders with good intentions to find themselves moved away from a grand mission into political conflict and contentiousness.[11]

That's why Doug Rauch, the former Trader Joe's executive, struggled so long with the name for his venture to end hunger while solving environmental problems, which eventually became the retail stores named Daily Table. He had pinned his dream down into a new retail concept to use otherwise-wasted (and greenhouse gas–emitting) healthy food to feed lower-income communities nutritiously and affordably. He could find board members and funders with a PowerPoint pitch deck with numbers, charts, and arrows, but getting community support was much more delicate. What if the people you were trying to help didn't want your help? That's a familiar dilemma for advanced leaders, especially those viewed as outsiders. He had to make sure that the narrative about his intentions and the outcomes truly included community members in welcoming ways.

That meant he had to have the right story about the community in his own mind so that they would see that in him. He had to treat people with respect and honor their dignity—the poor were wary of handouts and suspicious of outsiders imposing their own ideas. Many low-income people saw themselves as down on their luck, not as permanently flawed. The idea of leftovers would be insulting, so the environmental side of the story—reducing wasted food—couldn't be out front.

To understand nuances, advanced leaders can rely on focus groups just as businesses do to understand their customers, and on street data from wandering around and talking with people informally. A focus group helped Rauch settle on his innovation's Daily Table name. The Daily Table appealed to people in potential target neighborhoods who liked the feelings the brand name conveyed of freshness (Daily) and eating at home (Table). Rauch's story also had to explain the reasons for low prices and affordability, that Daily Table was not a commercial entity. But the idea of a nonprofit organization left people cold and even aroused more questions. Through interactions with local residents, he came to realize that using the word *community* or *neighborhood* in descriptions of Daily Table had far more resonance than highlighting the social enterprise's "nonprofit" nature. "That was an 'aha' for me," he said. "I thought 'nonprofit' really meant something. It does to me, but not to our customers." Daily Table stopped using the word in its marketing materials. Telling the right story helped Daily Table win friends and attract increasing attention in its first location.[12]

2. *Start a movement.* Simple stories told by a handful of people can swell into large social movements if they are spacious and empowering enough. Did #MeToo succeed in mobilizing people to oppose sexual harassment and assault where earlier waves of feminism stopped short because the #MeToo message was more capacious? Just two words and a hashtag (a social media digital-age-appropriate symbol) convey a capacious message inviting all affected women to tell their own stories—and men too. The accumulation of stories became a wave, provoking legal action and corporate change (firings, codes of conduct, webinars). This was the start of a movement that was bottom-up, grassroots-guided, inclusive of anyone, and self-organized.

Every successful change effort, whether a simple transition in a company or a more complex innovation project, rests on some sort of social movement. It includes a campaign to win people's hearts and minds. A campaign isn't a one-time event; it is a series of forays into support-building that gains momentum as more people join, whether actively as investors, sponsors, workers, and customers or more passively as allies who start seeing the world in a new way and internalizing a new narrative with new possibilities. This necessity is even greater for advanced leaders when they begin to elaborate on their ideas for addressing a big, intractable institutional problem and launch their ventures because of the very ambiguity and complexity of the current situation and the lack of clear goals and pathways. Advanced leaders must counter ideologies and belief systems that hold institutions in place. They must overcome inertia and skepticism, and they must be prepared to deal with outright resistance to change.

3. *Link self and others.* Social movements depend on voluntary participation, shared commitments, and ongoing motivations, which are elicited by the quality of the narrative people hear. Marshall Ganz, a past official of the farm workers' union turned academic and consultant, found that a key to an effective public narrative is that it links three substories: the stories of *self, us,* and *now. Self* is a leader's own story. Why was she called? What are the values that inspire her to lead, based on the leader's choices and lived experiences? Leaders must define themselves before others do. The story of *us* explains why *we* are called to action, including exploration of the shared values of *our* group—shared culture and community. Leaders interpret and make sense of shared experiences. And why now? Why is a call to action now? What are the challenges that require action and the choices that must be made? Is there a specific action that can be taken? In Ganz's public narrative framework, all three build toward winning people over and mobilizing them for change. Urgency counters inertia, anger helps overcome

apathy, hope rises above fear, solidarity does away with isolation, and encouragement that individuals can make a difference helps overcome self-doubt.[13]

Principles for persuasive narratives have endured through eons of Western thought. Aristotle's principles of rhetoric, as retold by politics expert Gary Orren in his work on persuasion, center on logos (a logical, coherent, cogent argument); ethos (a credible, authentic messenger); and pathos (an emotional appeal to the motives, feelings, and beliefs of the audience). Logos alone is a trap; it's possible to get stuck in one's own reasoning and fail to see how others view the world. The quality of the idea and the credentials of the leader alone cannot be persuasive without understanding what matters to the other people one is attempting to influence.[14]

4. *Make it about them and what they value.* When leaders are attuned to the beliefs and feelings of others and tell their stories in ways that appeal to those beliefs and feelings, they can effectively move other people to accept new narratives, including counternarratives that challenge previous positions. Studies of political attitudes provide compelling evidence of the possibilities. Research by Toronto Rotman School psychologist Matthew Feinberg showed the importance of appealing to an opponent's ethical or moral code. If a message is framed to fit the values of conservatives, for example, they are likelier to express support for such liberal causes as immigration and universal health care. At the same time, liberals are likelier to support the conservative position of higher levels of military spending if it is framed as a poverty-fighting tool.[15] In short, know the others' world and trade in the currencies they value, leadership experts Allan Cohen and David Bradford advised. Leaders must make sure that the others actually get something of value for allowing themselves to be persuaded. Seek quid pro quos and ignore the norm of reciprocity at your peril, they urged.[16]

5. *Convene in person.* To persuade others requires reaching and touching them personally. Social media is a powerful tool to amplify protest but not necessarily to organize longer-term change efforts, as the Arab Spring protests made clear; such social media–fueled movements destabilized existing institutions without building new ones. Books—which, by definition, are more message capacious than tweets—can lay out arguments and establish thought leadership, as Susan Leal did in writing *Running Out of Water* with engineer Peter Rogers. Leal had been the elected treasurer and appointed public utilities director for San Francisco County and had been instrumental in creating a coalition of utility officials across the western part of the United States to push action on the water front.[17] The book's credibility put her in position to speak and launch a project to test solutions to conserve drinking and household water. But it was her active organizing, first of the coalition and then of local initiatives, that gave her the potential for impact. Even more essential for advanced leaders is the use of convening power—gathering people face-to-face in specific times and places to gain a personal connection to the venture.

Face-to-face (F2F) communication remains important even when digital tools permit remote work and online interactions. Consider the fact that people who could work at home are flocking to coworking spaces dotted with frequent informal gatherings, formal programs, and civic meetings. If F2F matters for the ordinary stuff of daily living, imagine its importance for the complex challenges of social innovation. To exercise advanced leadership, convening is often necessary to establish the big idea and to create a robust movement even while the initiating leaders have not much more than a small demonstration underway. Even when City Year was just a small, embryonic local Boston program, cofounders Alan Khazei and Michael Brown invited significant national figures to visit, and they convened national conferences on service that included many similar organizations. One early visitor in 1991 was US presidential candidate Bill Clinton. His firsthand experience of the little local program with the big dream led him to make national service a key policy proposal in his campaign, which he enacted as soon as he became president, signing a bill to create the Corporation for National and Community Service and its AmeriCorps program.[18] Soon local became national.

The kind of convening and who gets invited is important for the change effort. Convening has its own establishment and castles in which they meet. Conventions, industry association meetings, civic lunches, annual addresses, or lecture series are institutional structures in themselves that can serve to reinforce the established order and conventional narrative by offering a more-of-the-same agenda and favoring people who are traditional insiders and incumbents. No matter how persuasive a story, innovative solutions won't be stimulated by talking to the same old people in the same old settings; in fact, that's a good way to unite the establishment against a new idea. Although advanced leaders can use those forums to tell a new story, they will be stymied if they are confined by them. Would-be advanced leaders who have risen to top elite positions could find themselves talking only to themselves and people like them. Their membership in exclusive clubs can tag them with the negative baggage of those groups and potentially deflect them from thinking too far outside the building. Doug Rauch had numerous speaking engagements in the food industry when he was conceiving of and building Daily Table, but he was careful about what he accepted, and his most effective convenings involved community members. Torsten Thiele spoke on conventional panels at the usual environmental organization meetings, but he had to convene a broader group across silos and sectors to bring new ideas for innovation to the oceans, as we'll see in chapter 5.

Raymond Jetson's Very Roomy Tent

Raymond Jetson understood the persuasive power of convening under a big tent. He offered a capacious, compelling narrative of community economic development and change that stimulated innovation outside the buildings (and divides) that had kept his city stuck. He had grown up on the mostly black side of Baton Rouge, became the pastor of an urban congregation, served in the Louisiana state legislature with Mitch Landrieu, and then, as a state official, presided over assistance to poor families and emergency relief after Hurricane Katrina. I met him when he was recommended as a speaker with valuable insights into the Katrina aftermath and the community rebuilding tasks that remained. I learned that he wanted to go well beyond those roles to propel transformational change throughout the city and level the playing field.

Jetson began Better Baton Rouge (BBR) two years later, eventually morphing it into MetroMorphosis, with a goal of citizen-led empowerment—not unlike the vision of chapter 3's Gilberto Dimenstein in São Paulo, Brazil. Jetson had two of the three Cs, capabilities and connections, and he could leverage those to raise the third, cash. As a preacher, Jetson could certainly tell a powerful story, and he had a pulpit to speak from. But the narrative he favored involved getting others to speak.

BBR started when he convened a broad cross-section of residents and officials to discuss how to act to shape a healthier future for the city. BBR began as a loose assemblage that would self-organize into smaller groups to tackle specific problems, whether in education, employment, or public health; some groups could become the basis for permanent or long-term entities.[19] Jetson thought of activities in four buckets: mobilized citizens, catalytic partnerships, activated assets, and thought leadership to promote a new narrative. He and his listeners needed a different story about life in inner-city neighborhoods. He needed to tell it early and often. He needed to enlist many others to buy into the narrative, embellish it, and disseminate it.

An underpinning of the story was that the status quo was not working for many residents. Despite the amount of philanthropic dollars being spent and the lip service paid in establishment circles, outcomes were still horrible, whether in education, employment, or health. Anecdotes about individuals, which were appealing and memorable, were backed up by abundant data (e.g., a high school graduation rate for black males of less than 50 percent, well below white rates and even black rates in other cities).

It was important to question and challenge the dominant narrative about causes and solutions and to find innovations that could be deployed quickly. Jetson wanted to build an inclusive narrative not only in the types of people to be involved in the framing of change but also to be capacious in its holistic view of the number of institutions and organizations that should play a role. Jetson's narrative, retold by a growing team of volunteers, was aimed at helping people see that the whole ecosystem was part of sustained change.

Highlighting the failures of established institutions, such as schools and philanthropies, was threatening to their officials. So how would Jetson and team get them to sit at the table? Public skepticism surfaced after the first statement—"Imagining a Better Baton Rouge"— was issued. Critics complained about an overly broad agenda and no formal entities to carry it out. Jetson recalled, "We had selected really challenging issues, wicked problems. There were no organized structures in place to make anything happen. There was a lot of skepticism at this whole idea of citizen-led innovation. That they did not need to be part of a blue ribbon commission. They didn't need authorization. They didn't need to run for office." And yet they were going to find and deploy new solutions? It didn't seem credible in the beginning.

Jetson persisted in telling that story and in convening, inviting the skeptics in established institutions to participate in discussions alongside average residents, sometimes on Saturdays before Louisiana State University football games or Sundays following church. After several repetitions and early indications of enthusiasm by working groups, momentum built. BBR was a tent with room for many sideshows. It was a portfolio intended to catalyze others' actions rather than act directly itself; for example, one year, Jetson and team oversaw the training of seven hundred mentors but didn't mentor anyone directly themselves. A multiplier effect from mobilizing others began to prove the idea. Jetson was attempting to address three main structural challenges that Marshall Ganz found plagued movements: going from a heroic leader to a team; group debate and consensus, not autocracy; and accountability among volunteer members.

BBR and MetroMorphosis events were innovative in getting people to think holistically as well as practically. One convening featured twenty-five compelling statistics from MetroMorphosis's background research. About 250 people showed up. First there was a "data-walk" around a large room with twenty-five stations, each with one statistic and a BBR volunteer telling the story behind that statistic. "They were totally blown away by the numbers they were exposed to," Jetson enthused. Then the group divided into twenty-five tables of ten each, with one table per statistic, to discuss root causes and drill down on the two most important. When every table reported, they saw that some core issues could be the basis for action projects.

In addition to such changes as healthy food markets springing up in low-income areas as part of a health effort, a centerpiece project was the Urban Congress on African American Males, begun in April 2016. Similarly based on research and community input, the group identified seven areas needing attention, including mentoring, reentry from prison, finances, and high school graduation rates. Those were big but conventional issues, ones for which numerous organizations were already engaged. But what emerged from Jetson's community self-empowerment were some highly innovative outside-the-building approaches to change. Novel and promising efforts were built on realities of black life on the street, where barbershops were more important than chambers of commerce. The hair and health initiative, stemming from the urban congress on men stimulated by MetroMorphosis, trained barbers in twenty barbershops to take blood pressures and to provide that and other relevant data to health partners for follow up. Barbershop Talks emerged from the realization that some black men were more comfortable talking in that setting. Over one month in the fall of 2018, more than one hundred men attended five talks across the city, a conversation about what it requires to build healthy lives, with follow-ups planned for the winter of 2019.

Projects began to complement one another. For example, with respect to business development to create employment, LaunchBR, another initiative seeded by the empowerment and self-organizing under Jetson's big tent, helped landscaping and lawn companies succeed as businesses and offered training with Southern University to make sure that inner-city businesses had the best and latest in innovative water technology. An accelerator helped black businesses with public bids. A prerelease curriculum was offered with the corrections department to prepare incarcerated black males for reentry and a shot at employment. Some things in the portfolio didn't work. A workforce credentials effort didn't have tangible impact, so Jetson and his team dropped it. Novelty was less important than getting actions underway that demonstrated community self-empowerment and encouraged additional projects to open opportunity and change norms and institutions. Although Reverend Ray Jetson had no formal authority, he persuaded people to embrace and act on a capacious story.[20]

An inclusive vision like that of Jetson is not only motivating; it is likely to get more done. Opting in and volunteering are looser forms of "membership" in an innovation effort than formal contracts or employment relationships, even though similar principles apply when trying to innovate across units in an established organization. A capacious story can include actions that anyone can take, because they embrace new possibilities without someone in authority telling them to take that action, and even while waiting for the bigger actions to change policy or allocate funds. Urban entrepreneurs Rebecca Fishman Lipsey and Marta Viciedo heard civic leaders' stories about getting more public transit to ease traffic congestion in Miami, and they saw this item emerge high on surveys they conducted about the issues that millennials cared most about. Impatient for action, they created a social media campaign for Transit Day in November 2016, a day when public officials and the public were encouraged to ride existing public transit. They lined up multiple sponsors, encouraged forty elected officials to use public transit across three Florida counties, had wide media reach when about sixteen hundred people posted about their rides, and nearly four million people were estimated to be reached overall. They were thanked by county officials for moving their efforts forward.[21]

Capacious framing invites more partnerships. More allies under the big tent can help advance the idea. To change a system requires many stakeholders to make their own contributions or to adjust. By definition, ideas for innovation are often much bigger than the resources or reach of any one organization. To get others involved, they must feel that they are part of the story. A big inclusive tent leaves room for a shared vision but many different expressions of how it can be put into practice.

Show More than Tell: Making the Future Tangible

The third big piece of telling the right story is less telling and more showing. What might the innovation look like in practice? A vision is a dream of what might be, but there are problems with leaving the story as a theory of change—how change X will result in outcome Y and impact Z. Rhetoric can be subject to misinterpretation, as different people think it means different things, especially as diversity is included in the big tent. Potential volunteers motivated to enlist in the cause or join the movement can be lost if they don't have a clear picture of what is expected of them and no specific goals and milestones to show whether the change project is getting anywhere. And potential recipients of help can have no idea what the leader is offering them, which can make it easier for skeptics and opponents to jump in with a counternarrative, saying that it can't work anyway. The solution is tangible demonstrations, models, prototypes, and pilot programs to make the promise of change concrete and to prove that it can work. The right story includes balancing a grand vision with prototypes and demonstrations that prove the possibility of quick wins and early successes.

The cliché that actions speak louder than words dates back to the seventeenth century, a longevity that, in this case, shows its enduring worth. The right story is not just talk. It's not just a great speech or a one-time event. The narrative is embodied in the leaders' actions. Informally, that's called walking the talk. Nelson Mandela was widely revered for more than his inspiring rhetoric. He served as a role model through actions that signaled unity over division, and then he also put new institutions in place that involved the victims of apartheid in defining a new constitution, governing, and growing the economy. The credibility of his narrative grew as he demonstrated what unity meant in his personal actions and made it concrete through specific programs. I call these the *MEs* of leadership: the message espoused (what a leader says), the model exemplified (what a leader does), and the mechanisms established (what a leader enables others to do). Leaders' actions and the tangible demonstrations and prototypes they develop are significant parts of the right story.

Stories can't be fairy tales. Narratives should be evidence based, meeting a plausibility test. Marshaling the evidence sometimes requires creating new evidence through pilot programs—something that people can see and touch, something that has "street cred" (visible on the street). Prototypes are fundamental. That's why the City Year founders started not a think tank, they said, but rather an "action tank" with programs demonstrating the meaning of national service in practice first, before trying to get new federal policies and legislation in place to authorize and fund national service.[22]

That's why Rakesh Khurana, Nitin Nohria, and I decided that our idea for a new stage of higher education to mobilize a new leadership force for the world would have no credibility unless we could show that our own university was doing it. In order to start persuading officials at our university, we created a narrative in the form of a long concept paper, complete with 105 footnotes, to show that there was evidence supporting the story we put forward. This also helped us with another important aspect of leadership storytelling: to use contextual intelligence to know the world of the stakeholders and to speak in the language of the targets of persuasion, using the currency of the dominant institution. In our case, we spoke the language of academic papers and footnotes. In business, one might need PowerPoint and financial jargon; in communities, perhaps the language of the street.

As marketers know, people vary in their willingness to buy into new visions and accept the idea of change. Some are early adopters who have been waiting for just this sort of thing, but many others are laggards who have to be convinced by seeing signs that the mission can be accomplished and that whatever it is will be good for them. Depending on how much the story challenges the conventional narrative, the show-me skeptics can outnumber the eager early enlistees. And those who are supposed to benefit from the change can be the most skeptical. Advanced leaders who genuinely want to help aren't always welcome, as Doug Rauch found. The right story is about their potential, not your largesse.

If telling the right story is so fraught with complications under benign and minimally controversial circumstances like those of Carol Hallquist's in Kansas City—a respected leader living in the same community, speaking the same language, and offering assistance that didn't require anyone to change anything to get the help—then imagine how much more difficult this is when the dominant narrative is deeply embedded in longstanding formal and informal institutions. That makes demonstrations and testimonials vital to getting any traction for a new story about new possibilities.

Dealing with Community Skepticism: A Health Story

Leaders simply can't swoop in from outside and lay their stories on people, even when they have a great theory of change. That's ironic, because turnarounds in companies and cultures, as I found in research for my book *Confidence*, tend to require fresh thinking and often a leader from outside the established leadership circles. Yet antibodies rise to reject those perceived as outsiders regardless of whether they are well connected inside. Even people who formerly occupied positions in traditional hierarchies inside established structures become outsiders when they step outside the building. I've seen this shift from once-one-of-us to suspicious outsider happen to those who go away to college or build their careers elsewhere and then try to extend a helping hand to their home communities. The inertial forces of culture and tradition are too deep. Resentment of those who have "made it" and want to "tell us what to do" is too strong among those who have been left behind. The right story must reckon with the past and provide benefits that people value in the present, and that requires early tangible demonstrations.

I saw these dynamics almost extinguish Anand Piramal's promising innovation to use technology to transform health care for rural India before it could gain traction. The idea was e-health, to be called Piramal e-Swasthya, signifying the tools for health workers who would connect villagers digitally to professional medical services. Anand Piramal thought that e-health could be as huge and democratizing as Henry Ford's Model T, which made the automobile and, hence, mobility, affordable by the masses.

Piramal was a member of a family that had left their rural origins to create one of the most prominent companies in India, a manufacturer of generic pharmaceuticals headquartered in Mumbai with a foundation and a long track record of respected philanthropy. Piramal and his family advisors didn't think of themselves as outsiders. Their village roots were in a part of the region he targeted for beginning his venture, and his founding team took the time to travel often from Mumbai's high-rise office towers to explore life on the ground for the rural poor. They weren't, they believed, carpetbaggers coming to exploit distressed people. Their foundation was separate from the generic drug company that had made the family fortune, and they had no commercial intention to build new markets or sell more drugs. They felt their motives were pure.

Piramal developed a narrative about how the rural poor could get access to modern health care through a totally new delivery model. Each village would have a set of health workers—women who were otherwise unemployed, often mothers, whose pay would augment family income. Each village would get a weekly physician visit. A call center in the city staffed by professionals would serve all the villages, backing up the physicians with sophisticated tools for diagnosis. Complex ailments would be referred to regional hospitals. This was an efficient proposal using the latest digital technologies to provide the best of care to places that lacked access. It was considered by advisors in Mumbai and beyond a great theory of change, one that was potentially transformative for India.

But as the first few village programs were launched, Piramal faced the opposing pull of a competing narrative. Villages already had healers, known as "quacks," who had been in business for generations. Throughout India, about 57 percent of the purported "doctors" are quacks who lack medical training. The situation was complicated because of a shortage of trained physicians in India (nineteen doctors and nurses per ten thousand people overall, well below the World

Health Organization benchmark of twenty-five per ten thousand), a situation that was worse in rural areas. As a result, some quacks received nods and winks that kept them in place.[23]

One common mode of treatment by quacks was steroid injections. This offered temporary euphoria but had severe long-term negative consequences and generally didn't cure most ailments anyway. Moreover, this was illegal based on national laws. The instant gratification from steroid injections proved strong competition for the invisible effects of modern medications, which had to be taken for several days to be effective. Every country, even the most medically sophisticated, shares the problem of people failing to take all the pills in a prescription once they start feeling better. This situation would be that much more difficult in villages that had never learned the story of modern Western medicine and its scientific reasoning. Faith in karma made it hard to listen to a new medical tale, especially when there was no visible connection between a little pill and a physical condition.

Piramal's good story was undermined by the dominant narrative about women too. They had low status in the villages. It was hard for them to be persuasive. Where they had personal relationships with other mothers, there would be a trickle of patients for simple ailments. But the clinics were barely filling their hours. This raised Piramal's costs per patient and could undermine justification for bringing this innovation to villages. The village quacks must have felt they faced no threat, that hundreds of years of history would continue to justify their privileges, and that the low status of women would remain intact.

But Piramal's e-Swasthya did not need large numbers to create proof of concept. The team knew that modern medicine (meaning Western medicine) worked and that treatment and medication at the village level could vastly improve health outcomes for a high proportion of the everyday ailments village adults and children faced. The question was merely how to demonstrate that in a credible way so that word of mouth from satisfied patients would produce stories of people even before formal data emerged. Anyway, if people in developed countries listen to stories more than statistics, imagine how little villagers would be swayed by numbers. They were persuaded by seeing people who would otherwise have been plagued by repeated illness returning to health. They saw that people did, in fact, get well soon. Mothers talking about their children's recoveries became the basis for Piramal telling the right story.

As a new narrative took hold, the e-health model attracted more patients in the few original villages. Learnings from the pilot villages could be taken to more villages, and that built its own momentum. One lesson was that Piramal needed a bigger tent, especially if trying to rewrite history and to counter traditions. The venture needed to include more stakeholders across sectors who would embrace the narrative; for example, village elders, who were the equivalent of local politicians; spiritual leaders; and teachers in local schools who could teach children who were already enamored with digital tools about the science of health and encourage them to bring that information home to their families. The vision wouldn't sell itself; people would sell it. Piramal's experience on the ground also showed that the story had to include other factors responsible for health outcomes, such as clean drinking water.

Later, Piramal could tell a more holistic story of improving village life when the venture merged with a bigger health initiative in another state that had included a package of systems change tools that also had a bearing on health: water purification tanks, job training, computer workstations for the schools, regional training centers, and strong involvement by the village elders. The merger put them on the map for providing an emergency response system and mobile vans. And then there were many other storytellers who could be mobilized to help villagers embrace the e-health/modern medicine narrative. Eventually, the package of changes were reflected in a growing number of users, accumulating data about health outcomes and a slew of national awards for making a difference on a major problem in India—work that is still ongoing.²⁴

As Anand Piramal, Carol Hallquist, and other leaders learned, the right story doesn't rest on the words alone; it becomes compelling because of tangible demonstrations of value early in the change process, demonstrations that constitute proof of concept. Even if advanced leaders can't solve the whole problem quickly, they can develop models, pilot programs, and prototypes that turn an abstract vision into a tangible result, something people can feel or experience. To use another time-honored cliché, seeing is believing.

As in lean start-ups of all kinds, the initial demonstration need not be more than is necessary to show what the eventual innovation will look like—a minimum viable proposition. To get off the ground, the project might not have widespread support—Mitch Landrieu and Anand Piramal didn't start with broad backing, if they had backing at all—but rather just enough to get started. But the demonstration does need to reflect key elements that are central to the idea. For example, if diversity is important to the effort, then there should be diversity from the beginning. Ray Jetson began the work on BBR, and its dream of shared prosperity for blacks and whites, with a multiracial team, reflecting what future leadership could look like.

Sometimes you can't persuade everyone with words. Sometimes you must just do it. Let the right story unfold as you get started. The first results will make the narrative the right one. Big visions become real as small wins and early successes demonstrate the potential. Demonstrations have many benefits: they are feasible, manageable, and cost-effective; they can be improvised and evolve with learning; and they can calm fears of radical change by appearing to be contained and reversible if they don't work. Try-outs also carry risks: they can look peripheral, trivial, and unsupported, and opponents can stop them or eliminate them.

That's why telling the right story is important—a narrative that inspires and illuminates through a big vision for repairing the world based on a new frame for history that creates a different path to the future.

* * *

The most compelling stories get the work of innovation started by enabling action that is open-ended, leaving room for others to join and add their sense of positive possibilities. After all, the stories of life, of institutions, and of communities are ongoing. That's why entrepreneurial leaders should learn to revise the unproductive stories and create new narratives that inspire people to join them in innovation and transformation. That's why advanced leaders must find and tell the right stories to gain support for their grand vision of change.

5

LIGHT A SPARK AND KEEP THEM FIRED UP

Activating Allies, Crafting Coalitions

urning big problems into innovation opportunities takes more than a village (as the African proverb about child-raising holds); it takes a cross-sector multistakeholder coalition. Advanced leaders must reach beyond the connections they already have to identify the most desirable backers and supporters among a multiplicity of sometimes competing stakeholders, often from far outside the building. They must light the fires of enthusiasm, align the interests of many diverse groups, and keep the embers glowing.

Crafting coalitions and holding them together requires full attention. It is not all hearty handshakes, hugs, and high-fives before moving on to the next agenda item. Even the staunchest allies can do unpredictable things to further their own agendas and, perhaps unwittingly, undermine the mission. Multiple stakeholders with diverse goals can be converted but not fully controlled.

Former Trader Joe's president Doug Rauch thought he had the allies he needed to launch his innovative new retail concept to end food insecurity in inner cities. Then, just when it looked like everything was lined up for success, a hungry policeman almost put the venture in jeopardy when Rauch saw a flash of metal near his face. It was the cop's gun.

Rauch told me about the gun scare a few years later, when we were sitting in almost the same positions as Rauch and the cop: at a tiny table near a microwave oven in the small employee break room at a Daily Table store in Roxbury, Massachusetts. The compact room was tucked away beyond bins of apples and avocados, yards from the major meat and banana bonanzas, down the wide, airy aisles with their simulated wood floors, adjacent to the dairy case near the refrigerated prepared foods. By the time Rauch recounted the gun incident, Daily Table had been in operation nearly four years, having effectively built a strong coalition of backers and supporters that helped the stores serve the community with affordable, nutritious foods that might have otherwise been wasted.

The officer was decidedly not among the malnourished, underfed people Daily Table was created to serve. The man simply wanted to heat his lunch, which he had grabbed on his way back to the break room. Despite the weapon he waved, he was not among those initially opposed to Daily Table. Just the opposite, he was a big fan who wanted Daily Table to succeed, one of a burgeoning number of allies who helped Rauch deal with opposition. Among the early opponents was a fussy city health inspector ready to pounce at the merest sign of an infraction. So Rauch wanted to observe all health department regulations carefully—including the one the policeman was about to violate by putting food from the store in the employee-only microwave. Hence, the gun. The cop brandished it with a big grin, saying, in effect, that the bureaucrats couldn't stop him; he was the police. (But he did put it back in its holster some slow-motion seconds later.)

Rauch related this as part of our discussion of how he mobilized resources and attracted allies for the Daily Table vision, with enough stakeholders on board to develop his venture—even if he couldn't keep them under control. Allies helped him fend off the critics and bring others to the table.

This challenge is what I call the Change Agent Rule of Three. In every situation requiring change, whether little tweaks or big innovations, stakeholders cluster into three groups: *allies*, *opponents*, and *undecideds*. That is, those for it, who can become allies; those against it, whose opposition can undermine the initiative; and those who are indifferent or undecided, who are sitting on the fence and either not paying attention or waiting to see how things go. It's not enough to have passive allies; leaders must make sure that allies continue to be committed to the mission and keep their own goals from getting in the way, whether an illicit lunch with a gun or other forms of self-interest.

Anything new and different must contend with these three groups. In the beginning, after all, the story is just a story, unproven and perhaps threatening. Getting backers, sponsors, and champions is a time-consuming task for innovators and entrepreneurs under any circumstances, even in a digital era with crowdfunding and social media. Imagine how much harder the task of crafting a coalition can be outside the traditional hierarchical leadership paradigms of single organizations.

To get even relatively straightforward things underway, like a new model for grocery stores in inner cities, leaders must mobilize a multiplicity of stakeholders beyond their direct sphere of influence. They can span every sector and include diverse, sometimes conflicting interests. Those people and groups may define the problem and the solution differently. They operate autonomously and have their own agendas. Bad blood may exist between certain stakeholders; they may be engaged in hidden or not-so-hidden turf battles. Moreover, as a project develops, the numbers and stances of allies, opponents, and undecideds change. Fence sitters can be converted to allies, but alliances can fragment and opposition can grow.

Thus, advanced leaders must know how to forge a dynamic coalition of support for institution-changing innovations—and to ensure that allies remain committed to a common goal. They must persuade, motivate, and energize supporters with their visionary story and relationship skills, keeping the spark of inspiration glowing.

Getting the Wheel Rolling: Coalitions at the Table

The need for allies and the important roles they play become clear in examining coalition-building for Daily Table. Rauch's allies were inspired by his big idea that one problem—wasted but perfectly edible food—could be used to solve another: hunger and malnutrition, with all their associated health problems. They became partners who could help attract the power tools that innovators need: resources (money, facilities, and supplies), information or expertise (including community knowledge), and support or legitimacy (high-level sponsorship). Allies helped Rauch sway undecideds and neutralize opponents.

Allies: Why You Need Them

Rauch's main allies included key advisors who provided more than advice; they opened doors to significant resources and support. Meeting Bill Walczak was fortuitous, because Walczak offered community legitimacy that could stop some potential critics from even thinking about opposing the innovation. Walczak was the founder and former CEO of the Codman Square Community Health Center, a Boston-based national leader in the integration of community health, education, and wellness. His successor as CEO, Sandra Cotterell, gave Daily Table its first space in their building in an underserved Dorchester neighborhood, which had limited access to healthy foods but was close to dense residential areas and transportation. The center enjoyed strong community partners. Daily Table could share a compact retail space with Healthworks Community Fitness, a nonprofit that operated a low-cost gym with a subsidized membership fee.

Other early allies helped Rauch raise money and proved critical later as events unfolded: Jose Alvarez, former CEO of the Stop and

Shop supermarket chain; Jay Martin, a lawyer who shared Rauch's values; and Tim Ferguson and colleagues at Next Street Financial, a group dedicated to building inner-city businesses to improve communities, a contact I made for him. Rauch also attracted some experienced managers, including a former Whole Foods executive and the former executive chef of a popular restaurant in Vermont who had experience with gleaned food. Though internal, and not the whole team, these hires signaled professionalism, which also proved important later.

Rauch attracted some donors through speaking engagements and media appearances, which he began even when Daily Table was nothing more than an idea. A panel on which he spoke got him Hain Celestial as a donor. Abundant early media was also a source of support and legitimacy. At the time Rauch started framing his narrative, he chaired the board of a local National Public Radio (NPR) affiliate; newsroom buzz led to an interview on *Weekend Edition,* a popular NPR program. The concept of recovering otherwise-wasted food and using it to provide affordable nutrition for the food insecure made a good media story. A short interview in the *New York Times Sunday Magazine* led to national television with Brian Williams and Katie Couric on *Good Morning America.*

Rauch also befriended Boston mayor Marty Walsh and showed him the prelaunch store. Rauch spoke the mayor's language, telling him about the community jobs he was creating. Rauch recalled that the mayor "loves what we're doing, he helps ride you through the flack," including calming down complaints from neighboring convenience stores concerned about the competition.[1] Rauch was an engaging, welcoming host; he told the story tirelessly, helping people like the mayor see the same potential he saw and come to share the vision.

Undecideds: Can Fence Sitters Become Allies?

It's not surprising that many stakeholders are undecided in the beginning. For Daily Table, some were relatively easy to tip over to become allies, with existing allies providing some of the push. But they all wanted different things.

Funders. Some potential funders wanted a social return, not just to see stores up and running, which was hard to prove until stores were up and running. Would Daily Table actually have an impact on reducing wasted food, limiting obesity, and improving health outcomes? Then there were some corporate funders who didn't want to be the first, such as a big national bank that only wanted to join if others did. Jose Alvarez's connections proved significant. Alvarez accompanied Rauch to a meeting with Sam Kennedy, Boston Red Sox president, whom Alvarez knew; Kennedy said the Sox were already committed elsewhere but introduced Rauch to Jim Davis, chairman of athletic footwear company New Balance, who invested in Daily Table. Rauch mused about his initial surprise that allies could come on a "dotted line," using corporate jargon for indirect relationships. He never would have thought of reaching out to a shoe company.

Suppliers wanted the tax deduction from donating food. Some might have liked the nobility of the cause and the chance to unload those overly ripe bananas. But the nonprofit charitable status mattered, maybe mattering even more to local farmers than to big chains like Whole Foods. That tax status could affect Daily Table's food supply. At the same time, Rauch had high standards; he wanted healthy, nutritious food, so he wouldn't take just anything or let suppliers unload their junk.

Community members. There was potential for tension and a wait-and-see attitude. After all, here was this white guy coming into a largely black and immigrant neighborhood, offering something no one was yet sure was good for them. Community members were not only the target market of customers; they were also the ulti-mate street-level legitimizers, especially the opinion leaders among them. Rauch started a community advisory board at his first store and intended to do this everywhere, to give local residents a voice in how the store operated. This is a form of what sociologists call *co-optation*, which entails bringing potential critics close to you, giving them a role, and listening to them in order to stem their opposition before it begins. Besides, they might have good ideas.

Rauch also made his main employment goal to create jobs for community members, jobs with a livable wage (starting at fifteen dollars per hour before that became a public goal) and benefits, and to provide life-skill training, including legal literacy, financial lit-eracy, interview skills, nondefensive communication presentation skills, and goal-setting. By the fall of 2018, Daily Table had created sixty-one community jobs. Legions of undecideds became converts.

Competing nonprofits. Daily Table competed with a vast universe of other nonprofit organizations for scarce funding. Closer to home, food banks could perceive Daily Table as a rival. To convert them into allies, he used his media platform and political connections to praise the good work of food banks. The Greater Boston Food Bank became a Daily Table ally from the first store's opening. The two entities supported and occasionally supplied each other. "This sort of relationship can happen when people see shared vision and stop thinking that you're in my space and competing," he said.

Opponents: Can Allies Quash Critics?

Despite a growing number of allies, Rauch still had battles on his hands. Stakeholders are not just useful sources of input and power tools; they also determine the right to exist. The presence of oppon-ents who could block the venture before it started was another reason

Rauch needed allies. Allies could run interference, neutralize critics, and sometimes even remove opponents from the scene. This is the political part of coalition-building. It sometimes involves maintaining a fighting stance.

Federal tax authorities. In 2011, to get underway, Rauch applied to the IRS for 501c3 status for Daily Table as a not-for-profit organization so that it could accept tax-deductible donations. Taking donated or subsidized food and selling it at low prices was essential to the model. Generating revenues could help Daily Table be sustainable and grow to significant impact. "If we can get it to break even, then it can be scalable. No other hunger relief project has truly been scalable because it's such a deep philanthropic hole," he explained.[2]

His IRS application coincided with the national media coverage his idea had received, which proved to be a mixed blessing. During the media buzz, Rauch found to his consternation that the key message was condensed to "the ex-president of Trader Joe's plans to sell expired food to the poor." Adding to the misfortune, one of the IRS examiners had seen the *Good Morning America* TV show about the Daily Table concept and stopped the approval process in order to conduct further analysis—including whether the model would really qualify as serving the needy. The IRS argued that it was just another discount grocery engaged in regular business activities that would ordinarily be carried out for profit.

Rauch drew on his inner circle of allies to get through the crisis. Next Street secured the Boston Foundation to serve as fiscal agent for cash donations while the IRS deliberated. Then, Rauch's team created an innovative membership concept through zip code tracking. Consumers were allowed to make purchases regardless of domicile, but their zip codes would be regularly analyzed to determine the percentage of customers who resided in at-risk neighborhoods versus those from affluent ones, whose use could be restricted. Rauch's group also provided the IRS with documentation about its service to a charitable class and funding through contributions from many sources that included the general public, government agencies, corporations, private foundations, and other public charities. It finally worked. Three years after first applying to the IRS, in December 2014, Daily Table got its federal 501c3 charitable designation.

Health inspectors. Just as one bureaucracy was out of the way, another popped up. The feds permitted Daily Table to take food donations, but a local city official was opposed to that very idea. Rauch said, "If you're in food, the Health Department is like the Supreme Court. Until they issue your Certificate of Occupancy, you're not doing business." Just before the planned opening of the first Daily Table in Dorchester, a field health inspection chief told Rauch that she didn't like the idea of selling donated food. He argued that the model depended on it, and anyway, it was perfectly legal. He agreed not to carry anything past its code date. Still, she delayed the opening about six weeks, carping about small details and threatening to continue opposing the store. She was a classic example of my theory that powerlessness corrupts; she was stuck in a limited job in an unappealing bureaucracy, so she took out her feelings of powerlessness on other people by holding her little bit of control over them as long as possible. This time, Rauch was on the receiving end.

As he expanded, he soon found allies to run interference. A VIP sneak preview for Daily Table's second store was attended by Mayor Walsh, the state commissioner of agriculture, and other officials. One man in particular complimented Rauch on a great idea, then offered his business card, saying that Rauch could contact him if he needed anything. The mystery man turned out to be Buddy

Christopher, the commissioner of Inspectional Services, to whom the Health Department reported. (Rauch felt like he had just scored a get-out-of-jail-free card in a Monopoly board game.)

That was on a Thursday. The opening was set for Friday of the following week. On Monday, Rauch's team called the fire department, the second-to-last approval, for the safety inspection, only to be told that they couldn't come for many weeks—which meant that Daily Table couldn't open after all. Rauch contacted his new buddy, Buddy, and got a return email. That same afternoon, the fire inspectors came to the store. Then the commissioner emailed again to say that he had asked another local health inspector, as a favor, to do a prelook. That informal inspection resulted in a list of about five things to fix. The next day the inspector checked those repairs and handed Rauch the final Certificate of Occupancy, just in time for Daily Table to open. The opponent had been removed.

Nearly four years and many millions of servings and grocery bags later, there were no health complaints, and there were thousands of satisfied customers with better nutrition, adding up to gradually improving community health. One sign of credibility: the city's field inspectors themselves stopped by to shop. The police shopped at Daily Table too; they could be counted on to come quickly if managers had a problem—say, a rowdy person. And the lunch-craving, gun-waving cop told Rauch that he loved Daily Table for having the best food for the best prices.

As Doug Rauch came to understand a wide array of diverse stakeholders across sectors, he used allies to neutralize opponents and convert fence sitters. In late fall 2018, we sat in an Asian fusion restaurant between his two stores as he sketched his thoughts about what was next. Momentum was building, and Rauch could contemplate growing his Daily Table model to more locations (clusters of five) and more cities (perhaps New York was next), feeling comfortable that he could apply his advanced leadership coalition-building skills to pave the way.

Power Tools: The Case for Coalitions

Even if an innovator is lucky enough to start out with the three Cs of cash, capabilities, and connections, this might be just a small portion of what is actually required. Leaders taking on big, messy problems must form alliances with multiple partners to access the bulk of what they need to realize their visions and overcome entrenched interests. Mobilizing allies can ensure supplies of three main power tools.

Resources: Paying the Bills

The most basic resource is money, without which it is challenging to obtain talent, technology, and other necessary items such as facilities or travel. Inspiring visions can attract volunteers, as Raymond Jetson found in Baton Rouge, and volunteers can sometimes help raise funds, making them key to coalitions. Some advanced leaders start with varying degrees of financial power, whether it is a budget from their job, from friends and family, or from the ability to bootstrap using their own cash. Self-funding, however, might not be sustainable for long, and it's not a good idea—whether you have enough money or not. Giving others the chance to invest also gives them a stake in the venture's success. It reinforces commitment to finding more investors, as Alvarez did for Rauch, and to providing other power tools.

Finding allies to provide resources is a way to show that you have support and can build momentum. It is a sign that others find the initiative viable. Tin-cupping, as I've heard some people call it, isn't just begging; it is a way to prove that there is backing. Moreover, those who invest in projects become committed to their success—an old psychological principle of cognitive dissonance, or, to put it more colloquially, having skin in the game.

Even where capital is scarce, hidden assets can sometimes be found that can get the project started. The creativity of outside-the-building thinking can help leaders find assets in unexpected places. To turn around the New Orleans Public Defenders office, for example, which faced a huge backlog of cases following Hurricane Katrina, Ronald Sullivan Jr., who took a year's leave from teaching at Yale to take this on, didn't wait for funding from the courts. He begged and borrowed. Law firms where he had law school classmates provided spare computers and furniture; law schools in the region provided student interns on spring break. The fact that he could tap those resources gave him valuable credibility and helped others to believe he could succeed. He still had to do a lot of housecleaning, and he faced great opposition from those benefiting from the status quo. Mobilizing formerly invisible assets helped him do the job. He also gained a cluster of backers who remained interested in ensuring his success.[3]

Information and Expertise: The Knowledge for Credibility

The cross-sector, cross-disciplinary nature of complex institutional problems means that the knowledge potential advanced leaders bring could be inadequate for the task at hand. So they need a second power tool: information and expertise. They need detailed knowledge of the various sectors that their solution spans: the players' strengths, weaknesses, priorities, and concerns. They need advice on how to gain those players' cooperation and continued involvement as well as on how to handle expected naysayers. They need validation from experts that their innovation can work and suggestions on how to tweak it to make it more effective.

Allies provide a way to get inside a different domain and learn. Leaders need both sector and technical expertise, such as classic legal, marketing, research, or other know-how. The founders of Thirteenth Avenue Funding, Robert Whelan, Casey Jennings, and Ed Lowry, envisioned a new way for students to pay for college in the United States via equity rather than debt (interest-free money today in exchange for a share of income tomorrow) to reduce the student loan burden, which was a particular barrier to college for low-income students. They needed to craft a "human capital contract," but there was no legal precedent, and none of them were lawyers.[4] Similarly, former marketing executive Shelly London hit upon the idea of a computer game to teach ethics to teenagers, but "right away, I was out of my element," she said. She found young techies to teach her. "The key is knowing what you don't know."[5]

Advanced leaders need translators to explain the languages of various sectors. They need insiders to provide experience. Learning from them not only provides essential information; it can also transform leaders from novices to experts themselves.

Support and Legitimacy: Sponsors Whose Endorsements Matter

Legitimacy is intangible but highly significant. The blessing of well-placed sponsors opens doors, signals trust, and provides an aura of acceptability. This is necessary especially when innovators are outside their own buildings, reaching into unfamiliar sectors, and advocating for solutions that challenge traditions. Mahendra Bapna, for example, was well connected and well respected in industrial circles after holding top roles in Indian conglomerate Tata Group. All it took to obtain commitments from business stakeholder groups for his technical education innovation was a phone call to a senior company leader and a thoughtful presentation, he said. But he lacked credibility with India's tradition-minded higher education leaders who were needed to champion his mission. He called on dozens to find the first few backers.[6]

Similarly, the Thirteenth Avenue Funding partners' finance backgrounds raised potential university allies' suspicions of their intentions. "We are three strangers coming into their neighborhood. By definition, there are biases against us," said cofounder Whelan.[7] A university supporter would give them legitimacy and enable them to demonstrate the success needed to attract more students or to convince lenders that Thirteenth Avenue Funding was a sound investment. Finding their first university partner in California was a breakthrough; others followed, including, eventually, a big champion at Purdue, which adopted their income-share model.

Legitimacy comes from bottom-up as well as top-down support. Innovators who seek direct impact on local communities but have no history there must gain the trust and cooperation of those stakeholders. Talking to people who will be affected is essential. Coalitions that include representatives of all affected groups are likelier to succeed.

Forming Allies into Coalitions

It's not surprising that advanced leaders need allies who will invest or contribute the power tools that can build momentum and neutralize opposition, and so they need to find supporters. But in addition, some projects inherently require coalitions to achieve their goals because the mission itself is to forge new connections.

The coalition Doug Rauch needed to launch Daily Table was a relatively simple, loose, and informal one. He and his inner circle dealt with each stakeholder group one at a time. Groups rarely intersected or interacted, and, for the most part, they receded into the background once his venture was up and running so he could focus on customers, the target recipients of Daily Table offerings. His priority was running the stores, not managing a coalition (although, as we've seen, it's best to keep allies informed and involved, lest they get in the way). Daily Table's scope was local, a neighborhood at a time. Political issues were relatively straightforward and manageable.

For other smart innovations aimed at institutional change, however, coalitions are the main game. Coalitions are not just a way for leaders to get what they themselves need to proceed in the interest of their own ventures. Coalitions can be the very goal of the effort—to create new vehicles for action by getting many otherwise-siloed groups aligned behind a similar big idea. Leaders might want to connect unrelated groups to work for a joint outcome, or they might seek to mobilize many groups for joint action. That can occur within a community, but it gets even more complex when the project has a national or an international scope and could be entangled in major political controversies.

The possibilities can seem hard to get one's head around, but coalitions of any size are just larger variants of small groups. Years ago, social psychologists studying small groups identified several configurations of group communication networks, with the goal of teasing out productivity differences. There are *wheels*, in which one central figure dominates all the others; *chains*, with one person mediating between people lined up on either side; *circles* of people with equal opportunity to contribute but who are linked to their neighbors rather than to everyone; and *connected circles*, where almost anyone can reach anyone else.[8]

Advanced leaders build coalitions taking analogous forms but with a size and complexity well beyond small groups. *Wheels*, with their hubs and spokes, are the simplest coalitions. Wheels describe the support systems needed by innovators who create new ventures. Independent spokes support the venture hub, providing resources, information, and legitimacy. Allies do not necessarily have to be involved beyond that; most might be passive investors. This type of coalition tends to characterize service programs or ventures intended to be ongoing. The social value leaders create lies largely in the project itself, in the center of an assemblage of allies.

Doug Rauch's Daily Table venture is a good example of a wheel. The array of allies didn't have to be connected to one another in order to be helpful to him; each played different roles aimed at supporting his innovation. In three other types of coalitions, the connections and complexity multiply: chains, simple circles, and overlapping circles of circles.

Chains exist to match unrelated parties—someone with an asset linked with someone with a need, helping both ends of the chain maximize their potential. In this case, leaders create a coalition that they manage as a platform for making the connections. Allies are needed at either end of the chain, but they don't have to get involved beyond the transactions that the leaders facilitate. The impact comes when the match is made and the newly matched people or groups are able to do something differently.

Chains are a bit like online dating sites, ride-hailing services, or sites helping people with questions find people with answers. The initiative matches previously unrelated people. The social value leaders create comes from the connections. The more people who are connected this way, the greater the network value and, hence, the greater the possibility of making a big impact on how the whole system works.

Circles form to support an activity that all coalition members believe in, enabling them to contribute or act toward a change in behavior or social norms. Mass mobilization campaigns, like political campaigns, tend to have this form. The leaders' role is to extend reach by aligning more interests and influencing others to join the circle and contribute. A circle encourages coalition members to identify with the whole community, maintaining independent identities but, ideally, acting with a common purpose in mind for the duration of the campaign.

Circles are like book clubs. Leaders can help guide them, but the important thing is that everyone reads the same book. Community alliances such as Ray Jetson's BBR tend to take this form. The possibility for innovation and impact derives from the many actions by circle members to use their own assets to change social norms and behaviors, but under a common tent with a common mission.

Connected or overlapping circles. Circles are taken to the next level, with a range of dense circles describing the possibilities for everyone to be involved with everyone else. This tends to describe situations in which formal coalitions exist in the form of associations or alliances, but it takes coalitions of coalitions to move them beyond silos toward a collective voice. Leaders seeking change tend to insinuate themselves into existing coalitions, plant a new idea, and make new connections across them.

Very big institutional issues with many groups already working on some aspect take this form—consider the many organizations devoted to public education improvement, women's rights, racial justice, or climate change. New social value comes from beginning to align many coalitions around a new direction.

Each type of coalition brings its own challenges, as we'll see in the stories later in this chapter. However, the leadership skills in attracting and energizing allies to join a coalition are remarkably similar. The process of finding allies and attracting resources, information, and support relies on enduring principles for selling ideas and sparking interest in innovation. Tackling huge, intractable institutional problems still comes down to individual leaders making relationships and winning support. Advanced leadership involves what innovators always need: the right backers to provide the power tools that leaders need to move ideas into action.

Having viewed Doug Rauch's wheel, let's turn to a second kind of coalition, a chain. Coalition-building skills helped two innovators who had an idea but no position or authority (and not even Doug Rauch's degree of experience in relevant sectors) launch a solution to the international refugee crisis.

Matchmaking Chains: Coalitions Beyond Boundaries

The idea for a chain to make connections across a big global gap was seeded at a glamorous Washington, DC, fund-raiser with famous performer Téa Leoni. Seeing beyond the glitz, Mary Louise Cohen and husband Bruce Cohen decided to travel to rough, slum-like refugee camps in Lebanon and Jordan.

Leoni, an American actor and a UNICEF goodwill ambassador, had just returned from the Zaatari refugee camp in northern Jordan. With nearly eighty thousand Syrian refugees in residence, Zaatari had quickly filled to become the equivalent of Jordan's fourth largest city. In her talk, Leoni said she was struck by how many of the refugees she met there had skills and had been leading very successful lives in Syria before fleeing in turmoil and having to rely on humanitarian aid.

The Cohens had already been thinking about the refugee crisis, which was all over the news that year. It was a huge institutional problem that was getting worse. In 2014, there were about twenty-five million refugees worldwide, about 48 percent of them of working age, but fewer than 1 percent of whom would find meaningful resettlement using conventional channels. The consequences included massive poverty, dependency, and limited education for refugees' children, not to mention political upheaval in refugee-receiving countries.

Leoni's discussion of the skilled people she met in Zaatari was the kaleidoscope shake that made the Cohens decide to dig further into the problem. If there really are skilled people, they said to each other, then there is a commonsense solution; somebody should match skilled refugees with talent that the rest of the world needs. They started to reframe a humanitarian problem as containing an economic dimension—as a labor market problem. They could create a new narrative about refugees and involve the private sector.

Both Cohens brought political capabilities and connections, as well as a little cash, even though this domain was well beyond anything they had done before. Mary Louise had cofounded a leading Washington law firm that represented whistleblowers and was known for the large amounts of money it recovered for the federal government. She had also cofounded a small NGO supporting girls' education in Africa. Bruce was a longtime US Senate staffer, eventually serving as chief counsel and staff director for the Senate Judiciary Committee. They were friendly with prominent people working on refugee issues, including former UN assistant secretary-general Gillian Sorensen.

The Cohens began exploring the potential for their idea: a matchmaking service named Talent Beyond Boundaries (TBB). TBB would establish a new pathway to employment, helping skilled refugees resettle with their families in friendly countries as self-sufficient, tax-paying jobholders. At the other end of the chain, TBB would help employers needing skills to tap a new pool of talent.

"We knew we couldn't become experts ourselves, so we had to find the experts and get them to be thought partners with us," Mary Louise said. They reached across their network for introductions and spoke with the UN High Commissioner on Refugees (UNHCR), Mercy Corps, and other groups that had on-the-ground experience serving refugees to get the lay of the land. Then, in January 2015, they traveled to Beirut to visit camps and get firsthand information, at the invitation of an acquaintance working with UNICEF on psychosocial supports for traumatized refugee children. The US ambassador to Lebanon introduced them to the regional UNHCR officials, and that led to an invitation to UNHCR headquarters in Geneva, Switzerland, a few months later. They left the Geneva meetings with the possibility of a cooperation agreement for TBB, which was ready by early 2016.

UNCHR was their first and, arguably, most important ally. Formal cooperation with the global organization charged with protecting refugees lent them instant legitimacy.

The Cohens began to flesh out the elements required to build the coalition to make TBB a credible and effective matchmaking chain. A matching service to fill a glaring gap could sound like an Uber or Lyft for skilled refugees. That wasn't the Cohen's main goal. They were adamant that they were creating a new solution for refugees that could greatly increase the number of refugees starting new, self-reliant lives, with the job-matching to demonstrate the viability of this labor mobility pathway. Though TBB was not meant to be a digital app, the Uber analogy was not far-fetched. Bruce Cohen said they studied the Uber-type problem of how to align supply and demand. Do they work on the demand side to line up employers? Or on the supply side to line up skilled refugees? They were proposing an economic transaction and a business match: people with skills to fill job opportunities. Conversations with corporate HR executives made it clear to them that first they had to prove that skilled refugees existed and could be found; that was not the conventional image of ragged refugees. And they had to describe skills very specifically; it was not enough to say *engineer* without details about what kind and what experience. The credibility of TBB's story required information.

With seed funding from their family foundation, the Journey Fund, and, eventually, a grant from the US State Department, they put together a team to reach out to refugees in Lebanon and Jordan. Some were volunteers. They sent young team members to assemble focus groups and listening sessions for thirty to fifty people at a time to learn how their concept would look to refugees. They were careful not to raise unrealistic expectations, but they wanted to learn.

On the Cohens' first trip to Beirut in January 2015, they wondered whether refugees would be willing to travel from Lebanon to distant parts of the world for work. A UNICEF coordinator who worked with

Palestinian youth arranged focus groups of young people ages eighteen to twenty-two to pose that question. "They all looked like my children's classmates in Washington—and expressed the same hopes and dreams," Mary Louise recalled. "A young mechanic, maybe twenty-one or twenty-two, said that he had recently held a temporary job with Caterpillar in Nigeria. We asked him how the job was, and he said that life in Nigeria had been very hard. But when we asked if he would go back, he said 'absolutely'—he would move wherever he could find work in his field."

They realized they needed data that would turn themselves into experts. In July 2016, they set out to create an online data portal in Arabic and English. They chose a Syrian refugee they had met on their first trip to Beirut to build it; he had resettled in Canada on a humanitarian visa and then found work for an online data company. To discuss the program and encourage refugees to post data, TBB sent teams to Jordan and Lebanon with protocols in hand and hired refugees as outreach volunteers, paying them about $250 a month, the maximum the Jordanian and Lebanese governments would allow. UNHCR helped TBB generate more data, as did some social media mentions and a Syrian expat NGO that hosted webinars.

About 10,000 skilled people signed up to be in the talent catalog in the first year, including 495 engineers, 875 trade workers, 340 computer professionals, 195 accountants, and 375 health professionals. About 2,000 were women, including teachers, pharmacists, social workers, accountants, and administrators, a third of them with advanced English language proficiency. "Creating a database gave us credibility," Mary Louise said. "We were real, we had assets, we knew what we were talking about, and we were committed. We weren't just two folks walking around talking about a good idea."

Now they had a significant sponsor, other allies, an entity of their own, and a valuable resource that could build the chain. The talent catalog included very deep data. Mary Louise ticked off the benefits: "A company needed a roofer who can do metal roofs; we were able to find one who spoke English. A company in Australia needed a butcher, somebody who could deal with large, heavy animal carcasses; we could fill that with somebody who spoke English."

English ability was important for the demand side of the match platform. Just as Jordan and Lebanon were the pilot countries on the supply side, Canada and Australia became the pilots on the demand side. For Canada, immigration was a growth strategy. To identify employers, the Cohens attended conferences in Canada about immigration with trade associations such as the Information and Communications Council and the British Columbia Construction Association. There the tone was pragmatic. The humanitarian aspect was all well and good, but mainly employers needed to recruit people into their industry. This was especially true for some SMEs (small and midsized enterprises) that eagerly hopped on board because they otherwise couldn't afford to recruit globally. TBB also enticed some global partners in accounting and consulting, such as EY, Deloitte, and Accenture, who were always looking for talent. In Australia, an entrepreneur with a similar idea took on employer-finding for TBB. John Cameron, who made his fortune developing electronic trading platforms and had formed Refugee Jobs Marketplace, joined TBB in 2016 as vice chair and chief technology officer.

Soon, TBB was working with about fifty companies, including Canadian e-commerce contender Shopify, a Canadian strategic sourcing software company called Bonfire, and an Australian software company called IRESS. More than fifty refugee candidates were in various stages of recruitment with dozens of private sector companies, including more than a dozen with job offers.

Some employers became enthusiastic allies. Robert Collier, president of Davert Tool, a tool and die manufacturer in Niagara Falls, Ontario, desperately needed to hire new workers for his manufacturing facility to replace retirees. He was having trouble filling the jobs in Canada as the company was not in a hot industry or location. He heard about TBB at an industry meeting, flew to Lebanon, met some of the refugees TBB was helping, and hired one of them, who then went to the Canadian embassy for an interview to get his visa. Collier became so convinced of the business case that he organized small manufacturers in Ontario and helped persuade the Canadian government to support TBB's work. "Interviewing these refugees had a profound effect on me," he said in a TBB report. "These well-educated candidates were impressive on so many levels. They are driven, persistent, and determined to succeed and would be an asset to any company. What is good for business is good for the community and the country. It would be a mistake, in my opinion, for any country not to recognize the value they bring with them."[9]

In 2019, TBB was still the only organization working with skilled refugees on a path to employment. Its mission was unique, although other nationally based organizations helped refugees who had already been relocated in their countries to find jobs, such as Upwardly Global in the United States, Refugee Talent in Australia, and multiple groups in Germany. "The big significance of our work," Mary Louise observed, "is that we are using skills needed by the private sector as a lever to move refugees to countries where they can have safe and productive futures." The Cohens were awaiting the results of robust demonstrations—the first twenty people resettled in Canada and the first ten in Australia. They would continue discussions with those governments about administrative changes in immigration laws to make the countries more accessible—for example, modification of fees or passport renewal requirements too stiff for refugees—without diluting security considerations. Unlike Uber, which initially tended to ignore government, the Cohens paid attention to the context surrounding talent-employer matches from the beginning, with governments involved as fundamental facilitators.

Government adoption was part of the end game—that more countries would tweak policies to facilitate skills-based, employment-oriented resettlement. The Cohens had begun to explore Morocco with the help of London-based Global Innovation Fund. But they had walked away from Saudi Arabia, because the kingdom did not offer refugee protections, and its involvement would send the wrong signal to other stakeholders. Private sector market adoption was also a goal—more employers and more pathways to jobs, perhaps through adding staffing agencies. In addition, the Cohens hoped that other NGOs would replicate the model, thus multiplying the number of matches that could be made between skilled refugees and eager employers a thousandfold. TBB would have impact not just by itself but through multiple coalitions, joined across sectors.

And that's how "two folks walking around talking about a good idea," as Mary Louise put it, became global change agents on a problem of great magnitude. They drew from their reservoir of advanced leadership skills to link unrelated parties in a chain of impact and garner committed allies: They showed up personally. They gained grounded firsthand information about both refugees and employers. They brought a learning stance, seeking to be taught before asking, and then kept their requests manageable. They appealed to potential allies' material interests, not just tugging at their heartstrings. And they minimized opposition by presenting their innovation as augmenting, not replacing, established approaches. That's always a good tactic.

Forming a Circle: Campaigning to Sell Change

Similar tactics for selling change are found in all coalitions, whether allies ever meet one another. In a third kind of coalition, a circle, people and groups join in to contribute toward a shared goal that none, including the leader, could accomplish alone. Members of a circle might sometimes meet, but convening them is not the major success factor. The effectiveness of a circle depends on enlarging the number of contributors, each of which might act independently toward the shared goal. This is especially true when the mission is to campaign for change in individual behaviors. There are numerous lessons about activating allies, converting fence sitters, and neutralizing opponents in the process by which a determined academic created a campaign to change social and cultural norms.

Establishing a New Social Role

Hug a teenager you care about, and thank Jay Winsten. The allies Winsten brought into the circle of support for the Designated Driver Campaign helped save millions of lives that might otherwise have been lost to alcohol-related traffic fatalities, particularly the lives of young people.

Winsten's work is a classic case of how advanced leaders can entice participation in ad hoc coalitions that campaign for change. The project goes back a while and has stood the test of time. Winsten, a former molecular biologist who joined the Harvard School of Public Health, mobilized with his team the designated driver effort in the United States. The goal was not to eliminate alcohol or dampen party spirits. It was to ensure that, at every gathering that included alcohol, each group riding together would name at least one person to act as a designated driver who did not drink at all and could transport people safely. As its famous slogan went, "A designated driver is the life of the party."

Before the Designated Driver Campaign got underway, alcohol contributed to 60 percent of all traffic deaths in the United States and to two-thirds of those involving sixteen- to twenty-year-olds, making alcohol-related traffic crashes the leading cause of death among young adults.[10] Mothers Against Drunk Driving (MADD), formed by Candy Lightner after her thirteen-year-old daughter was killed by an intoxicated driver, had helped lobby for laws that temporarily reduced fatalities, but when the spotlight dimmed, numbers bounced back up. Laws alone are not enough to change individual behaviors if social structures surrounding people don't also change—just as Mitch Landrieu learned in New Orleans and Anand Piramal saw in India when dealing with illegal steroid providers. Public education efforts that exhort people to change without changing the structures around them also don't work. That's why behavioral economists argue for "nudges" via structures that make it easier to choose particular actions over others.[11]

While exploring the problem of teenage suicide, Winsten stumbled on the successful use of the designated driver idea in Scandinavia to reduce teenage deaths. Norway and Sweden had tough laws about driving while intoxicated, and strong enforcement, but the creation of a new social role was intriguing. He also heard about a small pilot project in Washington, DC, using the designated driver concept.

Winsten thought bigger. Even if a small pilot worked, Daily Table style, it would never spread far enough fast enough to make a dent in a terrible life-or-death problem that needed to be stopped immediately. He decided to go to the biggest players reaching the largest audiences. He knew none of them. But he and a small team plowed ahead anyway. He succeeded in forming a wide circle of relationships with Hollywood moguls, television networks, advertising agencies, the press, and political leaders.

It worked. The high level of media exposure generated by the Designated Driver Campaign over four TV seasons and over 160 prime-time programs with an estimated $100 million a year of donated air time helped to rejuvenate an anti–drunk driving movement that had temporarily run out of steam. Moreover, it became "cool" to name a designated driver, as stars did on favorite programs. Young people didn't feel preached to; instead, they embraced this rotating leadership idea in which they became responsible for others' safety. This new social role could be mentioned with pride and social approval. The term *designated driver* even made it into dictionaries.

To mobilize the allies who would make this happen, Jay Winsten went everywhere, talked to everyone he ran into, and knocked on every door he could find. It was classic networking, the way all coalitions are built. You find the people who know people. One door opens another. You improvise, seizing every opportunity. On a flight from New York to Boston, Winsten told his story to a top advertising executive who happened to be sitting in the next seat by pure chance. She offered to provide her agency's services pro bono, which resulted in the Designated Driver Campaign's widely praised poster and slogan. Other contacts introduced him to top people in entertainment media in New York and Los Angeles.

Winsten was an academic transformed into an evangelist by the power of the mission; he had the right story to tell. Early in the campaign, Winsten dined at celebrity chef Wolfgang Puck's famed Spago restaurant in Hollywood. A companion recognized Puck and his then wife, co-owner Barbara Lazaroff, across the room and prodded Winsten to approach them. "I forced myself to do that," Winsten recalled. It paid off. Spago sponsored a Hollywood reception for the Designated Driver Campaign, and Lazaroff became an advisor.

In the course of door-knocking, Winsten was introduced to former CBS president Frank Stanton, a media giant who became an important advisor. Stanton then introduced Winsten to former NBC chairman and MTM Enterprises founder Grant Tinker, who proved instrumental in getting Hollywood's creative community behind the campaign. Tinker offered valuable expertise, particularly in how to communicate effectively with a sector far outside of Winsten's home building. Tinker edited the campaign's outreach letters to make sure they fit with the Hollywood creative community's values. Tinker advised Winsten to be very sensitive to screenwriters' core value of creative freedom and to ask for participation rather than demand it, to avoid raising hackles. Winsten also learned about how to appeal to the emotions of people in the entertainment industry who had been personally affected by the drinking and driving problem.

Small asks of many people can be powerful. The pace of showing up and door-knocking accelerated. Tinker introduced Winsten to

Hollywood's top television production company executives and brought them into the circle. A who's who from Paramount, Disney Studios, Columbia Pictures Television, and Twentieth Century Fox joined the advisory board. They enabled him to attend dress rehearsals. Overall, Winsten held face-to-face meetings with 250 producers, screenwriters, and other key individuals in Hollywood, mostly one-on-one or in small batches. He was careful not to ask too much of any one person. He made it clear that even a small, subtle mention in a TV show would be enough. This removed excuses for saying no and made it easier to get to yes. In successful coalition-building, no one ally—outside of the working inner circle—has to do too much or make much change.

To get major allies to join the effort, it's important to strike mutually beneficial deals—to give as well as get by creative horse trading. That's where the ability to read potential allies and understand their interests comes in—to be attuned to the needs of the potential allies, to what they want and need, and to see what you have that can get it for them. In short, coalition-building relies on leaders with sufficient empathy that they can see what matters to a range of stakeholders from a range of sectors. Giving sets the norm of reciprocity into motion (I give to you, and you feel inclined to give back to me), even if it takes a while to bear fruit.

To build a working relationship with ABC, Winsten acceded to executive Tom Dzodin's request for help reviewing advertisements' health claims, despite Winsten's disinterest in the task. A few years later, that deal secured the network's participation in the Designated Driver Campaign, the first of the major networks to do so. He did this kind of horse trading repeatedly. To create goodwill with the Hollywood creative community, he volunteered his center as an information source to screenwriters to improve the realism and accuracy of their scripts and offered prestigious seats on the center's advisory board.

Circles enlarge because they become attractive for others to join. People want to participate because others do. Those already on board sell others. Winsten leveraged ABC's commitment and then CBS's. When he cold-called Rosalind Weinman at NBC to obtain NBC's support for the campaign, he explained to her that two other major TV networks had already pledged assistance.

Despite a project's big-tent capaciousness, it is also important to maintain boundaries: whom not to include. The Designated Driver Campaign had neutralized some potential opposition of the alcoholic beverage industry by asking only the designated driver to abstain. Alcohol giants Seagram and Anheuser-Busch offered financing, with Super Bowl tickets thrown in. Winsten was already under fire from some public health advocates that the designated driver concept enabled abusive drinking among nondrivers. He refused the companies' offers.[12]

When seeking resources, it is tempting to strike deals with all comers with access to them, but advanced leaders think as carefully about who should not be in their coalition as about who should. They avoid bringing in stakeholders whose participation will provide ammunition to their critics. That's why Doug Rauch was choosy about the health values of the groups that donated food, the Cohens didn't consider Saudi Arabia's offer of refugee employment, and Jay Winsten said no to the alcoholic beverage industry. Advanced leaders also avoid stakeholders whose participation will scare off or dampen the enthusiasm of highly valued allies. They might exclude groups whose self-interest means they would be selling their own agenda rather than supporting the higher shared purpose. Who is on the list at events, for example, sends a big signal about an event's purpose.

Although those with mission-undermining stances should be kept away, mere critics shouldn't be written off. They can provide a sanity check, pointing to flaws in the model and, in essence, removing the bubble wrap described in chapter 2 that stops feedback. Furthermore, as a project develops and begins to show tangible results, challengers can change their minds and come around to support it instead. That's why coalitions are dynamic.

Winsten faced doubters, naysayers, and maybe a little envy. Prominent foundations initially declined funding requests or advisory council seats because "they didn't think it had a chance," Winsten said, but eventually, they were eager to join in.[13] It took a year of outreach to the federal Office of Substance Abuse Protection to convince the staff that the campaign didn't tacitly encourage passengers to overindulge, and then the office issued a statement praising the campaign. Some Harvard colleagues questioned the campaign's suitability and likelihood of success—sometimes in public—as well as Winsten's name appearing often in the press. Vindication came when Winsten received a letter from his most vocal critic praising the project's accomplishments and indicating his strong support. By not writing off any of these groups, he was able to convert the undecideds and fence sitters into allies and build momentum.

The big coalition—with its very large circle of contributors—succeeded in making a difference. Findings from national surveys strongly suggested that the campaign contributed to a sharp increase in the self-reported use of designated drivers in the United States and a marked decrease in the number of drinking drivers, as measured directly in roadside surveys using breathalyzers. Young people showed an especially great drop. Of course, even careful studies can't attribute results to any one cause—for example, many states raised the drinking age during the same period—but the designated driver social role was a key factor. A new social expectation could be enacted at every restaurant, bar, and house party in America—and, ultimately, anywhere in the world where people watched American popular media.

Enlarging the Circles: Toward a Coalition of Coalitions

When advanced leaders want to take on big, intractable institutional problems of wide scope, it can be daunting to realize the magnitude of diversity of the people and groups who have a stake in the problem and who control the wide array of resources needed to resolve it. This is especially true for climate change, on land or on the sea.

A fourth type of coalition addresses that diversity and complexity. When a problem is multidimensional, gathering allies one by one is insufficient. It becomes important to create big, overlapping circles, form new cross-sector relationships, and introduce a new idea all can use. Torsten Thiele's advanced leadership task included creating allies to support his innovation—financing ocean development projects—by joining existing coalitions into an even bigger circle. Without formal power or position, he wanted to mobilize faster action to establish the idea that "blue finance" could improve the health of the oceans. I described Thiele's banker background and passion for the oceans problem in chapter 1; here, we see what he did to make a few small ripples of an idea become big waves.

A New Trust: Can Blue Finance Tackle Climate Change?

Former banker Torsten Thiele didn't do anything as bold or as headline-grabbing as Bertrand Piccard. Piccard, a psychiatrist, flew a solar plane around the globe in mid-2016 with professional pilot Andre Borschberg to promote the enormous potential of clean technologies. But Thiele got to know Piccard and his Solar Impulse Foundation as an advisor on oceans for the foundation's search for one thousand innovative climate change solutions. Thiele had gained experience on the selection panel for the National Geographic Marine Protection Prize and worked with a prizewinner, a drone company from Morocco.

Neither did Thiele do anything as simple and easy to explain as a crowdfunded campaign to support a machine for collecting plastic from the ocean, which didn't work anyway (as Thiele concluded it wouldn't from reading the 450-page plan). He didn't do anything as straightforward and exciting to consumers as the Parley for the Oceans campaign with Adidas, started by personal friends of his. Parley, a network of artists, musicians, fashion designers, journalists, and architects, founded in 2012 by German-born New York designer Cyrill Gutsch, partnered with Adidas when Adidas decided to make running shoes out of marine plastics, creating commercial value from ocean debris.

Thiele was serious rather than flamboyant, and he thought about whole systems rather than simple gestures. But his dream was big: to create a new sector of blue finance. He wanted to stimulate new financing mechanisms to unleash innovation that could speed up saving the oceans. "The ocean world is particularly slow because it was driven in the past very much by governments," he said. "I felt that innovation should be at the heart of this. Conservation technology innovation is a new emerging space." He also said, "Ocean finance is now in the millions. It must scale up to the billions and trillions. We need a very different way of looking at the ocean."

Thiele's international project finance experience got him started. He formed the Global Ocean Trust (GOT) as a nonprofit organization in the United States and a foundation in Germany, which gave him a basis for donations and, more important, an affiliation to list on the rosters of key conferences and events. He envisioned that GOT would encourage the launch of a Global Ocean Bank for Sustainability and Development to facilitate attracting significant private sector investment in ocean-related projects that would also mitigate climate change. To go from entity to impact, Thiele needed a big coalition of allies who would adopt the concept and influence their own organizations to change their thinking. He needed to connect otherwise-siloed stakeholders, who were suspicious of one another, had little history together, or fiercely guarded their own interests. Moreover, there were national and geopolitical divides, including tensions between developed and developing nations, bureaucrats who sometimes felt powerless and pushed around, business leaders who felt powerful and entitled, and civil society activists who felt morally superior and disdained the very idea of business.

To stimulate a market where little really existed, Thiele felt he needed to influence all of them. That took him to the fourth type of coalition, a series of circles—in essence, a coalition of coalitions across sectors and nations working toward a new agenda that could unlock capital for blue technology and innovation to save the oceans.

Although the oceans have no sovereignty, they do enjoy a head-spinning array of multilateral organizations and alliances concerned with their state, plus a calendar-jamming array of international meetings. That meant a lot of talk and questionable amounts of action. Thiele needed to exercise several key advanced leadership skills.

Showing up. The first necessity is being there. Thiele wasn't too proud to beg for a personal seat at every event he could. He went to the UN COP (Council of Parties) meetings, including the well-publicized Paris talks and the 2018 follow-up in Katowice, Poland, and injected more mentions of oceans at the discussions. He joined the Ocean and Climate Platform, a coalition of seventy different organizations, from science to business, formed during World Oceans Day in 2014, with the help of UN agencies. He participated in the International Union for Conservation of Nature, formed in 1948, an association of thirteen hundred government and civil society organizations and thirteen thousand experts. That led to GOT's membership in the High Seas Alliance, founded in 2011, with nearly forty NGOs. GOT was initially an observer to the working group on high seas biodiversity discussion for the UN General Assembly, then bringing expertise on finance issues to the official treaty negotiation. Thiele was asked to brief Pacific Island states at the UN in New York on blue finance and was deployed to Chile to talk to Latin American states. He even spoke at the International Boat Show in Dusseldorf, Germany, in January 2019.

Helping your way into inner circles. Showing up paid off because he also offered to help. He became a reliable worker who could be counted on to contribute without seeking credit, though he was willing to be a speaker. He wrote briefings on ocean finance, introducing the idea of blue natural capital. He joined working groups for behind-the-scenes planning. He was part of a big group that laid the groundwork for seven Arctic states, including Russia and the United States, to sign a joint moratorium on commercial fishing for at least sixteen years. He provided expertise to an ocean action initiative under the prime minister of Norway and to the European Union's blue strategy, acting as a team member to support others' efforts. He organized a conference for the German government in December 2018 while staying in the background. He helped found the Coalition for Private Investment in Conservation and the Ocean Data Alliance with technology companies.

Learning before asking. Thiele took a learning stance to his contacts. He didn't inject his point of view or agenda as a finance expert but indicated interest in understanding theirs. He recalled meetings with major global NGOs such as the World Wildlife Fund (WWF) and how he allayed their concerns that GOT might be competing with them. "I'm learning from you," he would say. He was genuinely interested in learning about ecology, biology, and conservation components of climate change with consequences for the oceans. Gradually, he added his agenda to the discussions, which he could then present, he said, as "very much aligned to yours." He could say, "Maybe there's another language, around economics?" He concluded that "this sort of deep immersion is key to get over some of the siloed approaches that come if you look at it just from your own perspective."

In turn, WWF officials listened to Thiele and invited him to tell his story about the value of establishing blue finance at a summit on economics at the World Ocean Summit. That was just one example of building trust by seeking to understand potential allies' points of view. Asking questions has an added bonus; the people you ask tend to think you're smarter than people who don't ask, as recent social psychological research shows.

Planting seeds and preselling. On contentious matters, it's wise to hold private conversations before seeking public commitment. Lining up new relationships behind the scenes, before anyone even comes to the table, is one of the secrets of great negotiators, as my friend and expert James Sebenius found in studying top global leaders. It's dangerous to walk into a meeting without knowing where people stand—that is a sure way to build a community of people totally united in opposition to your own agenda—and it misses the possibility for side deals.

For multistakeholder meetings, Thiele's mode was one-on-one advance discussions. For a blue finance launch event at COP, he invited senior bankers, but rather than bringing them into the room right away, "where they wouldn't have understood each other (or felt it was a good use of their time)," he said, "I met with them separately, then slowly brought the parties together." The event included a senior banker from Citibank speaking on the program with senior officials from an NGO and two governments. "The curation of that interaction was really fascinating," he observed. He talked with each group to explain it in their language, contacted the others for their input, circled back, and then slowly got buy-in. Using those principles, he held other cross-sector discussions with business leaders, development bankers, and conservation organizations.

By being a connector and mediating and translating across silos, he also became an expert. Thiele had gone from begging to attend, to offering to attend, to being invited to attend, to being part of the planning, to speaking as a key figure on the agenda.

Delivering new results. Now known as an effective connector and business expert, Thiele worked on arousing private sector interest for

the *Economist* newspaper's World Ocean Summit in 2017, including
an innovative finance challenge won by the Seychelles Blue Bonds
proposal. This launched in 2018 as the world's first sovereign blue
bond, supporting marine and fisheries projects, with help from the
World Bank and $15 million from international investors Calvert
Impact Capital, Nuveen, and Prudential Financial. Insurance companies came on board at a May 2018 Ocean Risk Summit in Bermuda, resulting in a scheme for "Blue Carbon Resilience Credits,"
a cross-sector collaboration between XL, a major insurer, and The
Nature Conservatory, a leading NGO. Wary adversaries found a
common task that made them allies.

Accepting failure and rethinking approaches. It wasn't always smooth
sailing. Not every outreach was a win. It never is. In the high seas
negotiations, the issue of marine genetic resources came up. Phar-
maceutical companies understood how to use them for medical progress, but developing countries saw this as their heritage and wanted
to share in the financial returns. Thiele and his colleagues held separate discussions with each group first before there could be agreement. But sometimes agreement was elusive anyway. When Thiele
began a project on human health and ocean health, he started out
thinking that "we all see it the same way," he said. "But I found that
the medical community didn't think the quality of water made a big
difference."

His aspirations still encountered doubters; some thought that the
scope was too big or that there would not be enough investible projects. People who understood the concept of an ocean sustainability
bank wondered where the $10 billion would come from. In his own
mind, Thiele himself sometimes sided with the skeptics. He knew
his work was hard to explain, and he kept honing the message to
get the right story to tell. He refined the narrative by listening to

stakeholders and incorporating their reactions. He looked for small, carefully chosen propositions.

From Ripples to Waves

By 2019, about four years after he formed GOT, Thiele was changing the conversation and enlarging the numbers of people in it. Thiele's coalition-building efforts were enabling others to think and act differently. He had formed a cross-sector coalition of coalitions, helping other groups and organizations connect across boundaries more effectively to move to action even faster. He could multiply the impact of Bertrand Piccard's Solar Impulse Foundation, Parley for the Oceans, and numerous other private sector activists. His efforts spanned the large and small. In early February, the Nordic Investment Bank issued the first Baltic Blue Bonds. A month later, Thiele was able to report on the first funding for a seaweed and marine plastics project in the Philippines. He planned soon after that to introduce a company with a new filter for washing machines that would help keep toxins out of the water supply and, ultimately, the oceans, at the *Economist* World Ocean Summit in Abu Dhabi, as an example of commercially viable business opportunities. He had also gained the connections and legitimacy to find resources for his envisioned Global Ocean Bank for Sustainability and Development.

Few people who care about the fate of the oceans—a group that includes Salesforce founder and CEO Marc Benioff—would want to do exactly what Torsten Thiele undertook. Instead, they might want to fly a solar plane, create products with marine plastic, float bond issues, or offer insurance for shipping risks. But that's not the point. Regardless of the project to be undertaken, the skills for assembling backers and supporters are similar. How Thiele went about mobilizing allies for a new angle on an urgent but intractable problem reflects advanced leadership lessons about how to use coalition-building and overlapping circles of contributors to open new opportunities that accelerate innovation and change.

Following the Rule of Three

Leadership for change can be tough going, even more so when tackling a large problem that spills across sectors. Indifference or passivity can be the kiss of death. Lukewarm support isn't good enough. It can slip away. Leaders must be energizers who light a spark and keep people fired up.

This chapter has looked at the coalition-building process to solve problems and make a positive difference by visiting neighborhoods, nations, Hollywood, and the high seas. In all cases, advanced leaders face the Rule of Three: there are potential allies, undecideds, and opponents. To get the power tools needed to turn a good story into a successful initiative for institutional change, they need skills to deal with all three groups.

Finding allies is the first step; then their backing must be firmed up. It's not enough to secure a one-time contribution and lose contact. Sometimes allies don't even know how their actions can support or undermine an innovation—recall the friendly gun-waving policeman at the start of this chapter who didn't realize that his joking could harm Daily Table. Keeping allies informed as well as involved is a good idea at any point. Advanced leaders must keep cultivating their coalitions to increase activism and support and to keep them from splintering into subgroups. After all, support is voluntary, and perfect agreement about details is unrealistic. So leaders can:

- *Appeal to larger principles.* Keep the mission first and foremost in everyone's minds. Highlight shared values, but be careful of superficial agreements in principle accompanied by continuing squabbling over specifics.

- *Bring allies closer.* Find roles for them, perhaps on advisory groups where they can join other allies that they find attractive. Open a channel for their ideas and feedback. Potential critics can be co-opted by moving them into the inner circle where their voices are heard. This works well when allies are opinion leaders who can sway others, or they have relevant expertise and something to contribute. But make sure that it doesn't slow decision-making.
- *Offer a bigger stake.* Share the benefits of a successful innovation. Make sure that allies and the groups they represent keep getting what they need and value. Benefits can include access, contacts, recognition, reputation, new resources, or financial returns.

Undecideds who are sitting on the fence can go either way. The task is to move them closer to support. Leaders might encounter many fence sitters in their initial sales process. Building relationships with them can leave the door open for future contact as the project develops. Of course, it's impossible and unnecessary to convert every last soul and answer every last critic, and it's a big waste of time to try. Still, leaders can:

- *Reduce the costs.* Minimize the number of affected areas and the number of losses or changes implied by the effort. Do this when the project can afford to be flexible or when some elements aren't necessary. But don't let the initiative get too watered down or lose what makes it innovative.
- *Send emissaries to pave the way.* Deploy diplomats. Use allies to keep key undecideds informed. Sometimes it helps to have someone else represent you. For women, in particular, research shows that they do a better job negotiating on behalf of others than for themselves.[14]
- *Display support.* Ask sponsors for a visible demonstration of backing. It helps when important sponsors are willing to speak out and put their own reputations on the line. But be careful not to ask them

for too much, or you risk finding that they are suddenly not available
or that they damn with faint praise.

- *Wear them down*. Repeat arguments and don't give ground until
  skeptics get tired of the battle. There are some virtues to being tenacious. This is useful when you are confident of the rightness of your
  ideas, time is on your side, and progress is clear. But watch out, in
  case criticism goes underground only to surface later.

Outright opponents are a challenge, especially if they can't be
ignored. The goal is to get them out of the way and decrease their
activism—neutralizing them by removing weapons or by encouraging
dissent and splintering opponents into weaker subgroups. Leaders can:

- *Confront them in public*. Denounce opponents in front of powerful
  people and opinion leaders. Do this when stakeholder opinion is
  largely on your side and favors project goals. But if critics and skeptics are embarrassed in public, they are likelier to hold their ground
  and try to sabotage the effort in other ways.
- *Force exits*. If you or your sponsors have position power and are willing to use it, remove them from the scene. (Get them sent on an
  expedition to Labrador, perhaps?) But beware of backlash. If opposition hardens, threat of retaliation grows.
- *Wait it out*. If you don't have the means to counter opposition, then
  stop arguing and let the project proceed slowly and quietly. Just keep
  plodding along patiently. But be careful not to put the initiative in
  danger of losing momentum or support from allies, who could begin
  to drop off. Sometimes patience is not rewarded.

Innovations are fragile in the beginning, and many things can go
wrong. The quest for support is ongoing. Big successes come when
allies are united, opponents are weakened and divided, and those on

the fence are gradually converted. The opposite is dangerous: when allies become divided, opponents are united, and undecideds are written off. Those mistakes could put a promising high-impact venture in jeopardy, especially when it encounters the inevitable setbacks that can arise in the middle of leading an innovation.

6

CROSSING THE DESERT TO THE NEXT OASIS

Mastering the Miserable Middles

Jeff Bezos and Junko Yoda have absolutely nothing in common. Except perhaps one thing. They each faced the murky, messy, miserable middles of change and then had to decide whether to persist, pivot, or pull the plug.

Bezos is a household name. Amazon, the company he founded and leads, is a daily presence for hundreds of millions of consumers. The fate of Amazon's deal to put part of its new second headquarters in Queens, New York, promising twenty-five thousand jobs, made big headlines. In contrast, very few people have heard of Yoda, despite her successes as a global investment banker in Hong Kong, a rare feat for a Japanese woman, or her partnership to change community life to get girls thinking about jobs—any jobs—in poor parts of Southeast Asia. The comparison is a stretch, I know—well beyond apples to oranges and more like apples to cloud computing.

But the one thing they shared is significant for leaders seeking change at any level: the near inevitability that cross-sector, multistakeholder initiatives will encounter surprises and setbacks. This happens regardless of the fame of the leader or the size of the enterprise. The founder of Amazon, one of the world's most valuable companies, and the founder of CLinked, a social venture to reduce sex trafficking of girls in Asia, both saw their perfect plans for community action—plans, by the way, that had been agreed to by key stakeholders—derailed by unexpected bumps in the road just as success was in sight. Even the richest man in the world and his legions of leaders could not suppress a group of politicized community activists, who, well outside any actual buildings, held protest rallies on the street. The establishment—a set of elected officials and chambers of commerce championing Amazon's plans, which the general public supported too—couldn't help much either.

The upshot: Bezos gave up while Yoda persevered. The Amazon team walked away without even trying to modify their proposal to consider the activists' objections or work with supporters on alternatives. This will be studied for years as a business and politics case. But Yoda's team pivoted and continued. You'd think it would have been the other way around. Amazon had resources and time. Plus, its reputation with consumers could be on the line. For Yoda, no one outside of a small circle of regional NGOs knew her and her work partner, Pam McCambridge. Whether she continued her embryonic project didn't matter to anyone beyond the small communities she intended to serve or the young girls themselves.[1] But maybe that's the difference between money and mission. Amazon's motivations, including its interest in millions of subsidy dollars, seemed purely commercial, no matter how many jobs it promised to create. CLinked, in contrast, had a mission too big to stop. Yoda and McCambridge dreamed of showing how to save young girls from a terrible fate and shut down a reprehensible criminal enterprise.

Obstacles do not have to be deal breakers. They are simply part and parcel of what I call Kanter's Law: that everything can look like a failure in the middle. The middle is that long phase after the burst of energy and excitement that characterizes beginnings subsides and before the satisfaction of endings begins. It is the period when the hard work of change takes place. I have yet to see a new idea that has not run into trouble at some point during its journey to realization. The more ways an innovation deviates from inside-the-building thinking, the more obstacles it will likely face. Give up, and it's automatically a bust—game over. Adjust accordingly, find a way to work around the obstacles, plow ahead, and the initiative could be back on track toward success.

Advanced leaders face the messes and muddles of middles all the time. Who knows how many promising innovations never make it beyond the first contentious argument or loss of support. Lost opportunities matter more when the goal is breaking through an impasse on a big, intractable institutional problem that threatens lives. New York City will probably be fine without HQ2 in Queens; Amazon will undoubtedly add tech jobs in NYC anyway. But would children get enough education without Jeff Dunn and *Sesame Street* taking Big Bird to refugee camps? Would New Orleans be able to confront racism without Mitch Landrieu's courage? Would venture philanthropy and impact investing have as much traction if Vanessa Kirsch had given up when her first partner left New Profit? And to give Jeff Bezos credit, would the quality of journalism in America be as high if he hadn't bought and rescued the *Washington Post*? The middles imperil great ideas. How to get over, through, or around them is a major test of advanced leadership.

Why Innovation and Change Can Be Miserable in the Middle

One of the ironies of innovation in the world of established organizations is a seeming lack of desire to get in early or to be original. Corporate executives would often ask me for help with a culture of innovation, saying that they want more innovation, and in the next breath ask, who else is doing it? Or they'd claim to want more innovation but just not to be the first. Imitation is easier than innovation. Institutional change can encounter similar reactions. Doug Rauch, seeking business funders for Daily Table, was told by Citibank to call back when he had other funders. Bob Whelan felt that everyone Thirteenth Avenue approached wanted to be "the third," not the first. This was surprising, because Whelan and partners were not strangers to fund-raising. The three founders had a combined seventy-five years of experience raising money. And the dozen relevant foundations they approached included some with reputations for innovation. But the universal response, as Whelan described it, was "Grow bigger, get established, become more accepted, and then we'll get involved."

Hard as it can be to break through the reluctance to try new approaches in the beginning, especially ones that question the established order of things, it can be even harder once an initiative is underway. Innovation is inherently uncertain, and things do not always go as planned. There can feel like long dry spells where nothing seems to bloom and there's no oasis in sight. Allies might turn out to be less committed; entities in the coalition might disagree and even drop out. Initial assumptions and timetables might not pan out. Unanticipated roadblocks might loom. Entrenched interests and critics might prove tougher than expected. Milestones might be missed, commitment might flag, and momentum might stall. Beginnings can be exciting, and endings are cause for celebration. But middles are the hardest work.

Middles are vast stretches of desert to cross before reaching the next oasis, where you've earned the relief of knowing that you've made progress. These middles of the work can present four primary kinds of difficulties for advanced leaders.

1. Rhetoric Meets Reality:
Coalition Partners Disagree or Drop Out

The right story—the narrative that compels allies to support the quest for change—is just a lot of words whose meaning emerges in the course of action. An imagined party with diverse allies under the capacious big tent can mask the fact that there are triggers for dissent in every cross-sector and multistakeholder coalition, even among members of the same group who are theoretically in favor of the same things.

Diverse stakeholders are essential for getting institutional change projects off the ground. But that also implies multiple conflicting goals, priorities, and loyalties. Knowledge bases and approaches to solving problems might also differ. Even when working together makes sense, disagreements are to be expected. Moreover, coalition partners' interests and priorities are not static; they can change with circumstances. Interests that were once aligned can diverge over time. In the Amazon case, it's not clear whether Amazon ever had the support of community leaders in Queens, but once new voices entered the discussion, dissension among elected officials as well as the general public put the deal for HQ2 in Queens in contention.

This scenario is all too common. People you thought were aligned behind the grand vision turn out to disagree on the details, and they start withdrawing their support. You remind them that they were consulted early in the process and given a chance to voice their objections. But then you remember that mostly what you got in all those meetings and conferences were smiles and nods. Once in the middle of implementing the idea, they start seeing what the inspiring narrative means in practice, and then they quibble. "Sorry," you might hear, "we didn't think *that* was what you meant."

Tom Santel, whom we met in earlier chapters, encountered coalition fracturing in moving his Raising St. Louis early childhood health and education innovation from concept to execution.[2] The hospital and medical education leaders backing RSL started to argue among themselves. Some saw it as an outcomes-based effort where method didn't matter, perhaps as a chain-like matchmaking navigation service to guide parents to appropriate health resources. One wanted to assign medical, nursing, pharmacy, and social work students from

Washington University and other nearby colleges to work with families as part of their training, which would keep costs down and enable faster scaling, while others preferred hiring full-time professionals for home visits despite the higher price tag. Community input became the tiebreaker. Mothers from three low-income neighborhoods, surveyed in focus groups, expressed serious doubts about using students as home visitors, preferring local provider organizations. This was another reminder of the value of including the community to be served. But the scars of contention could have undermined the whole effort.

Former corporate lawyer Paul Lee faced many such kerfuffles when he took on the task of leading a coalition for Asian American rights known as Asian Americans Advancing Justice.[3] The Advancing Justice coalition was composed of four organizations that had previously been collaborating for years but wanted a more unified national voice on civil rights, despite their differing priorities and approaches (not to mention the hundreds of ethnic groups and places of origin comprising Asian Americans). San Francisco–based Asian Law Caucus, for example, provided social services to local low-income immigrant communities and undertook litigation, whereas Washington, DC–based Asian American Justice Center (AAJC), for which Lee served as chairman, focused on national policy. Asian Law Caucus challenged the compromises AAJC made during congressional discussions over immigration reform in 2013, complaining that AAJC hadn't fought hard enough or got enough. "That made us realize the substantial difference in perspective," Lee said. "We at AAJC don't do very much direct service, so we don't see clients who are suffering from having to wait for reunification with their family members, whereas the Asian Law Caucus deals with this type of disappointment daily."[4]

Dissension of that sort made the news. In November 2013, Asian Law Caucus student affiliate Ju Hong, a twenty-four-year-old University of California graduate, interrupted then president Barack Obama during a speech in San Francisco's Chinatown pushing comprehensive immigration reform—a policy that Advancing Justice had told the Obama administration it supported. To audience cheers, Hong challenged the president to prevent family separation because of deportation of undocumented family members. Lee had to handle the fallout. Obama's unhappy staff contacted Advancing Justice. "You're telling us that you're supportive of the administration on immigration reform while another part of you is publicly questioning our position," Lee recalled a staffer saying.[5] This embarrassment led the affiliates to engage in a series of trust-building conversations to share perspectives and reiterate Advancing Justice's mission of creating a single voice for Asian Americans. The postscript: A year later, Obama expanded DACA (Deferred Action on Childhood Arrivals), which Ju Hong had pushed, and the four Advancing Justice organizations became more aligned.

Disagreements among independent parties are risky in a formal alliance. Members tended to view their support as ad hoc, depending on how they felt about a particular issue, which limited the coalition's advocacy efforts and undermined working relationships with important national civil rights organizations, such as the NAACP. To avoid further fracturing, Lee convened discussions of common interests and created a consultative coordinating council made up of board chairs and executive directors from each affiliate, which he hoped would eventually evolve into an umbrella governing body with decision-making power over disputes. Cooperation paved the way for a unified Advancing Justice pro–affirmative action response to anti–affirmative action groups' litigation against universities in 2015.

Interests and priorities can be misaligned enough that coalition members drop out. Recall Christiana Woods's work, described in chapter 3, enticing pension funds to create and sign on to gun safety principles. So far, so good. But moving to involve other types of financial investors could bring long dry spells or perils in the middle if new groups were slow to get on board or wanted to change the principles, and others dropped out due to conflicting priorities.

Thirteenth Avenue Funding faced this kind of challenge repeatedly. The partners struggled to find and use more than $1 million in pro bono legal work from 2009 to 2012. One team of lawyers decided to quit over a philosophical difference, which Thirteenth Avenue partner Ed Lowry described as "an emotional inability to create a type of contract for which they could find no US precedent." They floundered for a year because of that defection. In another disappointment for Thirteenth Avenue, a partnership with a small New England college for a pilot project fell through just before a scheduled public announcement. The college insisted on framing the deal as a loan instead of equity. Acquiescing on this point would have corrupted one of Thirteenth Avenue Funding's core values, which the founders were unwilling to do.

If stakeholders demand terms for participation that undermine the effort in the middle, or their behaviors are so incendiary that they undermine the integrity of the mission, then good riddance. Vivian Derryck faced this middle misery during her second Africa Watch effort at Bridges Institute, which was aimed at strengthening good governance and democracy in Africa.[6] Mali Watch, which Derryck convened following the seizure of territory in the country's north by rebel fighters, a military coup, and a humanitarian crisis, was already more challenging than her successful work in Côte d'Ivoire. Derryck had to figure out how to respond when a key participant in the effort vehemently objected to the use of the words *rebels* and *jihadists* in group messages. This contrarian emailed other Mali Watch participants, including ambassadors and State Department officials, to voice his strong opposition. This was a breach of the Watch's well-established mechanisms for managing disagreements, which were important for building and maintaining trust among coalition members. Rather than bending the rules for one disgruntled participant, no matter how important he was, Derryck reiterated the proper dispute resolution procedures and did not object when he subsequently decided to no longer take part. Despite this setback, the US State Department ultimately integrated Mali Watch's strategy and communications materials into its policy toward Mali.

2. Forecasting Problems:
Time and Money Run Out Too Soon

It's human nature to make overly optimistic forecasts about projects that seem so obvious and inspiring to the leaders promoting them. And sometimes leaders must sound optimistic in order to get allies to support them in the first place. Although some are wary of overpromising—recall Mary Louise and Bruce Cohen speaking in refugee camps—cautious statements sprinkled with *maybe* and *not certain* hardly motivate anyone to write a check, call a key contact, join the board, or take a job. So optimistic forecasts rule. But those plans—in fact, any plans—are difficult to fulfill. Innovations, especially those targeted at institutional change, don't unfold on a predictable timetable or with a predictable path (and if they did, then they couldn't take advantage of unexpected opportunities, either).

Forecasting is a dangerous occupation—especially when it's about the future. That's not a joke. Forecasts work best when they are really about the past—extrapolating from something done before, where parameters are known and can be projected into the future. But for innovations of any kind, including simple product innovations or the business plans of start-up ventures, there is too much uncertainty for accurate predictions, especially if the new item is truly different and has never been done before or if something done in one context is simply being applied to another.

A classic truism among innovation observers is that new things generally take longer and cost more. That's not always the case; sometimes innovators do it faster and cheaper. But it's true often enough that advanced leaders face the consequences. Raymond Jetson thought there would be more change sooner in Baton Rouge. Marissa Wesley saw that it took longer than she had anticipated for her Win-Win Coalition— designed to unite grassroots women's organizations from many countries to aid in finding corporate support—to get agreement on even simple actions, even though she knew they had joined the Win-Win Coalition because of similar goals. One overly optimistic former top military person waited too long to start fund-raising for a health initiative, thinking the family's own seed funds would last longer than they did and that grants would be easier to secure than they were.

Overoptimism plagues entrepreneurs and innovators of all kinds. They assume they can do things faster and produce more. For advanced leaders, this is a particular peril. Missing milestones can further fracture coalitions, jeopardize support from allies, and set a vicious cycle in motion, because righting the situation by reselling allies on the virtues of the project could take still more time.

Inaccurate estimates about time, money, and nearly everything else are inevitable not only when a model is new but also when its assumptions have yet to be tested in a new context. Robert Meaney and Richard Berkland were seasoned former executives at Valmont Industries, which manufactured irrigation systems in Nebraska to sell in developed countries. They knew how to forecast for big commercial farms, but as advanced leaders, they wanted to bring center pivot irrigation systems technology to smallholder farmers in Sub-Saharan Africa, with the dream of creating sustainable livelihoods for rural Africans.[7]

Meany and Berkland successfully activated stakeholders and mobilized sufficient technical, financial, and institutional resources to start pilot projects in Ghana, Tanzania, and Rwanda but hit different problems in each region. Irrigation work at a site in Ghana endured three years of delay due to tardy completion of both a government-funded canal and debushing of the site. In Tanzania, poor soil conditions at a site that initially looked perfect and an unexpected land ownership challenge at another slowed the launch of a pilot project there, giving them little concrete to show after two arduous years. Their Rwandan pilot project, on the other hand, went so much better than forecasted that overproduction became the problem; farmers' windfall maize yields overwhelmed existing transportation, storage, and drying infrastructures. The crisis was averted when the government provided an additional drying facility to handle the unexpected bounty.

Some leaders who have occupied top positions act on untested assumptions and face forecasting failures because of overconfidence in their own knowledge and capabilities. Michael Critelli was acclaimed as a great leader as CEO of Pitney Bowes, a Fortune 500 document management company with thirty-six thousand employees and a global customer base in an established market.[8] He had led employee health reforms there and had become passionate about health care quality. He decided to join Dossia Service Corporation to champion the cause of improving health care outcomes and reducing costs through personal health records, which was Dossia's specialty. With one office and only eighteen employees, cash-strapped for-profit start-up Dossia was miniscule by comparison to his former company. Critelli believed he knew Dossia and its challenges well, since Pitney Bowes was a founding member in 2006 and he had served on Dossia's board since then. Prior to taking Dossia's helm, Critelli had assumed that a more aggressive sales outreach effort would net more customers only to realize once inside the sales process that the solution was more nuanced and there was much less appetite for change in corporate benefits departments than imagined. He had also assumed he could facilitate sales by calling on Fortune 500 CEOs directly since he had been one himself and knew many of them, but that approach raised the hackles of underresourced benefits departments below the top, which viewed him as an outsider telling them how to do their jobs. For this and other sobering reasons, Critelli reassessed his forecasts. He opted to pivot Dossia's focus away from large enterprises and toward the universe of medium-sized enterprises that was less familiar to him—but with better results.

Related to underestimating the time it will take is overestimating how much support there will be—how quickly allies will join the coalition and how much they will be able to deliver once they do. Just returning phone calls or getting meetings scheduled eats up time. People don't show up—or if they do, they want to change the agenda.

Former agribusiness banker Inge Skjelfjord, a Netherlands native who had worked for Rabobank as well as the World Bank, thought he had lined up everything in Ecuador for starting the world's first cacao research center to help small-scale cacao farmers and find sustainable cacao production solutions.[9] Cacao was a major crop there (and Skjelfjord loved chocolate). An Ecuadorian colleague with political connections had promised to pave the way with government officials, who had expressed interest in the research center. While Ecuador met many of the site selection requirements for a proof-of-concept project—including workforce, geography, infrastructure, and need—it also failed to meet several key criteria. But like many overly optimistic leaders, Skjelfjord thought those other factors could be overcome. The recent policies of Ecuador's government, under President Rafael Correa, had not been favorable toward business or the United States and made potential American investment partners reluctant to work in Ecuador. Skjelfjord's colleague then failed to deliver on the promise of government support. Without close knowledge of Ecuador, Skjelfjord was slow to heed warning signs that the Ecuadorian government's expression of interest in partnering was not to be trusted and that the political risk of putting his pilot project there was too great.

Having spent nearly a year on the Ecuadorian possibility, Skjelfjord later commented on the disappointment of having fallen further and further behind in his goals. "This proved to be much more difficult than I imagined. I was trying to put a complicated project in a complicated country," he said.[10] Skjelfjord eventually redirected efforts toward Tanzania, having lost a great deal of time. He would still save chocolate supplies, just at a much slower pace.

By their very nature, cross-sector coalitions can suffer from forecasting problems. Sectors operate on different time frames, and the slower pace of large, established organizations can frustrate impatient business entrepreneurs. In Costa Rica, Carlos de Paco Alvarado, who worked closely with a pilot project to reduce global warming through hydrogen-fueled transportation, recalled time frame differences between private and public sector coalition members. Costa Rican Toyota dealership Purdy Motor Group wanted immediate action. "Okay, we've been talking about it for a week with everybody, and what are we doing now? What is the next move?" But government ministries, no matter how supportive, had slower response times—sometimes because of other priorities, sometimes because of the number of checkpoints before deciding anything. It's not just business versus government that suffer from timing clashes; big companies, too, are riddled with innovation-slowing processes and systems. But then, so are complex organizations of all kinds. I recall wishing for faster approvals from Harvard officials for some elements of ALI, only to face the fact that a nearly four-hundred-year-old institution might use a different time frame than a young, growing program like ALI did.

3. Unexpected Hurdles, Obstacles, and Roadblocks

Being in the middle of creating innovation can seem like playing Whac-A-Mole. Just when one thing is handled, another challenge pops up. If an innovation is truly new and different, then the path to get there is uncharted and a complete road map does not exist. There might be potholes, barriers, roadblocks, or sandstorms that are hard to anticipate because the path forward has never been tried before, but that must be dealt with before the journey can proceed. Or there can be unexpected detours because desert sands shift. The environment is changing while the work of change is taking place. Nothing stands still just to wait for a new initiative to proceed.

Many possible hurdles can slow an innovation's progress. There may be legal and bureaucratic snafus, such as Doug Rauch found when he tried to get nonprofit tax status from the US Internal Revenue Service and then to get a Certificate of Occupancy for his first store from the local Health Department. Leaders may run into obstacles hiring and maintaining staff. Planned funding may fall through at the last minute. Partners may overpromise what they can deliver. Logistics and scheduling can go awry in unpredictable ways. People come and go; allies get sick. They are discredited or caught up in a scandal or move on to something else. And then leaders have to tell the story all over again and relight the spark that engages allies.

In addition to obstacles that are specific to any particular initiative, there are macrochanges that throw up hurdles in the wider environment. The outbreak of an epidemic, such as Ebola in Liberia, can put a project on hold, as happened to Richard Fahey and Robert Saudek. The context may change due to a new governmental policy or the emergence of new players. Mary Louise and Bruce Cohen started TBB with funding from the US State Department only to see that funding stream dry up following a presidential election and a change of administrations.

Other changes in the environment can reshape the contours of the problem. New evidence is uncovered that shows that the problem is worse (e.g., sex trafficking or the opioid epidemic) and more urgent, but with a different twist. Or climate change action shifts from one challenge to another. There could be a technology advance; Gilberto Dimenstein, founder of Catraca Livre in Brazil, ended up shifting away from the idea of neighborhood or bus kiosks with citizen empowerment information to focus instead on mobile streaming and apps. There could be a change in the law. A troubling problem pops up that must be fixed before the action can proceed, such as the discovery of toxicity in the water that was to be used to help poor farmers with sustainable agriculture.

Crises can change what gets attention, the way school shootings or natural catastrophes do. A devastating flood in Baton Rouge diverted Ray Jetson from the steady progress of BBR and MetroMorphosis toward a side project in collaboration with Judy Perry Martinez and Anthony Barash to create a means for low-income people whose houses were flooded to find titles to their homes in order to qualify for FEMA (Federal Emergency Management Agency) money. That side project, which future American Bar Association president Martinez envisioned with a tech group and Barash's ABA innovation committee, turned out to be a smart social innovation. Called FloodProof, it involved increased routes to legal services for the poor and a mobile app that could access documents. The detour to handle a disaster would help in future weather events.

The list of potential hurdles that can unexpectedly arise seems endless. No matter how comprehensively advanced leaders research the ins and outs of their target problems, their solutions, and the stakeholders involved, they cannot foresee everything about such complicated cross-sector systems. I've sometimes led groups planning new initiatives through worst-case scenario exercises in which they try to identify everything that could go wrong with their projects. At one session, a participant who got into the spirit of anticipating negative events included nuclear war on his list—which would certainly undermine a change effort.

4. Criticism Mounts: Entrenched Interests Get Tougher

Paradoxically, critics' voices grow louder and objections stronger in the middle, just when innovations start showing signs of success. In the beginning, it's just a story, and it's too small and fragile to be a threat. It can fly under the radar unnoticed and therefore uncontroversial. But when an initiative begins to gain traction, then it can threaten incumbents, compete for resources, and arouse the ire of establishment stakeholders who prefer to stay inside the building. Vivian Derryck's work at Bridges Institute wasn't threatening until it looked like it could actually influence US aid to African nations; then critics carped. Doug Rauch needed help from the Boston mayor to quiet opposition from convenience stores in the neighborhood whose owners suddenly saw that Daily Table was real and, thus, real competition. The very popularity of Gilberto Dimenstein's Catraca Livre, which attracted fifty million users to its social media feeds, made it highly visible and thus a bigger target for those who were upset at how news affecting them was covered.

From foot-dragging to subtle subversion to direct revolts, there are many ways that people show their displeasure and many more channels to do so, including going viral on social media. There are also many reasons why they resist change. They might fear ceding territory or influence, or they might harbor historical resentments. They might be unsure where the initiative will lead, if it will work, or if it will displace them—like current popular fears of new robotic and AI technologies. They might resist a solution that threatens the dominant narrative and implies that they have been doing something the wrong way— like the ominous backlash by some groups against then mayor Mitch Landrieu's decision to remove Confederate statues in New Orleans.

People tend to resist changes that disrupt their ongoing activities or familiar patterns that have been taken for granted. They dislike innovations that create more work—work that perhaps they are not particularly interested in doing or that they are unsure they can handle. They might feel that the changes were sprung on them without providing adequate time to adjust, or they might feel threatened because they perceive that changes will indeed harm their positions in some way. Incumbents who enjoy privileges as members of the establishment don't cede their status without a fight—those castles are well defended.

Some leaders seem unprepared for the level of resistance from entrenched interest groups. Anand Piramal and his colleagues bringing e-health solutions to poor villages in India that lacked adequate care underestimated the hold of the traditional "quacks" on villagers; digital didn't overcome the human. Former auto manufacturing CEO Mahendra Bapna launched a pilot industry immersion program in 2014 to ensure that engineers were better prepared for the technical needs of industry.[11] He started at the Indian Institute of Technology Jodhpur, where he had historical ties and a strong champion in its director. He had expected the faculty to jump at the opportunity to work with industry, he said, but the vast majority would not sign up to participate in a summer program, despite extra pay and the director's exhortations. Instead, they preferred to spend their summers as they always had, researching and writing papers. He decided he had to work around them by recruiting doctoral and postdoctoral engineering students of Indian origin from US universities to demonstrate the value of hands-on industry collaboration.

Whelan, Jennings, and Lowry, Thirteenth Avenue Funding's partners, were unprepared for how many critics and resistors they faced. They had expected opposition from the highly profitable student loan industry but not much difficulty with finding a partner for their first demonstration. But it surprised them that some university administrators did not see an upside for their university in Thirteenth Avenue Funding's proposed solution, even if their students could benefit from being freed from onerous student loans and use income-sharing agreements to pay for their education instead. Whelan commented, "Very few in the college finance world want to talk about whether they are acting on behalf of the student or on behalf of the institution."[12] One of the slides in Thirteenth Avenue Funding's standard presentation clearly laid out the consequences of defaulting on a student loan. "You're going to talk to my students, but not with that page in your presentation," Jennings recalled some college administrators saying.[13] They found that their model stirred up some people's emotions and challenged their beliefs. "The issue has been uncertainty, innovation, threat," he reflected, adding, "we would have been better hiring politicians to help us with the traps than two finance guys."[14]

So the partners added politics to their repertoire. They began to focus on influencing the federal legislative agenda and the public narrative on the student loan issue and income-sharing agreements. By 2015, Whelan was traveling regularly to the US capital. More immediately, however, they continued to work their network doggedly to find a university partner for their pilot project. In 2012, they succeeded in leveraging one of their board members' close ties to a college near Santa Barbara, California, to finally start a pilot program. Then, of course, landing Purdue University was like reaching the oasis.

* * *

Maintaining momentum is challenging, especially during periods when one setback seems to follow another. Doug Rauch never expected to spend three years obtaining IRS approval of Daily Table's nonprofit status or five years before opening his first store. Carol Hallquist had not thought that school principals who would benefit from her Principals Connect project in Kansas City would drag their feet and make her prove that it was good for them. The grind of middles can be exhausting for everyone—for the leader, the core team, and other coalition partners. There is always a point, or many points, when the middles are so miserable that advanced leaders face a choice of whether to keep going or to be victims of the vulnerabilities of middles.

Why People Give Up: The Roots of Failure

A classic Kenny Rogers country song about playing poker, "You've got to know when to hold 'em, know when to fold 'em," is the calculation that leaders must make. Sometimes the hand—the idea—isn't a very good one, so folding makes sense. But before analyzing how to make that decision, let's look at three reasons people fold without even trying to make it work. These are failed projects, because stopping in the middle automatically means failure.

Rigidity and inflexibility. Some accomplished people are so accustomed to getting their way (one of those perverse career traps I identified in chapter 2) that they get stiff. They are unwilling to bend to circumstances, and thus they can't bounce back from setbacks. Sometimes they are so fixated on specific strategies to achieve their visions that they will not alter them to surmount roadblocks or pursue even a slightly different path. They might have big egos (overconfidence implies arrogance), so they prefer to give up rather than give in and modify their plans. (Jeff Bezos and New York City, anyone?) The skills and qualities that contributed to their past successes do not fully translate into success with their outside-the-building institutional change initiative.

Aram Sekel, a pseudonym for a highly accomplished and well-respected Mediterranean executive, did everything by the book but then fell prey to rigidity and the temptation just to get out. Sekel had big aspirations for an international leadership institute for younger potential leaders, ages twenty-five to thirty-five, from countries around the eastern Mediterranean. He proposed to locate it on a beautiful, remote coastal property that was perfect for reflection and relationship building. The idea was to create long-lasting ties among potential future leaders who would, later in their careers, be a force for peaceful conflict resolution in the region.

Sekel got off to an excellent start building his coalition and making arrangements for a short test project. He enlisted a retired global consulting firm partner to help develop a detailed business plan and approach chambers of commerce in other countries. He secured the support of his country's top political leadership and, possibly, a major US leader. He recruited forty-five other business leaders to donate $100,000 each. He built a relationship with a well-known US university by finding the right department where there was enthusiasm and models and by encouraging local universities to join the effort at the American university's urging. According to his vision, he would donate the land and fund-raise while the American university would provide faculty, hold the majority share of seats on the governing board, and operate the cobranded program.

Everything was going well. He had the essential elements lined up. But then, as a formal memorandum of understanding was being drafted, the US university made clear that it did not want to take full responsibility for running the program, which Sekel had insisted on. The partner preferred that local academics operate it after several years. Moreover, the university's institutional policy prohibited cobranding with other organizations. Months of frustrating negotiation later, the two sides' inability to agree on terms delayed the pilot's launch, during which time many potential donors took back their commitments. Disappointed and discouraged by these developments, and mourning the lost momentum, Sekel dropped the project entirely rather than explore alternative strategies, such as starting the institute with one of the local university partners or finding another American university. His blind spots prevented him from fully understanding the university's institutional norms. He didn't want to adapt his model. He gave up and turned his attention to other matters.

Naivete. A second cluster of would-be advanced leaders are simply unsophisticated about the challenges of social innovation. Their ideas seem so easy and straightforward to implement, resource requirements seem modest, and they are inexperienced at handling controversy and rejection.

"John Goodfriend," as I'll call him, was a successful entrepreneur who had grown a midsized technology company that dominated its market niche. He fervently believed in the power of entrepreneurship

to increase employment and alleviate poverty in struggling communities in the United States, like the one not far from his company's base. He knew that low-income people who could benefit from
starting businesses lacked the assets to get started, get education, or
cushion themselves and their families against losses. He planned
to launch an asset-building initiative, Goodfriend's Match (GM),
to unlock entrepreneurial potential and kick-start microenterprise
first in a small, distressed city, and then, if all went well, elsewhere
in that state and around the country.

The start was promising. He signed a partnering agreement with
the state's leading asset-building organization, ABO, that oversaw
a coalition of nonprofit community partners. Goodfriend thought
all would be smooth sailing because the numbers were very small.
He secured $5,000 from a donor to finance a study for ABO and
also provided $2,000 in matching funds to GM's entrepreneur,
which netted GM an invitation from an important local community
organization to provide matching funds for a cohort of entrepreneurs who would be receiving business and financial training. GM
announced it would provide $7,200 in matching funds for two par-
ticipants in that program. As part of the pilot, Goodfriend and ABO
submitted a proposal to a leading foundation for a grant to roll out
the pilot both regionally and nationally. "All we needed was a few
hundred thousand dollars to go to the next level," Goodfriend said.

Then, in the middle of the pilot, things started going wrong.
The proposal did not win the grant competition; Goodfriend's flag-
ship technology company struggled, diverting Goodfriend's attention; and his main contact person at ABO was out of the action
due to health problems, which cut the dialogue between GM and
ABO. ABO stopped referring entrepreneurs to GM, and the pilot
languished. An effort with other community nonprofits sputtered.
These groups were less interested in the social enterprise's offer of
"free money" for their clients than Goodfriend had anticipated. He

hadn't seen the need to help them educate their constituencies. He speculated that he was just a small player not aligned with their operations. His happy coalition basically dissolved. To make matters worse, the environment had changed significantly during the period of his pilot; in 2017, a new Congress unexpectedly stopped funding the matching grants program he had been counting on to help him identify good candidates.

Goodfriend had hit just about every obstacle that makes middles miserable. In retrospect, he regretted not having built mechanisms for regular reviews into his model. He was disappointed that he had not enlisted a group of people into an advisory board who would help it win over other allies or handle changes in the political environment. He still thought his concept was valid even if he had been naive about the difficulties of getting traction. But he put the idea on hold.

Sidetracked. The third reason would-be institutional change agents are tempted to give up is that they are too distracted by other matters. They give the venture only partial attention, neglect it, and then just let it wither and die. Accomplished leaders are often bombarded with opportunities—opportunities that are more comfortable, less ambiguous, and downright easier than implementing a solution to a big, intractable institutional problem. Everyone wants a piece of their expertise and prestige—often to sit on a board, speak at conferences, help with a one-off project, or manage an up-and-running entity. Would-be entrepreneurs attend more networking events or join more accelerator programs than they need, giving them the illusion of progress while siphoning off time and energy. It is easy to get sidetracked. Such options become especially appealing when innovations hit unexpected snags, which make some leaders realize that achieving their visions will not be as straightforward as they had hoped. If leaders are not careful, these activities can prove so comfortingly distracting that they no longer have sufficient time for their innovations or interest in pursuing them.

"Mary Howard," my name for one education leader, was determined to use her talents and experience to improve struggling public schools, drawing from her successes at the helm of several large urban school systems. As a former superintendent, she knew where the problems were. She set out to create an initiative to provide mentoring, support, and guidance for newly appointed superintendents, who turned over at a high rate in urban districts, ultimately undermining student achievement. Howard's two-pronged model foresaw a pilot project in a struggling school district, a partnership with a national-level education policy, and a research organization to facilitate the initiative's quick scaling. She set a 120-day timeline for launching both the local pilot and national roll-out for the superintendent leadership initiative. That proved wildly overoptimistic—not because it was impossible but because she became distracted by changes in the environment and numerous other opportunities to join boards, speak, and consult.

Howard enlisted an innovative education commissioner from a southern state to champion the local pilot, only to watch the possibility evaporate when he left his post and his successor chose to pursue other priorities. Later that year, she reached out to the director of a national education nonprofit, whom she knew well and who would provide an excellent platform for her initiative's national prong. The director worked with her to improve her proposal before submitting it to the group's board of directors early in the next year. Meanwhile, Howard invested her attention and time to help established education leadership organizations with their programs. A year after she first envisioned the initiative, the director of the national-level partner gave her the good news that the executive board wanted to move ahead with her project.

She didn't jump at this. She continued with her speaking and consulting. Months passed without her pursuing the superintendent leadership opportunity further or securing a new local pilot partner.

And by the end of the year, apart from the approval, her initiative had not advanced beyond where it was a year previously. Overdue to follow up with the director, she had been distracted by her commitments to the other groups' activities. After her dreams faded, she commented that she derived energy from working with a team, so she gravitated to consulting, where she didn't have to run things herself.

When to Persist or to Pivot

If some people are too rigid to try another tack to get over or around the messes of middles, there are others who are too stubborn to stop when they are clearly pursuing a lost cause. Knowing how to avoid these extremes is part of the art of advanced leadership. The answer to the question of whether to persist or to pull out comes from reassessing the factors that brought them to this point. That's like a trip through the preceding chapters of this book.

- *Tune in to the context.* Is the problem and need still there? Is the idea for a solution still valid? Is the playing field still relatively open, without much competition?
- *Shake the kaleidoscope.* Are there creative approaches or new combinations that haven't yet been tried?
- *Do a gut check.* Does your passion still match your aspiration? Are you willing to put yourself and your time on the line for this?
- *Review the vision.* Is it still the right story? Does it make sense out of the past, offer room for many people, and show what the future could be?
- *Look for quick wins.* Are there prototypes that work or demonstrations that provide credibility? Are there signs of more ahead?
- *Assess support.* Are initial allies still enthusiastic? Are the numbers and commitment of allies growing? Are undecideds tipping over to your side of the fence?
- *Examine the trajectory.* Is momentum building?

If all the answers lean toward *yes*, then it's not time to stop. But that doesn't mean you should hang on to the same tactics; seeking alternatives makes sense.

Some leaders do more than persist; they pivot. They feel there's enough promise ahead that they are willing to try another angle to create success out of the investments they've already made. They demonstrate the other side of Kanter's Law: if everything looks like a failure in the middle, then it can be turned into a success with some creative rejiggering.

Pivot has become a tech start-up term, since few ventures go in a straight line from first concept to success story. Stewart Butterfield, cofounder of Silicon Valley unicorn Slack, led an iconic example of pivoting. Butterfield redirected his original venture, to create a multiplayer online game platform—which proved to be too complex—into using the technology to make Slack a go-to workplace communication tool. He kept the technology but trashed the first application. Junko Yoda and Pam McCambridge pivoted CLinked, their anti–sex trafficking project. They went from their first idea, which was providing direct intervention and services themselves, through a period of offering public education campaigns by radio. Then they pivoted again, this time into multiplying their efforts by training facilitators who could work on the ground in villages with vulnerable girls.

It's not essential to change direction drastically. The key to success is being flexible and willing to explore new approaches while finding assets that should be nurtured and actions that should be continued. When Bob Meaney and Bob Berkland faced a multiyear delay that threatened the Ghana portion of their Africa irrigation project, they pushed forward at other sites while maintaining commitment to the Ghana project.[15] One of their contacts, the USAID embedded advisor to the Ghanaian minister for food and agriculture, championed the project with the Ghanaian government, which, in 2014, provided financing via the World Bank–funded Ghana Commercial Agriculture Project. Later, Meaney and Berkland's plans and cross-sector coalition in Tanzania lost momentum after problems made one site and then another unacceptable. "The partners were suffering from fatigue," Meaney reported.[16] Rather than giving up, they got back on a plane to Tanzania to meet with representatives of one of their NGO partners. While there, they visited a village that was located on top of an aquifer that looked to have sufficient water for irrigation, and farmers were excited about the irrigation system. They lost no time in forming a new plan and testing the environment, once again demonstrating the perseverance, flexibility, and creative problem-solving important for regaining momentum.

Doug Rauch cleared numerous unexpected hurdles on the road to opening Daily Table's first store. IRS recalcitrance was a blow, but it wasn't a knockout punch. Rauch had already found reservoirs of resilience and tenacity. He also demonstrated a strong stomach for suspense, which is particularly necessary when launching innovations, given the many unknowns, dry spells, and unexpected twists and turns that ventures might face. When Rauch suddenly lost an initially envisioned partnership with Whole Foods, which he had thought would make launching Daily Table a piece of (organic) cake, he had an important moment of reckoning. Rauch explained the internal dialogue he had with himself: "I had to stop and take a gut check. Hey, Doug—it's going to be a long slog now. It's going to be expensive. It's going to take a bunch of your money, take a whole lot of your time and energy. So are you in?" Rauch still felt strongly about the need for Daily Table and his ability to lead it. He determined that he still had it in himself to forge ahead. He recalled thinking, "Yeah, I'm in it. I believe this is a serious issue and think that my initial reasons for the project remain valid. I think this is a good idea; there might be something here that's of value." Having done the gut-check once, he could more easily weather other challenges of middles.

How to Persist

"Even when you think you have the right idea and everything in place, it is a marathon to effect systemic, big, institutional change," Bob Whelan observed.[17] During the marathon run to reach the next oasis, it helps to have used advanced leadership skills to find a compelling enough mission, offer an inspiring narrative, and build a coalition of allies who have invested in the venture themselves. Carrying out all the earlier steps well enables innovators to find the strength to keep going. That gives leaders people to lean on when the going is rough, commitment to keep running, a powerful sense of purpose to guide them, and a team to cheer them on that they can also celebrate.

Lean on Allies

We all certainly need a few confidantes, perhaps as an outlet for frustrations or a source of advice, but that's not enough to support advanced leaders as they find the inner strength to persist through difficulties. Wider groups of allies can be sources of accountability, keeping initiatives on track by reminding leaders of the obligation to do what they promised.

To avoid feeling small and alone, advanced leaders need many contacts. Doug Rauch reported moments of discouragement when he thought, "I have no people. It is only me. So how do I build this concept?" He found allies to lean on, people who would embrace Daily Table and encourage him to keep on going. Like many persistent advanced leaders, he attended hundreds of meetings with local officials, industry experts, academicians, and community leaders to learn and to enlist support.

Every indication of support was personally uplifting, and he identified people who could step in to help him overcome whatever hurdles lay ahead and stay committed. A robust coalition of allies won't let a leader fold his hand even if he is tempted to pull out.

To be able to lean on allies, it helps to invest in them and in keeping the coalition together in the face of possible dissent. Advanced leaders keep their ears to the street for signs that there might be fractures in their coalitions and act to repair any tears in the social fabric while learning ways to improve their ventures from feedback. Leaders might involve stakeholders in extensive discussions and participatory processes to make sure all voices are heard and opinions considered. If disagreement exists over strategy, the unbiased data derived from conducting focus groups, polling, and other fact-finding activities can help build consensus. Changing the coalition's governance structure may be advised if mechanisms don't exist for solving disagreements. All these steps solidify support that can help leaders get through the murky, messy, miserable middles.

Put in the Time

Those who initially think they can achieve their mission working on it casually inevitably come to the realization that they need to devote much more time to it, at least until it is fully formed and reaches a stable, institutionalized scale. Bob Whelan originally thought Thirteenth Avenue Funding would require only 20 percent of his working hours. At the time he cofounded it, he sat on the boards of four companies, chaired the board of a small nonprofit, and advised emerging companies through a consulting arm. But rather than be sidetracked, he reduced other obligations to focus on Thirteenth Avenue Funding. "It is a figment of your imagination to think you can do a start-up part time, especially of this scale and significance," Whelan said.[18] Howard Fischer, the founder of social impact investment venture Gratitude Railroad, was equally blunt about what it takes to get traction: "You have to believe it deeply and passionately and constantly. And you have to take the time. It can't be a hobby."[19] That's why what started as a hobby for Laura Dambier—visiting presidential libraries—became her full-time vocation: to use the libraries and other historic sites to teach democracy.

The big dream and the right story are powerful sources of the purpose and meaning that help people weather difficult situations. Although leaders cannot anticipate every momentum-sapping obstacle that will arise or opponent who will obstruct, they can embed elements into their work from the outset that help energize their own inner circles and motivate coalition members. To steer their ventures through tough times, advanced leaders can rely on their core values and strong sense of mission that motivated them in the first place—the stories that enticed others to join.

Dr. Donald Berwick, a physician who later served as administrator of the Centers for Medicare and Medicaid Services, a major national health policy position, was especially proficient at keeping mission at the forefront. He cofounded the Institute of Healthcare Improvement (IHI) to bring quality management and improvement tools to health care in the service of better patient outcomes. As a nonprofit, IHI took donations, but its main income was revenue earned from education and training programs. For example, thousands attended an annual conference in Orlando, Florida, where enthusiastic crowds filled every corner of an enormous Marriott Hotel. In the early 2000s, IHI's signature initiatives were two iconic mass-mobilization campaigns to reduce preventable medical errors in hospitals and save lives—a 100,000 Lives Campaign aimed at preventable deaths and a 5 Million Lives Campaign aimed at life-diminishing mistakes. Over four thousand hospitals signed on to join the campaigns and use the methods they featured.

Berwick's IHI was a highly visible, institutional change initiative that challenged the conventional organization, processes, and priorities of establishment hospitals. Not surprisingly, this outside-the-building venture was bombarded with criticism from inside the building, including questioning of the science and the measurements behind IHI's work. A few core values helped sustain IHI staff through difficult periods including financial downturns, as Berwick reported. The first was "keeping the face of the patient in front" (i.e., a constant focus on patients and the organization's work to save lives). The second was "Get out there: If you're in the office, you're in the wrong place." IHI team members derived energy from being out in the field, where practitioners worked directly with patients. According to Berwick, "That overcomes a tremendous amount of whining and attacks from others."[20] One other effective slogan IHI leadership used to center its team was "never worry alone," which focused staff on supporting each other rather than on skeptics' criticism.

Publicize, Recognize, and Celebrate

There is little more motivating than good results. Leaders seek to publicize quick wins in order to boost morale, provide coalition members with evidence that collaboration is mutually beneficial, and show evidence that there is progress toward the social impact goal. Leaders can use metrics, data collection, and feedback loops to demonstrate momentum, especially when there are evolving elements to add to the story. No matter how tiny the victories, advanced leaders can celebrate them with their teams and allies to keep participants' enthusiasm high. Advanced leaders can also acknowledge and express appreciation for individuals and for groups who contribute to small and large wins, understanding how important recognition is as a motivational tool. They dole out credit generously. When addressing coalition members, they say *we* and *our project's achievements*, not *I* and *my*.

Jay Winsten and his team made good use of recognition and celebration to maintain momentum during the multiyear Designated

Driver Campaign, sometimes in splashy ways.[21] They presented studio executives and producers with beautifully framed certificates, with a little resemblance to diplomas, to thank them for their support. They plastered billboard space on Sunset Strip with the message: "Thanks TV industry . . . for taking drunk drivers out of the picture." They held a reception in Hollywood for the creative community to thank supporters, which also helped recruit new participants.

Making everyone a hero becomes even more important during difficult middle periods, when keeping internal team members and coalition partners pulling in the same direction is most challenging. Through recognition of stakeholders' efforts and by nurturing a spirit of fun and celebration, advanced leaders encourage initiative and innovation in the best of times and in the worst of times, when those qualities are often in short supply.

* * *

Tackling big problems does not always proceed according to plan. The work of advanced leadership is more like improvisational theater, requiring intense listening to the audience, savvy interpretation of the context, give and take with partners, and flexibility to adjust rapidly. Knowing Kanter's Law—that everything can look like a failure in the middle—can be curiously comforting.[22] After all, other leaders have faced this, persevered, and thrived, reaching a refreshing, rewarding oasis. Sticking with it, reassessing the need and the support, relying on core values, staying flexible, making adjustments, recognizing contributions, and celebrating victories large and small can make the difference between a miserable middle, ending the mission prematurely before reaching the next oasis, or it proving to be just another leg of the journey to greater impact.

7

GOOD TO GROW

The Road to Impact

The street mechanics were the first saviors of Richard Fahey and Robert Saudek's affordable green energy innovation for Africa. Early in their venture, Fahey and Saudek experienced a self-evident truth about any innovation: first, the basic components must work, and then the rest can follow. They needed the street kids before they could prove or improve anything—before their innovation could be good to grow.

Forming LEN—the Liberia Energy Network, introduced in chapter 2—and positioning it to make a difference on a big problem had seemed straightforward at first. Import solar-powered lights from China and sell them inexpensively to provide clean energy to the 97 percent of Liberians who were not being served by the electric grid or who could not afford a generator. Fahey and Saudek had enlisted Abubakar Sherif, an experienced Liberian manager who had been a student of Fahey's wife when she had been a Peace Corps volunteer years earlier. Fahey and Sherif had stayed in touch—Fahey helped subsidize Sherif's education as well as his children's. In February 2012, after a painstaking five-month journey from China to Monrovia, Liberia, by way of

Hamburg, Germany, the lights were delivered. Fahey arrived in Monrovia, cleared the containers of lights out of the port with Sherif, took a look inside, and gasped.

"Not a single one of the lights worked. Not a single one," Fahey recalled. Facing the possible loss of the venture, Fahey contacted the manufacturer, who told him to talk to the electrical engineer in Denmark. This was already too globally complicated and would cause further delay, and why should they believe the lights would work next time? With a burst of inspiration, they went outside the building to find a solution on the street. The thought that the lights were like the electrical system of a car led them to seek out local car mechanics. "Abu says, 'Let's go to Benson Street,' which is where there are just kids, young men, former fighters, all up and down the street with their heads underneath cars up on blocks, filthy dirty."[1] They were hardly as credible as a Danish engineer at first blush, but Benson Street and the street kids were all they had at hand.

By asking around for someone who knew about the electrical systems of cars, they found David and then William. "Between David and William, they rebuilt all the lights and got them all working," Fahey said. That was a breakthrough. "The great outcome out of all of this wasn't just that we saved ourselves and rehabilitated all of the units, but we actually found that we have resources on the ground in Liberia . . . We can do product support with what's already there in Liberia. We don't have to bring in foreign technicians to sit around and oversee the project."[2] It was meaningful to discover that there were skills in the community.

The lights came on, modern appliances came alive, and life started to change for that corner of Africa. By 2018, at least seventy-six thousand people in more than fifteen thousand households were the first beneficiaries. Increased time to read and study at night improved educational outcomes. Low-income fishermen could stay on the water longer at night to increase their catches and their incomes. In remote areas, the hours spent walking to and from the nearest public electricity source just to charge a cell phone could be turned to more productive endeavors. Reduced use of fume-producing kerosene lamps and dangerous wood fires improved health. Making clean energy affordable for the poor also proved its value and viability—including nimble innovation off the grid, which offered benefits without hefty infrastructure costs.

Discovering the street kids was just the start of improvising to prove the concept and grow the project. Fahey and Saudek seized many opportunities to increase the impact and expand the scope of their initial idea. They developed operational expertise, devising a system for collecting payments from cash-strapped Liberians. They built a culture that engaged employees, creating a sense of solidarity and accountability after dealing with an embezzlement problem. They weathered an Ebola fever outbreak in 2014, which had caused their headquarters in Monrovia's commercial district to be quarantined for two months. "We got all our employees together, we gave them a bonus of a month's pay in advance, and we told them to buy everything they needed to survive for the next month or two, and to go home and stay safe," Fahey recalled.

The crisis slowed business expansion for as much as a year. But then, because of how they handled it, they found a commercial sideline in selling off-grid solar energy to companies that did not trust the regular electrical grid. In 2016, following the Ebola crisis, a big US entity contacted LEN about providing a large system for a research facility in Liberia. LEN won the contract. Sherif tapped a distant cousin to connect LEN to a small technical college that produced electrical engineers with knowledge of off-grid solar; LEN serendipitously hired some graduates to fulfill the contract. That also gave LEN a pipeline to engineers for the future.

Fahey and Saudek stumbled upon another system problem-solving innovation. They realized that LEN could address protein deficiency by solar-powering freezers in remote areas to preserve fish, which were abundant on the coastal fishing grounds but hard to access inland. For this and other follow-on innovations, the team formed a for-profit arm, LEN2, a Liberian-registered subsidiary of nonprofit LEN, which helped them get bank loans and not depend on foundations or the World Bank to pursue new activities. Any profits could be used to subsidize lights for people too poor to afford even LEN's low prices. The venture added products, moved to a new retail location in a popular market area of Monrovia, and deepened relationships with distribution partners, including a labor union. During this period of growth, Abubakar Sherif had become COO, and soon, they handed him day-to-day management responsibilities. LEN was positioned for sustainability and impact.

The journey was by no means perfect or finished. Logistics remained daunting in Africa, and there was competition. It's easy to imagine large government energy companies, including those from China, swooping in to complicate and challenge a vulnerable venture. But Fahey and Saudek had proved the LEN concept and its potential for impact, and they had built a platform that could take the enterprise to a significant scale. Their aim, after all, was not to have a viable small business that helped a few thousand Liberians but to open a path to solving a problem for many millions of people across Africa and beyond—and perhaps to have a positive impact on education, health, and climate change in the process.[3]

LEN is one example of a venture with the key ingredients for growth and sustainability, which can ensure impact on pressing social and environmental problems. The main growth aids include:

- a strong mission—to solve a meaningful, multifaceted societal problem and to accomplish more than one thing at a time;
- a positive, people-centered culture;
- the flexibility and creativity to improvise, including add-on innovations;
- management and operational expertise;

- a revenue model; and
- leadership development and succession.

If these sound like the lessons from any great company, such as the ones studied by Jim Collins and Jerry Porras for their book, *Built to Last,* or that I identified in *SuperCorp,* that's not accidental or coincidental.[4] That's the essential foundation, responsible for outputs, outcomes, and even growth. What advanced leadership adds is a focus on impact on the wider system. A venture, project, program, initiative, or campaign is not an end in itself; it is a means to a grander goal, making a difference in the world. An organization is a tool to be used in the quest for wider improvement.

Understanding Impact

Outcomes tend to be measurable, immediate consequences. Impact is more subjective and harder to tease out. It could be one of those IKIWISI terms—"I'll know it when I see it." Impact refers to longer-term, demonstrable influence on a system. The beneficial social or environmental results usually encompassed by the idea of impact are broader effects than outcomes, but for that reason, they are also harder to attribute to the actions of any one agent of change.

Advanced leadership is oriented to impact. It focuses on changing the institutional array, thereby opening new pathways and opportunities. It seeks to solve problems, improve situations, or reduce negative consequences in the system as a whole—changing the world one smart innovation at a time, with many innovations and adjustments adding up to a discernable shift. What I call "even bigger change" encompasses three system levels that combine to shape society: policies (laws, official mandates), programs (operating entities that serve as demonstrations or new forms of service), and public opinion (norms, social expectations, and people's consciousness and behavior). Impact comes from adding, influencing, or combining many elements that together create significant change. For example, while one set of leaders launches an operating organization demonstrating how something works in practice, another set might lobby to get new laws passed, and still others might mount a campaign to change social norms. Or these efforts can be joined.[5]

It's clear that action at one level alone is not enough for significant institutional change—or sometimes, even to keep the main project alive. Entrepreneurs with disruptive start-ups face this all the time. Uber, for example, started its ride-hailing service as a stand-alone enterprise but ran up against unfavorable laws. Uber later added staff working to get local and state governments to pass new ones. Uber mobilized public opinion to counter officials' attempts to block its use, and it succeeded in changing behavior by making ride-hailing a routine expectation, but it also ignored negative public opinion and disgruntled stakeholder relationships needing repair. Neglecting these other elements of change left room for rivals to make inroads. At the same time, changing the law is not sufficient to change behavior. As Charles Ogletree pointed out in his book about the landmark Supreme Court decision in *Brown v. Board of Education*, passing laws ending de jure school segregation didn't end de facto school segregation; social ventures and new programs are also necessary to change residential patterns and educational opportunities for underserved black students.[6]

Thus, the road to impact might start out as a narrow path trod by a small set of leaders. Then, as projects grow, so do the activities, allies, and unplanned companions, which widen the path into a road and add more lanes. The ecosystem supporting the projects becomes ever more favorable. Eventually, there might be a superhighway with branches in many directions. What starts as the road not taken can turn into the new route for doing things.

Making a difference in the world can't be "one and done." Some form of growth is central to the very idea of impact. Without reach, and a growing base of support, it's nearly impossible to change institutions. There are many ways to scale an initiative to gain critical mass for institutional change, as Kash Rangan and others show.[7] These are not mutually exclusive.

- Grow by adding members, users, or customers (like Gilberto Dimenstein's Catraca Livre in Brazil, Fahey and Saudek's LEN, or Mary Louise and Bruce Cohen's Talent Beyond Boundaries).
- Grow in geographic scope by adding sites (like Doug Rauch's Daily Table or Wendy Kopp's Teach for America).
- Grow in activity scope (like LEN, Anand Piramal's e-Swasthya health work in India, or Ray Jetson's Baton Rouge community portfolio).
- Grow the number of partners for a movement or a campaign (like Jay Winsten's Designated Driver Campaign or Don Berwick's 5 Million Lives Campaign).
- Grow the idea by inspiring others to take up the cause or by providing incentives for action (like Susan Leal's *Running Out of Water* book or impact investors such as Howard Fischer and Eric Jacobson's Gratitude Railroad, which encourages investments in green start-ups).[8]
- Grow the ecosystem by partnering with or supporting several complementary initiatives that fill in the field's missing pieces (like Vanessa Kirsch's New Profit venture philanthropy investments, which group the initiatives supported into themes such as education, early childhood, health, and economic empowerment).

The Rules of the Road: Driving to Scale

Growth begins with a robust demonstration that puts advanced leaders on the road to impact. There are three key phases of the development and diffusion of innovation—similar to what is needed for innovation in any field.

1. *Proof of concept. Can you do it and do it well?* The first test is whether it works at all. This is more than a rough prototype or small demo; it involves a full-fledged pilot program.

2. *Replication. Can you do it again?* Can you reproduce it? Can it thrive beyond the first trial, when the excitement of beginnings provides an extra boost? The next test is whether the model can work without the extra support and attention that come with the first demonstration, especially because of a potential Hawthorne effect—that people might perform better when knowing that they are in a special program and are being observed.[9] Replication also offers the opportunity to incorporate learning from the first offering. "Do it right the first time" is a mantra of total quality management, but for innovations, I prefer to substitute "do it better the second time."

3. *Expansion. Can many others do it?* When large numbers adopt the innovation, it has impact. The third phase is diffusion to grow in scale, scope, and importance to become a new institutional pathway. Expansion and diffusion also require the ecosystem to become more favorable over time. The innovation should become a safe, routine expectation, complete with supporting activities—such as a supply chain, a labor market, a distribution mechanism, official authorizations, and so forth. In effect, an innovation might become an industry.

Consider the case of a particularly big idea that whizzed through these phases to scale rapidly. It illustrates key principles that can help other institutional innovation projects gain traction and grow to impact.

P-TECH Reinvents High School: The Fastest-Scaling School Model in America

Six-year high schools? When I first heard that idea from people working on it, I had a visceral flashback to how much I had wanted to get out of high school fast, not to hang around for a few more years. But then I heard more and was sold—and, of course, got over those common nightmares about being in high school again, since this high school was designed for an entirely different purpose and population and came with benefits for the extra time. The six years were intended to combine high school with two years of college that would offer technology skills and employer connections, solving many problems at once. It was a structural change in education that could also close opportunity gaps for lower-income minority youth and grow a diverse tech workforce. It would simultaneously address the middle skills shortage—not enough tech workers in jobs that don't require a four-year degree—and give disadvantaged kids access to jobs of the future.

This venture's backers claimed that it scaled more rapidly than any single structural innovation in public education in American history—indeed, perhaps since the invention of free public high school itself. It holds many lessons about ensuring that advanced leadership initiatives grow to powerful impact. At first glance, the specific situation can seem unique and out of reach. But take another look: the principles are widely applicable and lie behind every start-up venture that grows to accomplish big changes.

The big idea was seeded at a tennis match. New York City schools chancellor Joel Klein sat with then IBM CEO Sam Palmisano at the US Open championship in Flushing Meadows, New York, as they often did. This time, in mid-2010, Klein was concerned about new solutions for the woes of public education: uneven quality, inequity and race disparities, low high school graduation rates, and poor skills that didn't translate into jobs. He asked Palmisano if IBM could help him. Palmisano turned to Stanley Litow, president of the IBM International Foundation and a corporate vice president, who had spearheaded numerous other outside-the-building social impact initiatives for the company and had once been deputy schools chancellor. He understood the multistakeholder ambiguities of large-scale systemic change, and he had the three Cs—capabilities as a change agent and coalition mobilizer, connections throughout the public sector, and cash from the foundation, although he had deemphasized cash grants in favor of bringing human capital (employee time and expertise) to problems.

Litow came back to Palmisano the next day with an idea he had been pondering with his team, which included education experts Robin Willner, Ann Cramer, Maura Banta, and Grace Suh. The idea was to connect public high schools and community colleges for a six-year employer-connected educational experience that would tap new talent by preparing average students to be job ready—especially jobs-of-the-future, tech-jobs ready. It was a kaleidoscope moment: there were bits and pieces of this model scattered in many places that Litow wanted to rearrange in a bigger, bolder way.

Litow knew well the silos and gaps. Industry and education were unconnected, and even the public community colleges operated in isolation from the public high schools. He immediately thought about connections as a solution: a new partnership among businesses, the K–12 bureaucracy, and the two-year community colleges. He was ready to enlist the chancellor of City University of New York, which ran the community colleges. New York City had a very small early college program for some high school students, and that provided a springboard for the much bigger idea: make high school six years instead of four years; give students both a high school diploma and an associate's degree; and have corporate partners available to mentor, guide, and offer jobs or at least first-in-line job interviews to the graduates, who would work in highly competitive STEM fields or go on to four-year colleges. Palmisano, whom Litow always made sure to credit, gave the go-ahead.

Like Doug Rauch's Daily Table and Fahey and Saudek's LEN, Litow's idea would solve many problems at once. Like Mary Louise and Bruce Cohen's Talent Beyond Boundaries, it would require a great deal of matching and support from groups that didn't necessarily know one another. Like Jay Winsten's Designated Driver Campaign, it required support from within Litow's own home base, so key departments at IBM had to be brought in and kept on board. And like Torsten Thiele's Global Ocean Trust, this venture was surrounded by numerous overlapping and competing stakeholders—the education sector holds its own daunting array of overlapping government officials, bureaucracies, associations, foundations, interest groups, consultants, change agents, and conferences—who had their own agendas that sometimes coexisted uneasily in particular schools. The business community backed a wide variety of education reform efforts, some of which were proprietary programs developed by individual corporations.

One challenge facing Litow and his team was how to make a radical idea seem safe and easy to support—how to get the mainstream to support actions that might undermine that very establishment. That's key to the success of getting through the barriers to try experiments that couldn't be stand-alone. My studies of thousands of innovations in many sectors showed that the ones likeliest to succeed were the ones that could be cast in familiar terms so that key allies could understand, embrace, and support them. Make the radical seem safe.

Litow and team went into action. Numerous phone calls, door-knocks, and meetings later—classic advanced leadership coalition-building on a very fast track and with IBM leaders and backing—the concept was ready to move from dream to pilot project. It was called P-TECH, for Pathways in Technology Early College High School. P-TECH opened with its first class of ninth graders at the start of the school year in September 2011.

From the beginning, P-TECH was designed to scale. The idea for P-TECH was much bigger than a single high school in New York City; it aimed at significant reinvention, making the six-year high school, combined degree, and employer involvement a new possibility and expectation throughout America and the world. With thousands of public school districts in the United States alone, operating with their own governing boards, the change challenge was daunting. But the need, interest, and credibility of the partners were sufficiently high that cities and then states jumped on board while the pilot was still underway.

This social innovation went through proof of concept and replication to diffusion in record time. Ten principles, applicable to any venture-building effort, account for the speed and effectiveness—even without the power of IBM.[10]

Proof of Concept

You want the innovation to succeed, but with an eye toward its later growth and impact. You thus don't want to make the first iteration so exceptional that it can't continue or expand elsewhere without extraordinary support. There's a delicate balance between loading an initiative for success and proving that it can work under tough circumstances so it could grow on its own merits. There's also a balance between an immediate, laser-like short-term focus on what needs to be done to get the pilot project underway and a longer-term perspective on what needs to be in place to expand the idea later.

Principle #1. Organize for decision-making. Formalize an advisory and governance process, including key resource providers and legitimizers.

Litow and team set up a steering committee of the three partners to engage together in school creation issues, such as principal selection, curriculum development, and school identification, to make joint decisions when relevant, and to assign tasks to specific partners. Within IBM, Litow established a small cross-department team to ensure enthusiasm for the pilot and asked for the human resource department's input to understand the company's needs and to ensure the department prioritized the hiring of P-TECH graduates.

The steering committee sought ideas, but only what was needed to launch the pilot. They convened twenty-five school principals, including highly regarded Rashid Davis, the principal of Bronx Engineering and Technology Academy (BETA), who had worked in New York City public schools for fifteen years. Community-savvy, dreadlock-adorned Davis was asked to be the P-TECH school's principal and join the project's steering committee. He became an important liaison to Crown Heights's neighborhood leaders, ranging from ministers and congregations to the police, and could allay concerns that P-TECH was simply another vocational school that put students on a second-class track. Litow also brought city council member Al Vann, whom Litow had known for many years and was then representing Brooklyn on the council, to help reassure community members.

Principle #2. Start lean. Ignore the complexity, and do only as much as necessary to get underway. But build into the model's design critical pieces you'll need later to grow the venture.

The planning team focused on their minimally viable proposition: the basics of classroom space, a principal, teachers, students, and a curriculum design. Space was available in a section of the old Paul Robeson High School building in the urban-problems-plagued Crown Heights area of Brooklyn. That was good enough for planning to accelerate toward a fast-track opening. Criteria were identified for an innovative long time-block curriculum and company involvement, because those were unique elements that could be taken elsewhere later. Because of the focus on tech jobs of the future, the learning model included technology and workplace skills in addition to math and English, augmented by company mentors, workplace visits, and internships. The curriculum was kept lean but deep, stripping out courses that would not contribute to the main goals.

Principle #3. Keep it familiar rather than jarring. Don't rock too many boats. Minimize the ripple effects. Change as little as possible, and don't require too many others to change.

Despite all its differences, P-TECH was a regular public school, working through and not against the system. It did not require increasing per-pupil allocation of funds. It was not set up as a charter school exempt from the rules, which allayed the fears of the teacher unions. P-TECH used the existing labor framework, procedures, and work rules for teacher selection and for Davis's appointment as principal.

Students were identified randomly through the regular open enrollment lottery with no achievement criteria. They were mostly from low-income, low-education minority families, mirroring the whole of the public school system. The first P-TECH school was 96 percent black or Hispanic, with 80 percent of the students qualifying for free or reduced-price lunch. For some students and parents, P-TECH was not even among their choices. Like all innovations, no one had heard of this, so how could they be sure it would be compatible? But that was the process; they had to take it if they wanted to stay in the public school system.

Principle #4. Deploy dedicated people who can manage effectively and offer a ubiquitous presence. Ensure a management backbone.

The design team incorporated into the pilot a focus on measurable outcomes and the ability to manage by information. In collaboration with faculty, it measured student performance incrementally and then swiftly adjusted based on feedback. The operations team documented everything, including principal selection criteria and coursework, compiling it into a guidebook to facilitate growth if teachers and staff turned over and to facilitate start-up at new sites. IBM—which, by the way, was not providing any funding—deployed a liaison person in residence who oversaw the mentor program and connected teachers with industry experts to help make curriculum more relevant for employers. IBM also had a very visible and tangible presence at the school via the IBM professionals who volunteered to mentor students during the school day. These activities underscored the innovation's employment-boosting potential on an almost daily basis for teachers, students, and parents.

Principle #5. Be open. Welcome observers to hear the story and see early results. Collect data, but give data a human face. Make the narrative persuasive and enlist powerful storytellers. Be transparent and encourage transmission.

Principal Rashid Davis's willingness to open his school led to a parade of visitors, which eventually included governors, mayors, and US president Barack Obama. This education about the model also raised P-TECH's profile and accelerated national demand for P-TECH-modeled schools. President Obama liked P-TECH's story so much that he mentioned it in his 2012 State of the Union address and in subsequent addresses.

Nearly all students in the pilot's inaugural class, some 30 percent of whom started their freshman year at P-TECH below grade level, did well enough to enter the sophomore class the following year. More than 50 percent of students took college-level courses at CUNY's City Tech before the end of tenth grade. These results quickly made P-TECH a model for the STEM movement, with other states and cities clamoring for its replication in their school districts. The first cohort to finish the program graduated at quadruple the pace of community college graduates and five times the rate for low-income students.

Star student Radcliffe Saddler, from a low-income black family of Jamaican immigrants, was asked to tell his personal story about why he hadn't wanted to come to P-TECH (he had been rejected by his top twelve high schools) but then later felt he had "won the lottery."

He was an impressively poised ninth grader when I visited the school in Brooklyn in its first winter and invited him to speak at a large event at Harvard, which could have been intimidating—but he flew to Boston on a Saturday with his mother and Davis by his side. He was on his way to being a major representative of what P-TECH could bring to young people. After Obama's visit, the school featured a large poster of Saddler with the president.

Experiences became legends. There were frequently told stories about how students started taking college-level courses before it had been anticipated and how a handful graduated from their six-year program after just four years, including Saddler, who took a high-paying job at IBM while planning to apply to a four-year college to complete his bachelor's degree and maybe go on to graduate school. Rashid Davis became a hero, frequenting the education speakers' circuit. When flaws in the model were discovered (e.g., that some students struggled with and failed the college math classes), he was the one who declared that he would do everything possible to make sure that every student succeeded and graduated with both degrees (which they mostly did).

P-TECH proved the concept under tough circumstances with students who hadn't been expected to succeed. Champions could sing the "New York, New York" song lyrics: "If you can make it there, you can make it anywhere."

Replication

The next efforts must show that the pilot is not just an anomaly—that it can, indeed, work anywhere. Replication is a major step forward, showing that the proven concept is more widely applicable. Otherwise, any success enjoyed by the pilot project can be written off as due to the extra attentions enjoyed by the pioneers—the Hawthorne effect again.

Principle #6. Seize opportunities. Don't overplan. Choose the next site or wave of action based on enthusiasm and commitment. Let new allies take on some of the work.

Some friendly rivalry between big city mayors helped Litow and the P-TECH coalition find an unplanned opportunity for replication almost before the first school year in Brooklyn was well underway. After New York City mayor Michael Bloomberg praised the innovation in a meeting with Chicago mayor Rahm Emanuel, Emanuel wanted it for his city too. Emanuel, a former US congressman and chief of staff to President Obama, contacted Palmisano and then Litow to discuss possibilities.

Litow sprang into action again. He spoke with the CEO of Chicago Public School Systems, J. C. Brizzard, who had previously worked with Litow at the New York City Department of Education, and to the chancellor of the Chicago City College System, Cheryl Hyman. Litow sent a six-person team to meet with local government and business stakeholders to start planning and to offer IBM's partnership for one school. Emanuel wanted five new P-TECH high schools, so the mayor personally called the CEOs of tech companies Cisco, Microsoft Corporation, Motorola Solutions, and Verizon Wireless to ask each to partner with one of the other four schools.

Principle #7. Learn from the experiences. Accept differences and adjust quickly. Enlarge the coalition. Stay closely involved.

Already there were tweaks to the P-TECH model, with five new schools and five business partners. The schools were of varying sizes. Some were conversions of whole buildings; others were situated as tenants within other schools. They used names other than P-TECH. The five neighborhoods had distinctive, sometimes severe, problems. The additional companies had their own staffs and ideas. Chicago's labor unions were more cantankerous than New York City's, and its community colleges had lower graduation rates, so it was an even tougher environment.

Launched in 2012, all five schools showed some improvement within a year, but there were shortfalls and variations. Results were better in some schools than in others, and best in the Sarah Goode School, the IBM partner school that most closely resembled the original Brooklyn model. Replication is always difficult without extra attention. Litow's team quickly realized that this was no time to declare victory and move on. They needed to work closely with their new partners to give them a playbook—which they put on the web—and help them succeed. They saw that the model could still work even when some elements were changed. They realized they had to work on the process of scaling rather than the process of school design, and they saw that the right "authorizer"—an elected official with the power to create new schools—made a difference in how fast the initiative could grow. New York City, which had been discussing adding more P-TECH schools since the start of the Brooklyn demonstration project, decided to move forward in August 2013—undoubtedly to try to outdo Chicago.[11]

Expansion and Diffusion

Proof of concept and fast replication were very important milestones, but not enough for the big impact Litow and team had envisioned and not enough to quiet all the critics, even with an appealing story and VIP endorsers. But the work had generated big demand to take the model elsewhere.

At this point, it was clear that the hands-on, labor-intensive nature of the work, city by city, would start bearing fruit as long as the structures for scaling were in place.

Principle #8. Find the fastest, most efficient path to scaling and the partners who can get you there.

Litow and team adjusted P-TECH's scaling strategy for more rapid diffusion. Rather than work with individual cities and their mayors, they decided to enlist state governors as P-TECH champions, given that some education funding, regulations, and standards were decided at the state level. Even before New York City greenlighted new sites, in early 2013, New York State governor Andrew Cuomo announced ten more P-TECH-modeled schools across the state and later added another twenty-three sites to touch a total of ten thousand students during the 2016 school year. The speed with which governors could act, and the incentives that could be provided to cash-strapped schools, were noteworthy.

Litow began traveling to governors' mansions and state houses, sometimes alongside the next IBM CEO, Virginia Rometty, to describe the P-TECH model and enlist support. It was the right move. By 2018, the P-TECH model was being used in 110 schools in eight US states (New York, Illinois, Connecticut, Colorado, Maryland, Rhode Island, Texas, and Louisiana) and three other countries (Morocco, Taiwan, and Australia), expanding the model under a variety of names. Litow anticipated that fall 2019 would bring over two hundred P-TECH-type schools in twelve states and twelve countries.[12]

Principle #9. Keep your eye on the main idea, not the details, and keep selling the mission and vision. Maintain core elements, but let others be modified by circumstances. Know what's key and what isn't.

Moving beyond New York City and Chicago showed the need for flexibility and creativity. In less urban areas of New York State, it was not easy to find employers as large and tech-savvy as those in major cities, with jobs to offer and credible mentors. But those areas were included in Governor Cuomo's plan precisely because they were economic development zones that needed to increase employment opportunities. Litow and the team created consortia of employers to work with P-TECH-style schools, such as groups of hospitals in the region, or to include companies that were not in tech industries but were heavy tech users, such as the supermarket chain Wegman's, headquartered in upstate New York. And as with all public education programs, the quality of principals is key (which is why Carol Hallquist started her Principals Connect program in Kansas City, as we saw in chapter 4).

Ensuring P-TECH program quality while scaling rapidly to schools of varying sizes, locations, and employer types were key challenges. Litow and the team homed in on seven core components that were integral to the Brooklyn P-TECH model and stressed those over and over again. Beyond that, they gave each location leeway. Of course, this entailed a massive education effort in itself. They tried to meet extensively with state teams to help them understand the model's components and implementation, making it clear that the model was more a set of goals and inspiration than an exact, detailed recipe.

Principle #10. Work on the surrounding ecosystem. Get elected officials and laws on your side. Grow the number of allies and supporters. Influence public policy and public opinion.

Litow's team led the charge to pass a new version of the Carl D. Perkins Vocational and Technical Act to improve the quality of technical education. The Perkins Act, which had not been updated since 2006, underpinned federal funding for Career and Technical Education (CTE). Forming a four-hundred-group-strong coalition and meeting regularly with legislators, Litow and other IBM leaders advocated for revisions reflecting the P-TECH model to the act, which Congress finally reauthorized with bipartisan support in 2018. By working on a legislative level and enlisting other corporate partners, Litow and his team strengthened government, private sector, and public support for CTE for impact beyond P-TECH's direct outcomes.[13]

By 2018, the more than 110 P-TECH-style six-year high schools in the United States worked with 550 industrial partners and 70 community college partners. "Pathways" is the right first name. A new institutional trail had been blazed along the road to major impact. P-TECH went from pilot project in Brooklyn, New York, to replication in Chicago, to massive national expansion and international adoption in its first five years. Litow, Davis, and P-TECH's designers consciously made strategic decisions in the conception stage in 2010 to facilitate replication, rapid scaling, and potentially transformational education system impact.[14]

And Radcliffe Saddler, who started in the first class in 2011 and completed the six-year program in four years (along with five other fast learners), was hard at work at his $50,000+ job at IBM, which he landed while still a teenager. He was thinking about graduate degrees.

A Culture for Impact: Innovation, Collaboration, and Scaling

The P-TECH project had a powerful corporate champion that lent staff (including P-TECH's lead architect), a global team with key relationships, and employees who wanted to volunteer. Such favorable conditions seem formidable and hard to duplicate. But social innovators, take heart! If you're not born with similar assets, you can make them yourself. Keep in mind that Wendy Kopp—one person, all on her own—conceived of Teach for America as a Princeton undergraduate and made it a force in American public education as well as a central player in the movement to establish civilian national service as an expectation for young people, joining the coalition that City Year forged.

Idea size matters more than anything. What's important is not the size of the resources; it's the size of the idea. With a big enough idea and bold enough people skilled in advanced leadership, it's possible to go from zero to impact, collecting assets and allies along the way. If you don't start out knowing VIPs, you pull out your best persuasion and coalition-building skills and befriend them. It might take longer, but the same principles that got P-TECH whizzing from concept to expansion in record time lie behind the scaling of every social change initiative that has stood the test of time and is well along on the road to impact. That's true of City Year, a thirty-year-old force for change that mobilizes young people, eighteen to twenty-four years old, for a year of service, working in schools with large numbers of at-risk students to help them stay in school and on track for graduation.

City Year started in Boston in 1988, but from the beginning, cofounders Michael Brown and Alan Khazei, who met as college roommates, had their eyes on America and the world. These recent graduates, with their founding colleagues, Jennifer Eplett Reilly and Neil Silverston, dreamed of establishing national service in America. While finishing college and law school, Brown and Khazei worked in Congress and on presidential commissions; like Torsten Thiele, they wormed their way into the right circles.

Despite their youth back then, their leadership was advanced. They knew how to tell an engaging story and to activate allies for their start-up. They found corporate sponsors and got VIPs and elected officials of both parties behind them, including US president Bill Clinton and Governor (and later presidential candidate and senator) Mitt Romney. Others followed. They played a big role in getting a law passed and federal funds allocated for national service in 1993. After Clinton left office, Brown and Khazei sat with him on a Delta flight to South Africa to stand with Nelson Mandela in 2003 as he sang the virtues of youth service (and helped establish City Year in Johannesburg).

City Year hosted presidential candidates Barack Obama (Democrat) and John McCain (Republican) on the same stage for a big audience at Columbia University in 2008—albeit one after the other rather than together (which, as I recall from a second-row seat as a board member, made for a very late evening). And they were instrumental in getting another law passed in 2009, the Edward M. Kennedy Serve America Act. Starting small, with just one's own vision and hustle, can lead to big accomplishments when the idea is big enough and the leadership determined enough.

Growing to Impact by Knowing
What—and What Not—to Change

The ten principles behind proof of concept, replication, and expansion can also be found in City Year's growth story. Brown and Khazei ran a pilot program in Boston for five years and then improvised their way opportunistically to the next three sites. For example, Columbia, South Carolina, wouldn't pop up in any analysis of the right place to go next, but enthusiastic young lawyer Mary Louise Ramsdell simply pestered the team into getting a City Year site in her hometown, which she could lead. Early on, the cofounders learned to manage by information, using data to drive the performance of the red-jacketed City Year corps members (yellow in California, where red is a gang color) who demonstrated national service in action.

Growth requires change. Along the way from those early years to twenty-nine sites in the United States at the thirtieth anniversary (plus South Africa and the United Kingdom), nearly everything was altered.

People and the work. Early volunteer staff became professionals with advanced degrees. Corps members who once could have included high school dropouts became better educated and were given training tools to make them valuable to teachers. The work had started as a hodgepodge of any kind of service—renovating homeless shelters, cleaning up vacant lots, helping in food banks, painting classroom walls, after-school tutoring. But in the mid-2000s, City Year pivoted to become exclusively school-focused, where much of the service was happening anyway. Corps members served as near peers who could be success coaches, supporting students' achievements in schools under teachers' supervision, guided by a big LTI—a long-term impact goal of reducing the high school dropout rate, which had skyrocketed to crisis proportions in low-performing schools. Led by Brown and president Jim Balfanz, a former corps member and Philadelphia site founding codirector, the pivot to education and LTI was a way to show that national service was not just nice to have but also essential to solving a major national problem. (Khazei had left by then to try two runs for public office and then founded other organizations while remaining on the board.)

Organization and funding. The organization model wobbled from control from headquarters to more autonomy for sites and their boards, with a formal charter, back to tighter integration into a national organization with central standardized processes, which were high quality and professionally led. The coalition circle enlarged to include national sponsors who could sponsor multiple teams rather than sites having to scramble for numerous smaller local team sponsors, although sites were still responsible for community support. Funding changed too. City Year went from refusing government money to getting some support from AmeriCorps (along with continuing private sector funding and a trickle of revenue from selling service days to companies) to charging school districts $100,000 or more for the work of a team of corps members in the classroom and schools.

Culture and values. One thing built in from the beginning did not change: the culture and values. Every new venture that scales to impact needs to think culture first. Everything else can vary and can be modified by innovation, but the culture continues. Building a culture around a set of core values helps people and organizations navigate strategic pivots and leadership transitions as well as weather messy middles. Like every human organization, City Year had its share of squabbling, turnover, and stumbles, but the aspirational culture guided choices about what to do, or not. The unique "idealist" organizational culture that City Year founders Brown and Khazei introduced glued the organization together as it added sites, changed partners, shifted focus to the high school dropout crisis, revised personnel needs, and made other adjustments over the course of its thirty-year history. That culture included special rituals, colors, logos, practices, principles, management techniques, founding stories, and a guidebook explaining it all, called *The Idealist Handbook*. Every meeting began with ripples—good news named after a famous Robert F. Kennedy speech about ripples of hope. Embrace of the culture was among a few items that were nonnegotiable for new sites. Another must-have was diversity. One of the most dramatic sights at schools served by City Year was morning greeting: rows of clapping, cheering, chanting red-jacketed corps members, young women and men of all sizes and skin colors, welcoming students to the school day as they entered the building.

Wider circles and coalitions for big change. From the beginning, Brown and Khazei also collaborated extensively with similar groups, building a big circle-like coalition. The goal was to go bigger: to build a movement to establish national service as a routine expectation for young people. While City Year was still small and new, they worked on enriching the ecosystem and building coalitions for service. The first national conference was held in Columbus, Ohio, and called Cyzygy—a play on syzygy for City Year, aligning the planet and stars—when there were just four fledgling sites. There, other nonprofits were invited for learning sessions. City Year continued to convene, invite, and participate. They met with Wendy

Kopp when she started Teach for America and offered her tips. They incubated other service organizations and shared materials. They were central participants in a presidential summit on America's future in Philadelphia in 1997, which was chaired by General Colin Powell and featured all five living US presidents. Although national service remained controversial despite this high-level sponsorship ("Pay volunteers?" critics sneered), the City Year team persisted in championing the big dream of national service by collaborating with every related organization they could find and mobilizing local leaders at their growing network of sites.

In short, Brown, Khazei, and their growing senior leadership team of Balfanz and others understood that their success in getting to impact required bigger coalitions—enriching the ecosystem for many other initiatives and organizations whose efforts would combine for systemic change. They knew it was unlikely that they could grow big enough to do it all themselves—the same reason that other cause-oriented innovations decide they need to create or join groups to try to influence lawmakers, resource holders, and opinion leaders to get behind the cause.

Through all this coalition-crafting, Brown and colleagues were building a movement. They harvested the fruits of their efforts in 2003, when AmeriCorps faced cuts in government funding. City Year was at the center of enlisting nonprofits, champions, and thought leaders to launch a Save AmeriCorps campaign, led by City Year policy and strategy chief AnnMaura Connolly, who was based in Washington and was well acquainted with Capitol Hill. Funding was restored, though there has been a battle over AmeriCorps funding in every Congress since then. Connolly then formalized the coalition as founding president of Voices for National Service while also serving as a City Year top executive.

The importance of this coalition was proven again in 2018, when a mobilization of numerous allies who had seen the value of service for themselves encouraged Congress, which had tried again to eliminate all funding, to increase its allocation. "We were successful because we mobilized both grass top leaders (donors, board members, leading voices in the media) and the troops on the ground," Connolly summarized to me. "We were able to help members of Congress see why the federal investment in national service mattered to the states and communities they represent in a very specific, localized way." She also praised bipartisan support from Republican senators Roy Blunt and Bill Cassidy—both from states with active City Year sites—and Democratic senators Chris Coons and Patty Murray. The combination of mobilizing community organizations and well-known and highly connected leaders who understood the value of AmeriCorps was powerful—and it worked.

The other ecosystem-enriching, outside-the-building actions by City Year leaders involved education. They realized that their ability to have an impact on the high school dropout crisis depended on many variables City Year didn't control, including the quality of schools. To influence the districts they served, and perhaps beyond, City Year set up its own laboratory to test "whole school, whole child" best practices in the form of a grade six-to-twelve charter school in Denver in a formal partnership with Johns Hopkins University's Everyone Graduates Center serving mostly low-income students. To avoid the problem of mission drift distraction, the school was kept isolated from City Year's mainstream operations. For the rest of the City Year universe, Balfanz led the formation of school improvement networks that would encourage discussion with many innovators in school districts—and City Year.

By 2018, City Year's 3,000 corps members delivered services to 223,000 students in 327 schools in 29 US cities. More importantly, the strategy appeared to be making a measurable impact on student performance. A 2015 study found that City Year schools in the study cohort were twice as likely as non–City Year schools to improve student outcomes on state English exams and three times as likely to improve outcomes on state math exams.

Its long-term impact strategy was named as among the best investible big bets for social impact. This was a valuable endorsement by consultants from Bridgespan, a major advisory firm.[15]

Thirty years is a long journey to impact, but there were many oases of achievement along the way that refreshed the leadership team and nurtured enthusiasm for continuing the quest. City Year avoided getting stale because of constant innovation and change, collaboration for dynamic ecosystem-building coalitions, and culture and values that reminded everyone around City Year about its core purpose: to make national service a routine expectation for young people by demonstrating its power in practice.[16]

Does the Road Ever End? Renewing Impact

The itinerary for the road to impact has taken us from start-up through proof of concept and replication to expansion and diffusion, with advanced leadership actions at every point. It's inspiring to know that small, smart innovations can have widespread impact on a variety of problems, gradually shifting institutional patterns. But in a changing world, the quest for impact is ongoing. Even if one set of problems is solved, it's inevitable that new problems surface, so innovation, change, and renewal are a constant imperative. And along the way, there are common dynamics and dilemmas of organizational life and societal change that can start undermining impact.

- Leaders of change initiatives might succeed in getting a law passed or a policy changed, only to find that their allies decide that the work is done or that the problem is solved and that their support is no longer needed, so they then reduce their support.

- Social movements might build a membership that has to be serviced, so a loose, informal movement becomes a professionalized organization, adding operational efficiencies and distance from the passions of members.
- Charismatic leaders who engage people in an inspiring mission might find that growing the initiative requires bean counters and administrators, so the charismatic founders leave and inside-the-building bureaucrats take over.
- Innovators might change the conversation about solutions to big problems, only to find that unless a new array of organizational possibilities also emerge and they can demonstrate viable programs that work, the conversation is just talk, there is little meaningful action, and the effort loses credibility.
- Innovators who start well outside the building and succeed might become celebrities, and soon they are attending all the elite meetings of establishments, going from critics of the dominant narrative to members of the club of those who maintain it.
- Institution-challenging ventures might grow to the point where they become entrenched establishments themselves, smug and inward-looking, failing to acknowledge the changes swirling around them. They become the new entrenched institutions that a new generation of radicals will want to disrupt.

Thus, over time, innovations that begin as outside-the-building challengers often become established structures themselves that are hard to change. Innovators leave the street and go inside. When this happens, the journey to impact must begin again: having a dream of changing the world, finding an idea that challenges old models, telling the right story, and mobilizing new resources and new coalitions for change. Let's take another trip to *Sesame Street*, which we visited in chapter 1, and look at its history to see how advanced leadership can renew a significant social enterprise falling on hard times precisely because of its success. Winning streaks end when complacency sets in; then a venture or a team can easily slide downhill.[17]

Did Big Bird and Friends Go Over the Hill? And Could They Come Back?

In the early years, Joan Ganz Cooney, Peggy Charren, Big Bird, and Cookie Monster seemed to have everything in place for a big and continuing impact on early childhood education through television. Then Dora upended it all.

Sesame Workshop, as indicated earlier, became an American and international social icon almost overnight, exemplifying advanced leadership for innovation and institutional change. In 1968, Joan Ganz Cooney, a then thirty-six-year-old Emmy Award–winning television producer, and Lloyd Morrisett, an experimental psychologist, founded what was first called the Children's Television Workshop (CTW) with the idea of developing cutting-edge educational television programming that appealed to young children and adult caregivers to remedy the lack of early education opportunities for low-income children.

Using television as a teaching tool was not common practice. As executive director, Cooney recruited a top team of producers and staff to create innovative content for a new television program, *Sesame Street*. Puppeteer Jim Henson created for the show a soon-to-be-famous cast of Muppet characters, including Elmo, Bert, Ernie, Big Bird, and Cookie Monster, to interact with a multicultural cast of adults and children. Nonprofit CTW made a deal for exclusive distribution on the Public Broadcasting System, so any family in America, regardless of income, could watch the show for free. Almost immediately, *Sesame Street*'s viewership among two- to five-year-olds reached some 30 percent and continued to climb.

The show was much praised, and Cooney became much honored. Demand for commercial licensing of *Sesame Street* toys and other merchandise soared. Despite objections within the organization that commercial marketing was antithetical to Sesame Workshop's mission, Cooney and her team seized the opportunity. They later added home video and DVD sales to create steadier revenue streams to enhance the organization's financial sustainability. The team expanded Sesame internationally, first in Mexico and Brazil, then in Germany and the Netherlands, and eventually to about thirty nations.

Other actions, including a well-led social movement, complemented Sesame's goals. Over the same period, in suburban Boston, Peggy Charren, who often described herself as a "Newton housewife and mother," was also watching children's television (and the zeitgeist). I got to know her much later, after she had become one of America's best-known early childhood advocates—a savvy, feisty, outspoken, and very effective ecosystem builder who enriched the environment in which *Sesame Street* flourished. With three cofounders, she formed Action for Children's Television in 1968. At its height, twenty thousand members were its primary funders, augmented by grants. Through the 1970s, ACT lobbied and litigated to remove or limit television advertising to children. Every broadcaster and most legislators got to know her well. In 1973, the National Association of Broadcasters revised its code to limit commercial time on children's programs. In 1990, Congress passed the Children's Television Act, which included guidelines for content and advertising.

Taking Success for Granted: Getting Stuck and Failing to See Change

So far, so good. Children's television was established as a force in preschool and outside-of-school education. But disruptive change had been coming and was soon visibly undermining the coalition that worried about limiting commercial aspects of television for children.

Wandering cheerily onto television screens were the new animated characters Dora the Explorer, SpongeBob SquarePants, and their friends on cable TV channel Nickelodeon, which was part of a growing pay-TV industry. Nickelodeon had launched about a decade after Sesame, and in 1991, targeted children with an experiment called Launch Box with NASA, part of a defunct Cable in the Classroom effort. So *Sesame Street* couldn't rest easily at the top of the hill after all. Dora appeared in her first episode on Nickelodeon in 2000, and *Sponge-Bob SquarePants* surfaced at about the same time. Dora, bilingual in English and Spanish, appealed to preschoolers sometimes more than Muppets did. Moreover, she and her friends did not require rehearsals, retakes, or paid human actors, so she brought financial advantages too.

And if that wasn't enough, screens moved far beyond TV sets to include computers, the internet, smartphones, and other devices. There were changing audience demands, even on the part of three-year-olds. During that same period of Dora's dominance, and despite its highly creative core, Sesame Workshop, the new name for CTW, grew complacent and stuck in its ways. It's as though the characters on the street had gone inside the building and closed the doors, forgetting to take any new media with them. Sesame did not evolve fast enough to keep up with the changing technological and competitive landscape. New, more agile competitors entered the market, consumer tastes changed, and the digital revolution increased viewing options, while Sesame Workshop's leaders and team continued to operate as they always had.

Beset by a culture of complacency, weak collaboration, and poor accountability, which are responses to losing streaks that also perpetuate them, the organization watched their once-steady revenue streams dwindle. *Sesame Street*'s ratings slipped, and the show started losing millions of dollars annually. It was close to the point where it could no longer produce new programs, let alone remain relevant to the still-significant challenges for early childhood learning, especially for families in impoverished situations who could not afford to buy or pay. As it rounded the forty-five-year lap, Sesame Workshop was in dire need of fresh, outside-the-building thinking.

There is always a question of whether organizations should be propped up just because they once contributed innovative solutions. Joan Ganz Cooney and colleagues demonstrably changed early childhood education; ecosystem partner Peggy Charren was among those agitating for changing the policy framework. At forty-five, had Sesame Workshop reached the end of the road to impact?

There's an old truth about the life cycle of organizations. Max Weber observed long ago that social movements grow into bureaucracies. What began as a force for change forgets how to change. Charismatic leaders who drive innovations give way to administrators, and that's when organizations or movements get stuck. In fact, for some charismatic founders, such as Gilberto Dimenstein at Catraca Livre in Brazil, growth to fifty million social media users meant tasks that he didn't want to do, involving processes, routines, and meetings, so he turned over the CEO role to his CTO son, Marco. It undermines social purpose when the head office starts to count for more than the front lines. The iron cage of career success that I described in chapter 2 starts confining people and limiting their thinking. Complacency reduces the willingness to take risks or to try anything big and bold. It becomes easier to repeat or to tinker around the edges than to press for change. The potential for further impact is lost when people try to hang on to a glorious past that no longer exists.[18]

Fresh Air, Fresh Thinking: Going Outside the Building Again

Fortunately for Sesame Workshop, Jeff Dunn—who had worked at Nickelodeon as well as HiT Entertainment (originally the distribution arm of Muppet creator Jim Henson) and was eager to make his next phase one of social purpose and impact—became Sesame Workshop's fifth CEO and first from outside the organization. We started to talk about it just after he had spent a summer as a consultant at the request of the board; he was subsequently offered the post. He saw the potential for a turnaround to even greater impact.

As noted in chapter 1, Dunn shook up the culture. He removed silos, added a five-year broadcasting agreement with for-profit HBO, renegotiated the PBS deal, and encouraged open dialogue and big thinking. He closed the organization's largely ineffective four-year-old internal innovation lab in favor of forging external partnerships with start-ups and major technology companies to develop viable, innovative digital products with Sesame Workshop's education experts.

Equally important, Dunn elevated Sherrie Westin to innovate in philanthropy in the newly created role of president of global impact and philanthropy. This focus had significant payoff. Together with the International Rescue Committee, Sesame Workshop won the $100 million McArthur Foundation competition for a very big societal mission: preschool education for children in refugee camps in the Syrian conflict areas, including new media. Another $100 million grant from LEGO Foundation in December 2018 helped expand this work in the Middle East and beyond.[19]

On the eve of the fiftieth anniversary, Big Bird and friends could swell with pride. The team was fired up. Sesame was not only relighting its creative spark; it was taking on even bigger impact goals. With advanced leadership skills, it's always possible to smash bureaucratic barriers, move outside the building, and get back on the road to impact.

* * *

If it takes many villagers to raise a child, it takes an army of advanced leaders and a continuing flow of new ideas to tackle a big, complex system problem and have an impact. Over time, the success of one attracts others, and an ecosystem cluster develops to support change.

When thinking outside the building, leaders from many sectors inevitably bump into one another on the road to impact. Consider a few of the many intersecting new partners for the revitalized Sesame Workshop. A digitally based Sesame partnership appealed to education technology start-up leaders such as Maxeme Tuchman, cofounder and CEO of Caribu, an app enabling reading to children from remote locations to build vocabulary and brainpower in early childhood. She included Sesame content on the app, knowing that the missions were similar.[20] Stanley Litow was nearby when IBM's education group partnered with Sesame to bring its Watson AI software to Sesame online learning products. Perhaps Mary Louise and Bruce Cohen of Talent Beyond Boundaries (TBB) will cross paths with Jeff Dunn and Sherrie Westin in a refugee camp in Jordan or Lebanon, where skilled refugees waiting for TBB-facilitated resettlement know that Sesame will help their preschool children learn. And maybe Rich Fahey and Bob Saudek's LEN will give Liberian children the ability to watch *Sesame Street* programs on fully charged mobile devices.

Such intersections enrich the ecosystem of institutional change. Other players fill in the field's missing pieces to hit all three levels of change, including laws and public policies, additional programs and organizational options, and public opinion. New connections encourage advanced leaders that their projects will find allies and coalitions of support, opening new conversations and new possibilities for action. Innovation, change, and renewal are way stations along the journey to impact. The reward for advanced leaders comes not just from the outcomes of their efforts but also from the purpose and meaning generated by their commitment to make a difference in the world. By improving the health of the oceans, the community, or the world, they improve their own.

The quest for impact is not just about scaling Daily Table, LEN, Catraca Livre, or City Year but also about how those innovations, and the investors that back them, can inspire many other Daily Tables and LEN-like innovations that accumulate to change the world. A movement is not a monolith; it consists of many independent actors. Other competing projects create an industry. One smart innovation at a time adds up to changing the world. For advanced leaders just starting down the road to impact, and maybe entering the desert, the best combination of strategies is a grand long-term impact goal, quick wins and milestones to measure along the way, and connections with many others with similar goals and values. As long as there's progress, there's momentum for impact.

CONCLUSION

AN ARMY FOR CHANGE

The Call to Lead

In perilous times, when bad news travels fast and swamps the media, advanced leadership can be a source of good news. With trust low and social division high, it is encouraging to know that there are numerous leaders in a variety of fields who take it upon themselves to find smart innovations to make a difference in the world. Advanced leaders work to build trust and increase social capital by making new connections and standing for positive action.

Some analysts think that democracy itself is on life support. Many nations suffer from this condition; the American version is sometimes said to be caused by a new Gilded Age of especially high and intractable inequality. Clearly, systems are challenged. But I think that advanced leaders form a division of a new army of democracy. They vote for change with their feet and work for it with their time and effort. They do not simply argue about problems; they deploy their capabilities, connections, and whatever cash they can muster to demonstrate change in action and seed new social institutions to tackle big problems. They are builders rather than destroyers—more like the Army Corps of Engineers than weaponized soldiers.

When big government, big business, and even big philanthropy are attacked for their domination of the agenda and pilloried for stale thinking and questionable results, advanced leaders take another tack. Rather than get stuck in expectations that little can change (so you'd better live with it!), advanced leaders venture outside existing structures to find new approaches that fill gaps, connect otherwise-unconnected activities, and show what's possible. They acknowledge the magnitude of big, intractable problems but want to act rather than merely whine. Their optimistic utopian dreams of a better world provide an alternative to apocalypse now and forever. The fresh ideas they find on the streets outside the building can change old institutions and give some of them a new lease on life.

Consider the range of social, economic, and environmental issues the leaders depicted in this book have tackled: racial and gender equity, ocean health, refugee resettlement, gun safety, college affordability, education innovation, community empowerment, and much more. This work is not charity; it is change.

With a few exceptions, the people whose stories I tell are not the stuff of legends, but they can inspire others. They are not famous and are not classic heroes tested by fire, although they are all accomplished leaders who have managed to overcome numerous barriers. For example, Reverend Raymond Jetson, whose Baton Rouge project appears in chapter 4, had been an elected legislator and state official, yet he still risked racism and rejection when telling the white establishment what they might not want to hear about the condition of their region and their complicity in problems. Head outside the building, and risk looking like an outsider even to people you've known for years. The strength to take this step is fueled by clear values and a sense of purpose, as David Brooks noted in *The Second Mountain*.[1]

For all that personal presence matters to success, advanced leadership is not a solo effort. I've shown pairs, trios, and groups working together to launch change initiatives, including married couples, college roommates, and some leaders who start with teams close at hand. The numerous people I've highlighted were resolute in their conviction that they could do something. And for all the hard work and inevitable setbacks they encountered, the ones who stayed with it seemed highly engaged—more so than employees who are notoriously unengaged with work. Regardless of generation, they were full of the energy that comes from a mission they embrace wholeheartedly. They often joined forces with others to create movements for change.

Changing the World?

"Never doubt that a small group of thoughtful, committed citizens can change the world. Indeed, it's the only thing that ever has." This quote is widely attributed to the late anthropologist Margaret Mead, although I couldn't find where she might have said it. This oft-repeated saying adorns plaques, wall hangings, and "on hold" phone messages at organizations seeking social change. The words are inspirational and motivating, but are they true?

Do the kinds of social innovations and entrepreneurial ventures I've described actually make a dent? Or are they just nibbling at the edges as interesting fringe efforts while establishments and elites continue on their merry way, singing the dominant narrative and growing more fortified and formidable? I certainly don't want to exaggerate the potency of the projects I've highlighted. Only history can tell us whether entrepreneurial institutional change initiatives such as these and their counterparts are harbingers of the future and initiators of waves of positive change or just intriguing blips.

In some cases, the numbers of lives touched get big quickly, especially when technology is involved. By social media, Gilberto Dimenstein's Catraca Livre reached fifty million people in Brazil relatively quickly and helped seed other movements, from community upgrades to action campaigns to alliances with groups seeking inclusion and justice. Clearly, the venture's immediate impact involves big numbers, but whether it will help transform a politically troubled Brazil remains to be seen.

Taken one by one, most of the stories I tell are about ventures that are still small. There are just two Daily Table stores in Boston neighborhoods (albeit with twenty-three thousand customers). No matter how inspiring, colorful, and publicity attracting they are, and no matter how ambitious Doug Rauch's scaling plans are (clusters of five in Boston and then in other cities), that is still very small. Or consider TBB's early result: just fifty resettled refugees out of twenty-five million. That might not sound like much against the magnitude of the problem, but, like Daily Table, it is one of many innovations that open new pathways, challenge the dominant narrative, and reach many large stakeholders through cross-sector coalitions with much larger organizations, including the governments of Canada and Australia. Thus, despite the small size of each project, when they are considered together, there is the prospect of developing into a significant force—that army of democracy I'm proposing.

Of course, many cases I discuss are small because they are new. Their initiators have every intention of growing and creating significant change. Some bootstrap, but others start with significant funding, whether private capital, foundation money, or governmental support. Haifa Al Kaylani envisioned a venture in Jordan to employ otherwise-unemployed women in greenhouses growing vegetables hydroponically—green in many senses—and got $300,000 from the World Bank while still in the idea phase. It's harder for not-for-profit organizations or NGOs to find resources to scale than for profit-making and revenue-producing enterprises, which can access big capital markets. But increasingly, models for investing in social change efforts are proliferating. Once Vanessa Kirsch's New Profit was nearly alone, but over the years many more vehicles have sprung up: impact investing groups and traditional private equity firms that create funds to invest in social change while making a profit, such as

Bain Capital's Double Impact Fund, cofounded by former Massachusetts governor Deval Patrick.

Societal change takes time—an obvious observation but one that's sometimes forgotten in an era of impatience. Messes that took decades, if not centuries, to make can't be cleaned up instantly. Along the way, many projects fail. That's a reality of anything entrepreneurial. Some never get off the ground, or they don't take hold, perhaps because of poor execution or maybe because they weren't great ideas to begin with. I give examples of failure in chapter 6. It's a truism of innovation that getting more successes stems from trying more things and tolerating more failures.

However quickly single organizations or marches or media campaigns can form, one-by-ones or one-offs aren't enough. Movements for change require an accumulation of adjacent and even unrelated efforts that help the new norms or social institutions reach a tipping point and the surrounding system to change. Ride-hailing services such as Uber and Lyft built their markets in a few stunning years, while a regulatory and labor framework has lagged and the autonomous cars they seek are taking longer and costing more. Sometimes technology can't live up to the hype, and, as mentioned earlier, sectors operate on different time frames. But the main reason for slow speed is universal: that systems change and ecosystem transformations take time. History teaches us this. It took waves of suffragettes over many decades to succeed in getting the vote for women. It took more than fifty years from major events in the US civil rights movement of the 1950s and 1960s to the removal of Confederate statues and flags in the South. In 1983, a major public warning about the problems in public schools, "A Nation at Risk," was issued during the late US president Ronald Reagan's administration; over thirty-five years later, many of the same problems remain on the table seeking solutions.

In short, we should look for the ripples rather than demanding finished results.

Small Pebbles, Wide Ripples

The small beginnings and need for patience don't reduce the significance of what advanced leaders accomplish well beyond their projects. The variety of projects and the number of problems touched speak to the potential of this mode of action to ripple through the world. The way leaders act to conceive and build innovative initiatives could represent a new paradigm of leadership, pushing conventional theories beyond walls to encompass all of society. They change the conversation. They reinterpret structures and constraints. They reframe a problem and show that new possibilities exist. Things that once seemed radical can become commonplace, part of the everyday discourse. Just saying it out loud makes something more real and, eventually, more likely. The initial efforts to enable women to drive in Saudi Arabia, which was banned by law and custom, could be considered dismal failures, until they weren't, and then laws changed to permit this once-heretical act.

Advanced leadership efforts can activate people who would otherwise be passive. The Asian American Justice Center gives voice to a range of concerns by immigrants. Other initiatives address the disaffected rural hinterland, such as Waide Warner and Susan Crawford's efforts to bring broadband to remote places; they listened to the economic needs of those who feel they have been left behind, ignored, or disrespected. Once mad as hell and not wanting to take it anymore (to paraphrase the famous shout in the movie *Network*), disgruntled community members can be empowered to join under a big, inclusive tent to create their own solutions.

These two benefits alone—changing the conversation and activating the passive—are important aspects of developing new narratives and mobilizing new constituents for making a difference in the world. It's not the size of the venture or its resources that matter; it's the size of the idea, as I've said. Advanced leadership involves thinking bigger than you are. Thus, this army for change might start with small numbers, but I predict that it will grow quickly in years to come.

One reason this leadership force will grow is because of values shifts among millennial and baby boom generations, both of which contain large numbers who want to make a meaningful difference in the world, as I showed in chapter 2. While cheering for innovators and entrepreneurs of any life stage, I'm betting on the boomers to rise to the challenge and show the way for generations that follow because of their large numbers and the likelihood that many will have the three Cs to invest in projects. In fact, some of the boomer elites who have unprecedented riches might decide to do this defensively because the embarrassingly large wealth and income disparities in America are under political attack, and they might want to assuage their consciences and join the movement to improve the world before being forced to. That's the cynical side. The positive side is that espoused values are changing.

In the United States, Europe, and Japan, an aging population and increased longevity presents an opportunity to engage people transitioning from their primary careers who want to do good works and leave a legacy. They might want to take an active role in change—if they hear the call, have role models, and see that they can adapt their identities and join a new peer group sharing the commitment to improving the world.

At the same time, one doesn't have to be advanced in age to practice advanced leadership; in fact, some are starting very young. Abby Falik went to graduate school to get ideas and skills and with the intention to start Global Citizen Year to send high school students to work in developing countries before attending college, changing their sensibilities with cross-cultural experiences in problem-solving for poor communities. Carolyn Casey started Project 351 in Massachusetts to deploy eighth-grade students as ambassadors for service in their communities and to organize service projects. Ashoka's changemaker initiative teaches micro versions of social innovation skills to children in schools throughout the world.

Another major reason that advanced leadership could guide a bigger change-seeking population is because it just might become the essential way of leading in many more places and many more situations.

An Essential Way of Leading:
The Broader Relevance of Advanced Leadership

The goals, sensibilities, and skills of advanced leadership have wide relevance. The significance goes far beyond the immediate numbers of lives touched by innovative projects. It extends to numerous institutional challenges and intractable problems that confront potential innovators in every sector and profession. The nature of change challenges, whether inside corporate offices or beyond the walls, increasingly requires more than traditional hierarchical leadership skills guiding teams inside the building; the new challenges require advanced leadership. For institutions that are threatened with disruption and displacement, this kind of leadership is essential because they simply can't keep singing variations of the same old refrains with a digital note added here or there. And as the routinized parts of jobs are replaced (or augmented) by technology, increasing numbers of people will find themselves working on tasks outside the building.

Advanced leaders are the ultimate silo busters. That alone explains why people employed by big, established organizations should embrace advanced leadership.

Breaking Through the Walls

Corporate giants and other established organizations need innovators and entrepreneurs for growth, renewal, and just plain defense against disruption. Every day, just to keep going, corporate executives and managers confront big, intractable institutional problems that necessitate breaking the constraints of convention. They can't be ignored by pulling down the shades and staying inside the building. Problems once considered external—someone else takes care of the schools or labor supply or waste management or supplier quality—have become internalized as a main locus of the action. Sometimes the problems are sources of business opportunities, as they are for insurance companies in Bermuda and beyond with a stake in preventing ocean disasters, or the small and midsized businesses in Canada that are eager to hire talented refugees.

Manufacturing and distribution companies are increasingly pushed to take end-to-end responsibility for their supply and distribution chains—pushed by business necessities, not just activist pressures. To ensure a continuing flow of supplies for its potato chips, PepsiCo Latin America had to improve the conditions of the small farmers who grow potatoes in the mountains of Peru. To ensure a supply of high-quality tiger shrimp for its US restaurants, Legal Sea Foods had to consider new kinds of partnerships in Thailand and get involved in projects addressing labor practices and sea level rises. A Brazilian bank found customers in inner cities by investing in neighborhood businesses and partnering with activists improving education so that students graduated and found jobs, growing the local economy. Procter & Gamble's baby care division worked on its mission to help babies thrive by sending mobile clinics to remote areas in Africa where babies could get check-ups and treatment for minor ailments and mothers could get education, incidentally distributing a few free Pampers diapers, reengineered to be less polluting.

No one is likely to say, "Now you're an advanced leader; go for it!" to the managers who get assignments to work in these domains. But whether they know it or not, they are being asked to think well outside the building and to break through walls—what Verizon called the "walled gardens" that hampered its progress in the smartphone and 5G world. These managers will confront and be measured on factors well beyond their direct control: Can they innovate so that they have impact on messy problems, and can they find new ideas, tell compelling stories, and create coalitions of conflicting stakeholders, inside or outside of the company?

Sometimes professionals act as self-appointed entrepreneurs inside the company and stretch well outside it—but if they are not schooled in advanced leadership, this work is at their peril. "Sandra Brown," for example, my name for a marketing manager at a biosciences company, decided to create an external social media campaign to bring attention to a disease for which the company had a product—not just by selling the product but by mobilizing a set of activists to stop the disease. The campaign attracted significant support, including enlisting rivals. However, Brown forgot to mobilize allies within the company. Senior officials shut down the campaign for undermining company policies and negotiated an exit package with her.

Top executives and average employees need to embrace advanced leadership principles every time they operate across boundaries or in unfamiliar settings, where stakeholder views can make or break the work. Indeed, Doug Rauch could teach a thing or two to his former employer, Trader Joe's, should it decide to open stores in inner cities to feed the poor nutritiously.

There's another benefit to bringing advanced leadership sensibilities to established companies. Because advanced leadership rests on mission and purpose, those working on change-the-world projects are highly engaged. Numerous human resource surveys show that traditional employers suffer from depressingly low rates of employee engagement. They have one foot out the door anyway, so they might as well be given the chance to do something meaningful for communities they care about. Giving more people the chance to work on projects outside the building can dramatically increase engagement. This would also encourage developing the leadership skills required for the future.

For example, IBM sent its first Corporate Service Corps—a field-based leadership-development program for high-potential employees—to

Ghana in July 2008 to spend a month solving an institutional problem with a diverse team drawn from many countries. Over the next four months, IBM sent a second group to Ghana and pairs of teams to Tanzania, Romania, and Vietnam, with three going to the Philippines. The teams were not marketing IBM; the point was to open their minds and enhance skills. The stretch in thinking was definitely advanced leadership in action. IBM took the risk of taking talented people away from their jobs for many weeks because of the benefits in sensibilities and connections, which produced enhanced engagement and retention. The program was expanded to more employees and eventually to executives, and IBM encouraged other companies to join them or start their own.

Advanced leadership skills are also essential when established organizations such as prominent nonprofits must adapt to new conditions. Sesame Workshop stretched outside its sector to work with commercial cable TV channel HBO and also with the International Refugee Committee. Educational establishments are among those that face challengers from well outside the building (e.g., Salman Khan's online Khan Academy for academic skill-providing videos, especially in math and science, which he said would reinvent education). Like Khan Academy, some ventures that start outside the building might be brought into it later, changing schooling in the process; David Weinstein formed Write the World as a digital platform with writing contests featuring peers as judges and coaches. After a few years, it was discovered by teachers who adopted it for their classrooms.

Just as corporate giants are eagerly seeking links to entrepreneurial ventures, if not outright acquisitions, NGO giants are partnering with digital start-ups that can propel them into the digital age before their arteries harden any further. Tech entrepreneur Sam Fankuchen started his for-profit, investor-owned venture, Golden, as a digital matching platform to connect people wanting to volunteer with volunteer opportunities. The ecosystem around Golden and its supply of coalition members included HR departments in big corporations, who want metrics on employee volunteering; global agencies such as UNICEF and NGOs, seeking volunteers; and states such as California, which have volunteer opportunities or crises such as wildfires that can sometimes use volunteers in the aftermath. Millennials and newcomers to an area were among the biggest early users, making friends as well as finding meaning. Golden opened new pathways and provided new data for its partners. This kind of cross-sector effort builds an ecosystem that changes the nonprofit sector in significant ways. Making it work requires advanced leadership skills in building coalitions and telling the right story with appeal across sectors.

The future of cities might also lie in using the advanced leadership tool kit. Giant Publicis Groupe wanted to turn Paris into a start-up hub, matching new millennial-led ventures with established companies that can use their innovations. Chairman Maurice Levy cofounded Viva-Tech Paris, connecting all of them with the highest circles in France. I sat toward the front when French president Emmanuel Macron touted the new partnerships. Throughout the world, cross-sector multistakeholder coalitions joining business, government, and nonprofits are vehicles for getting things done. They include the longstanding New York City Partnership and more recent coalitions in Columbus (the Columbus Partnership) and Minneapolis–St. Paul (Itasca Project). The Knight Foundation's CEO, Alberto Ibargüen, supported Miami director Matt Haggman in investing in an ecosystem for entrepreneurial start-ups, incubators, accelerators, and events to grow both for-profit start-ups and social ventures.

Establishments also need to acknowledge that advanced leaders want to take direct action well outside of conventional channels. It's not enough to dot a city with coworking spaces or to redecorate offices with whiteboards, long worktables, and snack stations—or to convene a few token cross-sector meetings. Advanced leadership is a mind-set that encourages multiple experiments by people who seize responsibilities without waiting in line. Make way for the new army for change.

Any Profession, Any Problem

Outside-the-building thinking spans professions and can enrich them. Big problems require many disciplines. Lawyers, physicians, educators, investment bankers, business executives, elected officials, entrepreneurs, and civic leaders can have a role in social innovation and social change.

Sometimes advanced leadership can be exercised within a profession to help others shed stale thinking and embrace new possibilities for making a difference in the world. While a young lawyer at large corporate law firm Akerman in Miami, Andrew Pompa developed opportunities for fellow lawyers to break out of their office routines and mingle with entrepreneurs. It was not a hard sell to encourage his civic-minded boss to reserve seats for Akerman in a burgeoning start-up incubator and let lawyers hang out there some days of the week. They could listen to stimulating ideas and learn to work across fields and sectors. They could see the value of innovations, such as software to create wills, and know the people who could create them. This was fresh air for lawyers.

The sensibilities and skills of advanced leadership can be applied to a wide range of deeply difficult societal and global problems. Consider a few other creative efforts that reflect courageous outside-the-building thinking.

- *New paths to solving perilous geopolitical conflicts.* Israeli Ohad Elhelo chose to connect entrepreneurs rather than work through the plethora of established governments and philanthropic organizations that had not solved the problem of Palestinians and Israel. After his army service, and while still a graduate student in Boston, he created Our Generation Speaks (OGS). It is a platform for joining talented young Israelis and Palestinians in joint business ventures to grow the economy, solve creative problems, and make connections that would provide a force for peace. Starting in 2016 with about thirty young people equally split by gender and Israeli or Palestinian status, and recruiting similar groups in subsequent years, OGS engaged a wide range of partners, avoided divisive regional politics, ran a summer boot camp in Boston, and created a portfolio of ventures—a few weaklings but many strong models. By 2018, a solar start-up company in Gaza provided more than eight hundred people with 24-7 electricity and had the infrastructure in place to support thousands of families. Another venture, Genesis, was poised to provide genetic testing for over a thousand people in the Bedouin community. Top regional and global professional and financial firms gave OGS pro bono services.

- *Expose Russian corruption and change the sports ecosystem.* Venture capitalists David Fialkow and Jim Swartz were coproducers with Dan Cogan and Bryan Fogel on the Oscar-winning documentary film *Icarus*, about the Russian Olympic doping scandal. They sheltered former Russian scientist Grigory Rodchenkov before he was put into the US Witness Protection Program and founded FairSport to lobby for change. They got an antidoping law introduced in the US Congress, entitled the Rodchenkov Act. All of this directly challenged Russian president Vladimir Putin. Swartz had the courage to go to St. Petersburg with his painter wife, Susan, for an exhibit of her art, despite having earned the enmity of the regime.

- *Help with menstrual periods and girls' education.* Another Oscar-honored documentary, winning in 2019, *Period. End of Sentence*, was part of a campaign to keep girls in school by making a taboo topic discussable and getting girls what they needed to be safe and comfortable. Under the slogan, "A period should end a sentence, not a girl's education," the leaders formed a nonprofit organization to get clean, affordable sanitary pads to girls in remote places where access was limited and traditions shamed girls as unclean. Distributing sanitary napkins helped girls stay in school all day. There are a growing number of efforts to address the previously unspeakable.

An Australian group, Share the Dignity, provides sanitary pads, tampons, and handbags to homeless women and girls. This could help menstruating women move from shamed and shunned to natural and dignified. Since girls' education and women's employment have been shown to benefit economies, destigmatizing menstruation (putting periods in the economic equation) has potentially large societal benefits.

Note that none of these three clusters of activities were undertaken by establishment organizations. None of them fit within familiar categories and structures. None of the initiators had a mandate. They didn't ask permission. They were volunteers, acting out of their own convictions. Their work had impact because they found allies who joined them—also voluntarily. And by being outside the building and cutting across institutional silos, they address not just one but several problems at the same time, just as we've seen in cases throughout this book. That's why I highlight them. Each of these sets of possibly game-changing, model-shifting initiatives came from leaders who bypassed officials, took responsibility, used persuasion, gathered allies, and formed coalitions. They definitely thought outside the building.

A leadership force guided by democratic principles can work on democracy itself. Emily Cherniack wanted to change the face of American politics by increasing the number of elected officials with service backgrounds, whether military or civilian national service. Cherniack was campaign manager for City Year cofounder Alan Khazei in his unsuccessful US Senate campaigns. She took the lessons from this failed experience to start New Politics. By 2018, her growing political organization and nonprofit leadership academy had succeeded in electing new members of Congress as well as state and local officials. Then Khazei started Democracy Entrepreneurs as a wing of his Be the Change organization; it mounted campaigns for change and sought to nurture additional groups that would find creative and innovative solutions to make civic life more participative and inclusive, solving problems such as corruption, suppression of voter rights, and apathy. With Khazei's help, veteran foreign correspondent Charles Sennott started Report for America with belief.net founder Steven Waldman to undergird democracy in left-behind areas by strengthening local news. This initiative of Sennott's GroundTruth Project deploys young journalists, using the Teach for America model, to work in local newsrooms and help high school journalists. This is a civics lesson in action.

Clearly, there is plenty of work to do and as-yet-unimagined ways of doing it—human work, that is. Data and technology can be powerful tools to help advanced leaders in the work of creating change, but robots, algorithms, and AI are unlikely to take over the work of imagining and leading that change.

Energizing and Mobilizing a New Leadership Force

#BeInspired, #GetMoving, #SolutionsNow. Can advanced leadership itself be a movement? Consider a few areas that could help enlist people in an army for change.

Educational pathways. People with assets who are burned out or less engaged in their main careers could use structured paths—and I'm not referring to ski slopes or golf courses. Colleges and universities have a significant role to play (and they might find themselves with a new market). Harvard ALI is one example of a new stage of higher education. This stage is not focused on enhancing primary careers, as executive education does, or providing another college-level program for a different career, as continuing education does, but rather moving leaders well beyond a career into a new realm of tackling messy systems change with multidisciplinary knowledge. Because the demand for this is increasingly clear, Stanford, Notre Dame, University of Texas's Tower School, and others have joined this embryonic movement with their own variations.

Human resource packages. Policies could also change to value this kind of transition to impact. Employers could provide incentives in exit packages for people to gain advanced leadership skills and embark on a new journey, especially if those people are holding down positions that a company wants to pass on to fresh talent. Laws could support tax benefits or deferments if people use savings to start entrepreneurial ventures, ones that could simultaneously create jobs and improve the world.

Innovative leadership development. Classic training could be enriched and improved by going outside the building and providing field (or far-afield) opportunities to tackle social system problems. High school and college students can benefit from more service learning, as would the rising talent from opportunities for service projects in their corporate careers. An important and highly scalable way to enhance leadership skills along with getting things done is national service itself. National service takes people out of their familiar milieu, puts them on diverse teams, imparts skills, and emphasizes values such as sacrifice for a cause larger than oneself. National service teams can work on urgent, pressing problems plaguing communities and nations, often finding new solutions but at least finding new awareness that can propel them into advanced leadership roles.

Recognition. To expand the pool of accomplished people willing to take on tough challenges, it would help to increase recognition and acclaim for traditional organizations that take people outside the walls of their buildings and encourage them to assume responsibility for improving the context and system around them. This is already happening with green certifications for positive environmental actions or with hospitals such as Boston Medical Center that take responsibility for improving life circumstances for poor people whose health involves more than their most obvious ailment—or with universities actively improving housing and other aspects of their neighborhoods, as Judith Rodin pioneered in Philadelphia as University of Pennsylvania president. Recognition is abundant and free! More of it can present models and encourage action.

Follow the money. Financial incentives matter too. Philanthropy has a major role to play in a shift from spare change (giving away a few leftovers for the needy) to real change (supporting innovative solutions that can be models for others, as Skoll Foundation and Draper Richards Kaplan do). Although big philanthropy sometimes stays too close to big establishments—it's easier to raise money if you already have money and are considered part of the traditional clubs of the elite—it's time for philanthropy to think outside the building too. Big philanthropy should focus on how to find the next wave of small but smart institutional innovations and then to build an ecosystem to support them, as New Profit does, so that they grow into major forces for change. Similarly, more venture funds could spend a portion of their investment on for-profit start-ups that also have a social mission along with a revenue model, thereby valuing the purpose-driven engagement that could make for-profit ventures with a social mission the success stories of the future.

Government partnerships. It's sometimes said that the private sector innovates in social and institutional realms, but only government has the reach and resources to spread those innovations widely. Government funding should seek creative new approaches, counting on the imaginations of advanced leaders rather than on well-worn and familiar but perhaps less effective solutions. For example, US Department of Education I3 competitions (investments in innovation) helped City Year mount a project to prove and improve its education efforts in low-performing schools. Donald Berwick, who founded the Institute for Healthcare Improvement and served as chief of Medicare and Medicaid, sought to find and encourage systemic innovations in health care that could be exemplars of significant change. Some states and nations provide grants, matching funds, or loan guarantees for promising innovations, including for-profit ventures. In India, Piramal e-Swasthya eventually grew to reach unserved millions of people in rural areas without modern health care by entering into public-private partnerships with state governments; government partnerships enabled it to provide so many services that it dropped the *e* from its name.

Reduce sector silos. To create effective movements to tackle big institutional problems, sector antagonisms must be overcome—including the skepticism about government indulged in by the spaghetti-dinner fund-raising ranchers in Montana I mentioned in the introduction. Cross-sector coalitions are likelier when people have already had experiences outside their professions or sectoral homes. Facilitating this can run the gamut from national service (again) to employers that encourage people to get involved in a community activity that might be unrelated to their day jobs but that would broaden their horizons. Portfolio careers, consisting of multiple projects simultaneously, could be encouraged by new forms of work arrangements.

Promote role models. Stories of leaders who cross sectors effectively can be told as role models. In addition to the stories in this book, others were advanced leaders almost from their early years. Schooled at West Point, Robert McDonald started in the military as a soldier with Army Ranger training and then joined consumer products giant Procter & Gamble. Deployed internationally when that was still rare, he rose to become CEO and reinforced the company's emphasis on its PVP—operating with purpose, values, and principles. Leaving P&G from the top position, he became the US secretary of Veterans Affairs, responsible for the nation's largest health care systems. This is just one example of someone from the real army who touched nearly every sector with an ethic of service and helped lay the foundations for an army for change.

* * *

This is the leadership paradigm for the future: the ability to "think outside the building" to overcome establishment paralysis and produce innovation for a better world.

When traditional approaches are inadequate or resisted, advanced leadership is essential. Advanced leaders tap big dreams and craft compelling narratives; they build coalitions and persevere through setbacks; and they lay the foundation for growth and impact. Rather than wait for elections or orders from on high, they step up to lead the hard work of change on the ground. With creativity and entrepreneurial adroitness, they tackle the complex, messy, seemingly intractable problems that plague us. They find fulfillment themselves while developing solutions for the world.

As advanced leaders become more numerous, they can start to shift the culture. Mission-driven men and women from diverse backgrounds and interests can unite in their conviction that positive change is possible. Their examples can foster a success revolution—a new definition of what it means to have a successful career and a successful life, equating success with service and measuring the magnitude of lives improved rather than the size of income earned.

Armed with advanced leadership skills and fortified by the courage to move beyond the castles of our time, this growing leadership force brings hope. They—and we alongside them—can blaze new trails and light new paths fueled by the abundant and renewable power of a positive purpose.

ACKNOWLEDGMENTS

It's said that success has many parents, but failure is an orphan. That means that I alone must take responsibility for any limitations or mistakes in this book, but I have many coparents to thank for important contributions to whatever works well.

First and foremost, special thanks are due to Rakesh Khurana and Nitin Nohria for their deep wisdom, breadth of knowledge, great values, and colleagueship. As Harvard ALI coconceivers, we mulled over the state of leadership in America and the world. Later, as HBS dean, Nitin provided steady encouragement and urged me to write this book. Rakesh, even when adding responsibilities as dean of Harvard College, remained an invaluable sounding board for decisions and ideas and an intellectual partner in many contexts.

Many outstanding colleagues served on the ALI faculty board at various times over fourteen years and provided insights from their range of fields—including law, medicine, public health, education, government, business, Chinese history, and social sciences. The list includes, alphabetically: Bill Alford, Julie Battilana, Don Berwick, Barry Bloom, David Bloom, Iris Bohnet, Frank Dobbin, Amy Edmonson, Bill George, David Gergen, Allen Grossman, Monica Higgins, Jim Honan, Bill Kirby, Howard Koh, Bob Mnookin, Charles Ogletree, Roger Porter, Fernando Reimers, Forest Reinhardt, Meredith Rosenthal, Guhan Subramanian, Ron Sullivan, and Pete Zimmerman. Listening to ideas across disciplinary silos from these colleagues and numerous others (including Jim Sebenius, Marshall Ganz, Jay Winsten, Dutch Leonard, and Kash Rangan) helped shape my thinking about problems and solutions. Ryan Raffaelli was cofaculty author of the Sesame Workshop case and always helpful in tossing around ideas about leadership for change. John McArthur, who enticed me to come to HBS, taught me about attacking castles when he was the dean, an image I carried through the years to this book.

My assistant, Russell Simons, officially known as a faculty support specialist, has been by my side for five years, facilitating getting the work done with good cheer, great people skills, and often above-and-beyond help, among many other things. Russ always managed to convince Technical Support Services to continue to support my out-of-warranty computers. (I should also thank Michael Dell, even though I've met him only in a crowd, because the aging Dell laptop on which I wrote the whole book miraculously survived being hauled from cold places to warm places so I could get some solar energy while writing.)

Matthew Bird and Ai-Ling Malone were valuable thought partners as research associates at HBS who became, at different times, research directors for ALI. Each helped explore ideas and produce cases, supervising numerous others who came on part time to conduct interviews and draft one case. They stayed in touch as Matthew moved to a professorship in Peru and Ai-Ling to a post at Netflix. Each provided comments on the emerging manuscript. Other great research associates included Kelsi Stine-Rowe, Dan Fox, Lance Pierce, Jonathan Cohen, Joseph Paul, and Joyce Kim; Joyce and Joe were especially helpful in later stages of book development. In addition to these full-time professional researchers, some talented people worked on particular cases and are thanked by being named as coauthors in the citations. Joana Canedo also pitched in with a key interview and translation.

Pamela Yatsko was especially critical to whether the book ever got written. The inimitable Pam has many talents as a researcher, writer, and editor. She first worked for me at HBS a few books back and then took on occasional assignments after moving to California. Pam can always be counted on to dig deeply, persist in seeking all facts, and integrate pieces into a coherent whole, complete with engaging writing. Pam had written several cases for ALI, so it was natural to bring her into this book project. Her research helped identify common themes across cases, and she provided an important foundation for several chapters. She always saw the big picture while being attentive to details. Pam was a constant source of much-needed and very welcome encouragement.

Research funding came from the HBS Division of Research and Faculty Development (thank you, Jan Rivkin, Teresa Amabile, and Cynthia Montgomery) and Harvard ALI (thank you, Jason Dyett, and many wonderful staff members, especially Bryan Panzano, who was always ready to provide info or stats). Thanks also for encouragement for ALI's growth to Alan Garber and Doreen Koretz, as well as Steve Hyman and various presidents and deans, plus some visionary corporate and individual donors who provided seed funding for the program at launch.

The ideas in this book were years in gestation as I observed the world and looked at problems and solutions. Long field trips to São Paulo, Shanghai, Mumbai, New Orleans, New York City, Miami, San Francisco/Palo Alto, and Baton Rouge included visits to companies and community organizations, both inside buildings and out on the streets. Adding to that was other travel for consulting and speaking (Melbourne and Sydney, Australia; Hong Kong; Xingdao, China; Nigeria; South Africa; Madrid; London; Tokyo; Austin; Kansas City; San Antonio; and Chicago, among others) provided valuable contacts, insights into how things worked on the ground, and a chance to test ideas. I'm grateful to more people than I can name for those outside-my-office-building experiences.

The first reader of a complete draft and the best critic was Matthew Moss Kanter Stein, who is a shrewd analyst, smart lawyer, and broad thinker. Very helpful comments and reactions were added by Frank Dobbin, Jan Rivkin, Matt Haggman, Maxeme Tuchman, Stephanie Khurana, Martha Nelson, and Charlie Silberstein, my honorary brother. I also thank the many leaders who were fast and responsive with fact checks for the stories I tell in this book that were not already approved via the HBS case-release process. And I am very grateful to all of the ALI fellows whom I taught and who taught me so much; each one deserves praise for his or her courage and convictions, even though space doesn't permit naming them all.

On the full disclosure front: I have served on the City Year national board of trustees for many years. I met Michael Brown and Alan Khazei soon after they founded the organization and thank them for the chance to help them make a difference in the world. I was backstage for City Year events with Senator Mitt Romney (who also served on the board when I did), Senator Ted Kennedy, President Clinton, President Obama, Senator John McCain, and others. David Gergen and, for a time, Wendy Kopp also served on the board, as did Rodney Slater, a former US transportation secretary who became an ALI fellow. I was a paid advisor to IBM for a number of years, via Stan Litow, during the Corporate Service Corps launch but not since the P-TECH founding, though my prior relationship provided great access. I am an investor in some entities mentioned in the text, including Golden and Bain Capital Double Impact Fund. I was a speaker at two Institute for Healthcare Improvement national forums and also spoke at events for Better Baton Rouge, Procter & Gamble, Publicis Groupe, and VivaTech. I am on advisory boards for New Politics, Report for America, and Our Generation Speaks. Knight Foundation helped sponsor the HBS Young American Leaders Program (thanks to CEO Alberto Ibargüen), and that's how I met Matt Haggman, Andrew Pompa, Rebecca Fishman Lipsey, Marta Viciedo, and many other outstanding millennial "advanced leaders."

On the fun but not necessary disclosure front: Gilberto Dimenstein provided hospitality twice in São Paulo, when I had the pleasure of staying with him instead of at an impersonal hotel. David Weinstein has provided the best-ever Red Sox seats at Fenway. The Dancing Elmo that Jeff Dunn gave to me (and others to Ryan Raffaelli and Jon Cohen) after visiting Sesame Workshop in New York occupies a place of honor at home next to the miniature Lombardi trophy from Philadelphia Eagles' owner Jeff Lurie. Jeff and his team's championship aren't mentioned in this book, but he symbolizes the many good friends not named here who cheered me on in this work, providing enjoyable events that were a welcome break from the writing grind.

John Mahaney, the book's chief editor, who previously worked with me on *Confidence* and *Supercorp* at another publisher, saw its virtues when the ideas were still raw and provided valuable feedback, chapter by chapter. I am also grateful to Pete Garceau, the creative designer who found a brilliant way to picture the title on the cover.

My husband, Barry Stein, is in a class of his own, always cheering me on. Matt, Melissa, Alison, Natalie, and Jacob Stein provide me with much joy and meaning, plus good dancing. Alison heard the title of this book and made some appealing drawings to represent it. Alison and Natalie asked when I would write a children's book. I said we should do it together. While still seeking the rainbow connection, we started putting together a story called *The Lonely Giraffe*. I confess we haven't gotten very far, but I am grateful for the people close to me who inspire me to write and help me get through the messy middles. *Ubuntu*: I am because you are.

—Boston and Cambridge, Massachusetts, June 2019

NOTES

A note on sources: If no citation to a publicly available source is provided for a particular quote, then it derived from firsthand observations or individual interviews. People quoted reviewed their stories for accuracy and consented to their use.

INTRODUCTION: TAKING LEADERSHIP TO A NEW PLACE

1. Warren G. Bennis, *Organization Development: Its Nature, Origins, and Prospects* (Reading, MA: Addison-Wesley, 1969).
2. Robert D. Putnam, *Bowling Alone: The Collapse and Revival of American Community* (New York: Simon & Schuster, 2000); Sherry Turkle, *Alone Together: Why We Expect More from Technology and Less from Each Other* (New York: Basic Books, 2011).
3. Alexis de Tocqueville, *Democracy in America*, trans. Harvey C. Mansfield and Delba Winthrop (Chicago: University of Chicago Press, 2000); Thomas L. Friedman, "Where American Politics Can Still Work: From the Bottom Up," *New York Times*, July 4, 2018; Alan Khazei, *Big Citizenship: How Pragmatic Idealism Can Bring Out the Best in America,* (New York: PublicAffairs, 2010); Report for America, "Who We Are," Report for America Company Site, accessed March 2019, https://www.reportforamerica.org/who-we-are/.

1. UP FROM THE DEPTHS: BIG PROBLEMS AND THE NEED FOR ADVANCED LEADERSHIP

1. "Global Shaper Survey," World Economic Forum 2017, accessed November 2018, http://www.shaperssurvey2017.org/static/data/WEF_GSC_Annual_Survey_2017.pdf.

2. "Living Ocean," NASA Science, accessed August 2015, http://science
   .nasa.gov/earth-science/oceanography/living-ocean.
3. Ove Hoegh-Guldberg, "Reviving the Ocean Economy: The Case for
   Action," World Wildlife Fund International, 2015, accessed June 26, 2019,
   https://c402277.ssl.cf1.rackcdn.com/publications/790/files/original
   /Reviving_Ocean_Economy_REPORT_low_res.pdf?1429717323.
4. Ove Hoegh-Guldberg, "Reviving the Ocean Economy: The Case for
   Action," World Wildlife Fund International, 2015, accessed June 26, 2019,
   https://c402277.ssl.cf1.rackcdn.com/publications/790/files/original
   /Reviving_Ocean_Economy_REPORT_low_res.pdf?1429717323.
5. Ove Hoegh-Guldberg, "Reviving the Ocean Economy: The Case for
   Action," World Wildlife Fund International, 2015, accessed June 26, 2019,
   https://c402277.ssl.cf1.rackcdn.com/publications/790/files/original
   /Reviving_Ocean_Economy_REPORT_low_res.pdf?1429717323.
6. Feeding America, "Facts About Poverty and Hunger in America,"
   accessed November 21, 2018, https://www.feedingamerica.org/hunger
   -in-america/facts; "Zero Hunger," WFP (World Food Programme),
   accessed November 2018, http://www1.wfp.org/zero-hunger; Julian
   Parfitt, Mark Barthel, and Sarah Macnaughton, "Food Waste within
   Food Supply Chains: Quantification and Potential for Change to
   2050," *Philosophical Transactions of the Royal Society B* 365, no. 1554
   (2010): 3065–3081; Frank Van Woerden, Lisa Yao, Perinaz Bhada-Tata,
   and Silpa Kaza, *What a Waste 2.0: A Global Snapshot of Solid Waste
   Management to 2050* (Washington, DC: World Bank, 2018), 31, https://
   openknowledge.worldbank.org/handle/10986/30317.
7. V. Kasturi Rangan, John A. Quelch, Gustavo Herrero, and Brooke
   Barton, eds., *Business Solutions for the Global Poor: Creating Social and
   Economic Value* (San Francisco, CA: Jossey-Bass, 2007); C. K. Prahalad,
   *The Fortune at the Bottom of the Pyramid: Eradicating Poverty through
   Profit* (Upper Saddle River, NJ: Wharton School Publishing, 2004).
8. Rob Reich, *Just Giving: Why Philanthropy Is Failing Democracy and How
   It Can Do Better* (Princeton, NJ: Princeton University Press, 2018).
9. Brian M. Stecher et al., *Improving Teaching Effectiveness: Final Report*,
   Rand Corporation, accessed October 2018, https://www.rand.org/pubs
   /research_reports/RR2242.html.
10. Gavin Yamey, "African Heads of State Promise Action Against Malaria,"
    British Medical Journal 320, no. 7244 (2000).
11. Gavin Yamey, "Roll Back Malaria: A Failing Global Health Campaign,"
    British Medical Journal 328, no. 7448 (2004): 1086–1087.
12. UN Climate Change, "WMO Report: The Escalating Impacts of Climate-
    Related Natural Disasters," accessed November 2018, https://unfccc.int

/news/wmo-report-the-escalating-impacts-of-climate-related-natural
-disasters; "Atlas of Mortality and Economic Losses from Weather,
Climate and Water Extremes (1970–2012)," WMO (World Meteorological
Organization), 2014: 1123, accessed November 2018, https://drive.google
.com/file/d/0BwdvoC9AeWjUd1RwQW5Ld2hqTDQ/view.

13. "WMO Report: The Escalating Impacts of Climate-Related Natural
Disasters," UN Climate Change, accessed November 2018, https://unfccc
.int/news/wmo-report-the-escalating-impacts-of-climate related natural
-disasters; "Atlas of Mortality and Economic Losses from Weather,
Climate and Water Extremes (1970–2012)," WMO (World Meteorological
Organization), 1123 (2014): 9, accessed November 2018, https://drive
.google.com/file/d/0BwdvoC9AeWjUd1RwQW5Ld2hqTDQ/view.

14. "Global Estimates of Modern Slavery," International Labour
Organization (ILO), Geneva, 2017, accessed November 2018,
https://www.ilo.org/wcmsp5/groups/public/---dgreports/---dcomm
/documents/publication/wcms_575479.pdf.

15. "Hotline Statistics," National Human Trafficking Hotline, accessed
November 2018, https://humantraffickinghotline.org/states.

16. Max Roser, "The Short History of Global Living Conditions and Why
It Matters that We Know It," Our World in a Data, accessed November
2018, https://ourworldindata.org/a-history-of-global-living-conditions
-in-5-charts; Hans Rosling, Ola Rosling, and Anna Rosling Rönnlund,
*Factfulness: Ten Reasons We're Wrong About the World—and Why
Things Are Better Than You Think* (New York: Flatiron Books,
2018), 52.

17. James C. Riley, "Estimates of Regional and Global Life Expectancy,
1800–2001," *Population and Development Review* 31, no. 3 (2005):
537–543; Max Roser, "Life Expectancy," Our World in Data, accessed
November 2018, https://ourworldindata.org/life-expectancy.

18. "U.S. Small-Area Life Expectancy Estimates Project (USALEEP): Life
Expectancy Estimate Files for Oklahoma 2010–2015, 2018," National
Center for Health Statistics, accessed October 2018, https://www.cdc
.gov/nchs/nvss/usaleep/usaleep.html.

19. Emily Zimmerman, Benjamin F. Evans, Steven H. Woolf, and Amber D.
Haley, *Social Capital and Health Outcomes in Boston Technical Report:
Center on Human Needs* (Richmond, VA: Virginia Commonwealth
University, 2012), 21, https://societyhealth.vcu.edu/media/society
-health/pdf/PMReport_Boston.pdf.

20. Hans Rosling, Ola Rosling, and Anna Rosling Rönnlund, *Factfulness:
Ten Reasons We're Wrong About the World—and Why Things Are Better
Than You Think* (New York: Flatiron Books, 2018).

21. "Homicide Counts and Rates, Time Series 2000–2012," United Nations Office on Drugs and Crime, accessed October 2018, https://www.unodc .org/gsh/en/data.html; Jens Manuel Krogstad, "Gun Homicides Steady after Decline in '90s; Suicide Rate Edges Up," Pew Research Center, accessed October 2018, http://www.pewresearch.org/fact-tank/2015/10/21 /gun-homicides-steady-after-decline-in-90s-suicide-rate-edges-up/.

22. "Education: Completion Rate for Primary Education (Household Survey Data)," UNESCO (United Nations Educational, Scientific, and Cultural Organization), accessed October 2018, http://data.uis.unesco.org/index .aspx?queryid=123#.

23. *2018 Edelman Trust Barometer Global Report* (Edelman, 2018), 6, https://www.edelman.com/sites/g/files/aatuss191/files/2018-10/2018 _Edelman_Trust_Barometer_Global_Report_FEB.pdf.

24. "Confidence in Institutions," Gallup, accessed November 2018, https:// news.gallup.com/poll/1597/confidence-institutions.aspx.

25. Steven Pinker, *Enlightenment Now: The Case for Reason, Science, Humanism and Progress* (New York: Viking, 2018), 48; Hans Rosling, Ola Rosling, and Anna Rosling Rönnlund, *Factfulness: Ten Reasons We're Wrong About the World—and Why Things Are Better Than You Think* (New York: Flatiron Books, 2018).

26. Roy F. Baumeister et al., "Bad Is Stronger Than Good," *Review of General Psychology* 5, no. 4 (2001): 325; Steven Ray Flora, "Praise's Magic Reinforcement Ratio: Five to One Gets the Job Done," *The Behavior Analyst Today* 1, no. 4 (2000): 64–69; Todd R. Risley and Betty Hart, *Meaningful Differences in the Everyday Experience of Young American Children* (Baltimore, MD: Paul H. Brookes Publishing, 1995).

27. Teresa M. Amabile, "Brilliant but Cruel: Perceptions of Negative Evaluators," *Journal of Experimental Psychology* 19 (1983): 146–156.

28. Edward N. Lorenz, "Deterministic Nonperiodic Flow," *Journal of the Atmospheric Sciences* 20 (1963): 130–141; Jamie L. Vernon, "Understanding the Butterfly Effect," *American Scientist* 105, no. 3: 130, https://www.americanscientist.org/article/understanding-the-butterfly -effect; Peter Dizkes, "When the Butterfly Effect Took Flight," *MIT Technology Review* (March/April 2011), https://www.technologyreview .com/s/422809/when-the-butterfly-effect-took-flight/.

29. Rosabeth Moss Kanter, *The Change Masters: Innovation for Productivity in the American Corporation* (New York: Simon & Schuster, 1983).

30. Mary Elise Sarotte, "How an Accident Caused the Berlin Wall to Come Down," *Washington Post*, November 1, 2009, http://www.washingtonpost .com/wp-dyn/content/article/2009/10/30/AR2009103001846.html;

Michael Meyer, "Günter Schabowski, the Man Who Opened the Wall," *New York Times*, November 6, 2015, https://www.nytimes .com/2015/11/07/opinion/gnter-schabowski-the-man-who-opened -the-wall.html.

31. Michael Meyer, "Günter Schabowski, the Man Who Opened the Wall," *New York Times*, November 6, 2015, https://www.nytimes .com/2015/11/07/opinion/gnter-schabowski-the-man-who-opened -the-wall.html.

32. Jerry Sternin, Monique Sternin, and Richard Pascale, *The Power of Positive Deviance: How Unlikely Innovators Solve the World's Toughest Problems* (Brighton, MA: Harvard Business Press, 2010).

33. Debra E. Meyerson, *Tempered Radicals: How Everyday Leaders Inspire Change at Work* (Brighton, MA: Harvard Business School Press, 2003).

34. Francesa Gino, *Rebel Talent: Why It Pays to Break the Rules at Work and in Life* (New York: HarperCollins, 2018).

35. David Bornstein, *How to Change the World: Social Entrepreneurs and the Power of New Ideas* (Oxford, UK: Oxford University Press, 2004), 42–46.

36. David Bornstein, *How to Change the World: Social Entrepreneurs and the Power of New Ideas* (Oxford, UK: Oxford University Press, 2004), 92.

37. Rosabeth Moss Kanter, Ryan Raffaelli, and Jonathan Cohen, "Sesame Workshop: Bringing Big Bird Back to Health," Harvard Business School Case 317-086, January 2017.

2. WHO WILL LEAD? HIERARCHY TO HUSTLE, CAREERS TO CAUSES

1. "Online Extra: Fred Smith on the Birth of FedEx," *Bloomberg Businessweek*, September 20, 2004, https://www.bloomberg.com/news /articles/2004-09-19/online-extra-fred-smith-on-the-birth-of-fedex.

2. Rosabeth Moss Kanter, Frank Jerome Lanasa, and Ai-ling Jamila Malone, "Advanced Leadership Pathways: John Dubinsky and the St. Louis Contractor Loan Fund," Harvard Business School Case ALI-316-041, November 2015.

3. Dana E. King et al., "The Status of Baby Boomers' Health in the United States: The Healthiest Generation?" *JAMA Internal Medicine* 174, no. 5 (2013): 385–386.

4. Terry A. Beehr and Misty M. Bennet, "Working After Retirement: Features of Bridge Employment and Research Directions," *Work, Aging, and Retirement* 1, no. 1 (2015): 112–118; Lynda Gratton and Andrew

Scott, *The 100-Year Life: Living and Working in an Age of Longevity* (London: Bloomsbury, 2016).

5. Corporation for National and Community Service, "Baby Boomers: Trends and Highlights Overview," accessed October 15, 2018, https://www.nationalservice.gov/vcla/demographic/baby-boomers.

6. Mark A. Davis, "Factors Related to Bridge Employment Participation Among Private Sector Early Retirees," *Journal of Vocational Behavior* 63 (2001): 55–71; Daniel Feldman, "The Decision to Retire Early: A Review and Conceptualization," *The Academy of Management Review* 19, no. 2 (1992): 285–311; Marc Freedman, *Encore: Finding Work That Matters in the Second Half of Life* (New York: PublicAffairs, 2007), 8; Kirsten T. Gobeski and Terry A. Beehr, "How Retirees Work: Predictors of Different Types of Bridge Employment," *Journal of Organizational Behavior* 30, no. 3 (2009): 401–425; Seongsu Kim and Daniel Feldman, "Working in Retirement: The Antecedents of Bridge Employment and Its Consequences for Quality of Life in Retirement," *The Academy of Management Journal* 43, no. 6 (2000): 1195–1210; Mary O'Hara-Devereaux, "Second Middle Age," Global Foresight, 2013, accessed October 15, 2018, http://trend-forecast.com/future-trends/video-second-middle-age/.

7. Anne Colby et al., "Purpose in the Encore Years: Shaping Lives of Meaning and Contribution," Pathways to Encore Purpose Project, 2018, accessed October 2018, https://encore.org/wp-content/uploads/2018/03/PEP-Full-Report.pdf.

8. Anne Colby et al., "Purpose in the Encore Years: Shaping Lives of Meaning and Contribution," Pathways to Encore Purpose Project, 2018, accessed October 2018, https://encore.org/wp-content/uploads/2018/03/PEP-Full-Report.pdf.

9. Bridget Hartnett and Ron Matan, *Generational Differences in Philanthropic Giving* (Livingston, NJ: Sobel & Co. 2014), 1–2, https://sobelcollc.com/sites/default/files/NFP%20Fall%202014%20Whitepaper.pdf; Sylvia Ann Hewlett et al., *Bookend Generations: Leveraging Talent and Finding Common Ground* (New York: Center for Work-Life Policy, 2009), 1.

10. David B. Grusky and Tamar Krichelli Katz, eds., *The New Gilded Age: The Critical Inequality Debates of Our Time* (Stanford, CA: Stanford University Press, 2012); Lily Rothman, "How American Inequality in the Gilded Age Compares to Today," *TIME*, February 2018, http://time.com/5122375/american-inequality-gilded-age.

11. Max Weber, *The Protestant Ethic and the Spirit of Capitalism* (New York: Charles Scribner's Sons, 1958), 181.

12. Thorstein Veblen, *The Instinct of Workmanship and the State of the Industrial Arts* (New York: Macmillan, 1914).

13. Marshall Goldsmith and Mark Reiter, *What Got You Here Won't Get You There: How Successful People Become Even More Successful* (New York: Hachette Book Group, 2007).

14. Rosabeth Moss Kanter, Douglas A Raymond, and Ryan Raffaelli, "The Making of Verizon," Harvard Business School Case 303-131, February 2004; Rosabeth Moss Kanter and Jonathan Cohen, "Verizon 2018," Harvard Business School Case 318-114, March 2018 (revised April 2018), 10.

15. Rosabeth Moss Kanter, "What If Lehman Brothers Had Been Lehman Sisters?" *Harvard Business Review*, October 25, 2010, https://hbr.org/2010/10/what-if-lehman-brothers-had-be.

16. Rosabeth Moss Kanter and Lance P. Pierce, "Still Leading (B5): General Claudia Kennedy—In Command of Life," Harvard Business School Case 308–037, September 2007; Rosabeth Moss Kanter and Lance P. Pierce, "Still Leading (B9): Hon. Colin Powell—A Portfolio for Powerful Impact," Harvard Business School Case 308–041, September 2007.

17. T. S. Eliot, *Murder in the Cathedral* (New York: Harcourt Brace & Co., 1935).

18. Simone de Beauvoir, *The Second Sex*, trans. Constance Borde and Sheila Malovany-Chevallier (New York: Random House, 2009).

19. Rosabeth Moss Kanter and Jane Roessner, "Deloitte & Touche (B): Changing the Workplace," Harvard Business School Case 300-013, September 1999, 8.

20. Rosabeth Moss Kanter and Patricia Bissett Higgins, "Advanced Leadership Pathways: Mike Critelli and Healthcare Solutions," Harvard Business School Case 316-053, November 2015.

21. Rosabeth Moss Kanter, Alexandre Naghirniac, Ai-Ling Jamila Malone, and Daniella Suarez, "Advanced Leadership Pathways: Gilberto Dimenstein and Community Empowerment in Brazil," Harvard Business School Case 316-116, Rev. November 2015, 1.

22. Rosabeth Moss Kanter, *Men and Women of the Corporation* (New York: Basic Books, 1993).

23. Rosabeth Moss Kanter and Anne Arlinghaus, "Advanced Leadership Pathways: Richard Fahey and Robert Saudek—Lighting Liberia," Harvard Business School Case 316-032, September 2012, 1.

24. Rosabeth Moss Kanter and Kelsi Stine-Rowe, "Advanced Leadership Pathways: Vivian Lowery Derryck and African Governance," Harvard Business School Case ALI-002, August 2016, 2.

25. Rosabeth Moss Kanter, Frank Jerome Lanasa, and Ai-ling Jamila Malone, "Advanced Leadership Pathways: John Dubinsky and the St. Louis Contractor Loan Fund," Harvard Business School Case ALI-316-041, November 2015.

26. Rosabeth Moss Kanter and Emma Franking, "Advanced Leadership Pathways: Garrett Moran and Scaling Year Up to Close the Opportunity Divide," Harvard Business School Case ALI-014, February 2017.

27. Rosabeth Moss Kanter and Kelsi Stine-Rowe, "Advanced Leadership Pathways: Marisa Wesley and Women's Empowerment," Harvard Business School Case ALI-004, August 2016, 3.

28. Rosabeth Moss Kanter, *The Tale of "O": On Being Different* (Cambridge, MA: Goodmeasure, Inc., 1993), video.

29. "About Posse," Posse Foundation, accessed March 2019, https://www
.possefoundation.org/about-posse.

30. Warren G. Bennis and Robert J. Thomas, *Geeks and Geezers* (Boston: Harvard University Press, 2002).

3. DREAMING BIG AND SEEING MORE: RANDOM WALKS, KALEIDOSCOPES, AND OTHER FIRST STEPS

1. Rosabeth Moss Kanter and Joyce Kim, "Gilberto Dimenstein and Community Empowerment (B)," Harvard Advanced Leadership Initiative Case No. ALI-024 (Boston: Harvard Business Publishing, June 2019), 3.

2. Rosabeth Moss Kanter, Alexandre Naghirniac, Ai-Ling Jamila Malone, and Daniella Suarez, "Advanced Leadership Pathways: Gilberto Dimenstein and Community Empowerment in Brazil," Harvard Business School Case 313-116, April 2013.

3. "Internet Usage in Brazil—Statistics & Facts, 2018," Statista, accessed December 2018, https://www.statista.com/topics/2045/internet
-usage-in-brazil/.

4. "Catraca Livre," Social Tech, accessed February 2019, https://www
.socialtech.org.uk/projects/catraca-livre/.

5. Rosabeth Moss Kanter, Alexandre Naghirniac, Ai-Ling Jamila Malone, and Daniella Suarez, "Advanced Leadership Pathways: Gilberto Dimenstein and Community Empowerment in Brazil," Harvard Business School Case 313-116, April 2013, 8.

6. Gilberto Dimenstein, "Um Robô para Combater Fake News," Catraca Livre, accessed January 2019, https://catracalivre.com.br/parceiros
-catraca/reciprocidade/um-robo-para-combater-fake-news/.

7. "About," Conversation Project, accessed March 2019, https://theconversationproject.org/about/.

8. Rosabeth Moss Kanter, Ai-Ling Jamila Malone, and Oludamilola Aladesanmi, "Advanced Leadership Pathways: Harvey Freishtat and Conversations About End-of-Life Care," Harvard Business School Case 316-050, March 2016.

9. Rosabeth Moss Kanter, "To Master Change, First Dread It," *Harvard Business Review*, accessed March 2019, https://hbr.org/2009/08/to-master-change-first-dread-i.

10. Liz Mineo, "Good Genes Are Nice, but Joy Is Better," *Harvard Gazette*, April 11, 2017, https://news.harvard.edu/gazette/story/2017/04/over-nearly-80-years-harvard-study-has-been-showing-how-to-live-a-healthy-and-happy-life/.

11. Teresa Amabile, *The Social Psychology of Creativity* (New York: Springer-Verlag, 1983), 99; Teresa Amabile and Steven J. Kramer, *The Progress Principle: Using Small Wins to Ignite Joy, Engagement, and Creativity at Work* (Boston: Harvard Business Press, 2011), 57; Teresa Amabile and Steven J. Kramer, *The Progress Principle: Using Small Wins to Ignite Joy, Engagement, and Creativity at Work* (Boston: Harvard Business Press, 2011), 106; Teresa Amabile, Constance Noonan Hadley, and Steven J. Kramer, "Creativity Under the Gun," *Harvard Business Review*, August 2002, https://hbr.org/2002/08/creativity-under-the-gun.

12. Rosabeth Moss Kanter, "Leadership for Change: Enduring Skills for Change Masters," Harvard Business School No. 9-304-062, 2005, 3.

13. Institutional theorists have proposed similar concepts about systems innovations that involve putting together pieces from different sources. See John Campbell, *Institutional Change and Globalization* (Princeton, NJ: Princeton University Press, 2004), 65. See also John F. Padgett and Walter W. Powell, *The Emergence of Organizations and Markets* (Princeton, NJ: Princeton University Press, 2012), 3.

14. Rosabeth Moss Kanter and Kelsi Stine-Rowe, "Advanced Leadership Pathways: Vivian Lowery Derryck and African Governance," Harvard Business School Case ALI-002, November 2015.

15. Rosabeth Moss Kanter, Grace Szu-Hua Chen, and Ai-Ling Jamila Malone, "Advanced Leadership Pathways: Tom Santel and a Community Based Approach to Early Childhood Health," Harvard Business School Case 316-048, November 2015.

16. Rosabeth Moss Kanter, "Kaleidoscope Thinking," in *Management 21C: Someday We'll All Manage This Way*, ed. Subir Chowdhury (London: Pearson, 2000), 256.

17. Rosabeth M. Kanter, "Leadership for Change: Enduring Skills for Change Masters," Harvard Business School Background Note 304-062, November 2003, 4.

18. Rosabeth M. Kanter, "Leadership for Change: Enduring Skills for Change Masters," Harvard Business School Background Note 304-062, November 2003, 4.

19. Cecilia Hyunjung Mo and Katharine M. Conn, "When Do the Advantaged See the Disadvantages of Others? A Quasi-Experimental Study of National Service," *American Political Science Review* 112, no. 4 (2018): 721–741.

20. Anthony J. Mayo and Nitin Nohria, "Zeitgeist Leadership," *Harvard Business Review* 83, no. 10 (2005): 46.

21. Howard Gardner, *Frames of Mind: The Theory of Multiple Intelligences* (New York: Basic Books, 1983); Robert J. Sternberg, *Beyond IQ: A Triarchic Theory of Human Intelligence* (Cambridge: Cambridge University Press, 1985).

22. Anthony J. Mayo and Nitin Nohria, *In Their Time: The Greatest Business Leaders of the Twentieth Century* (Brighton, MA: Harvard Business Press, 2005).

23. Tarun Khanna, Krishna G. Palepu, and Jayant Sinha, "Strategies That Fit Emerging Markets," *Harvard Business Review* 83, no. 6 (June 2005).

24. Matthew Kutz, *Contextual Intelligence: How Thinking in 3D Can Help Resolve Complexity, Uncertainty, and Ambiguity* (London: Palgrave Macmillan, 2017).

25. Anthony J. Mayo and Nitin Nohria, *In Their Time: The Greatest Business Leaders of the Twentieth Century* (Brighton, MA: Harvard Business Press, 2005); Tarun Khanna, "Contextual Intelligence," *Harvard Business Review* 92, no. 2 (September 2014): 58–68.

26. Rosabeth Moss Kanter and Sarah Patricia Vickers-Willis, "Citizen Schools (A)," Harvard Business School Case 300-061, January 2000.

27. Rosabeth Moss Kanter, Juliane Calingo Schwetz, and Patricia Bissett Higgins, "Advanced Leadership Pathways: David Weinstein and Write the World," Harvard Business School Case 314-030, September 2013.

28. Abraham Loeb, "Where Do Ideas Come From?," *Scientific American*, July 2018, https://blogs.scientificamerican.com/observations/where-do-ideas-come-from/.

29. Rosabeth Moss Kanter, "Zoom In, Zoom Out," *Harvard Business Review* 89, no. 3 (March 2011).

30. Ronald S. Burt, *Structural Holes: The Social Structure of Competition* (Cambridge, MA: Harvard University Press, 1992).

31. Rosabeth Moss Kanter and Joseph Paul, "Gun Safety in America: Three Leaders Propose Innovative Solutions," Harvard Business School Case 319-115 (Boston: Harvard Business Publishing, July 2019).

32. "Principles for a Responsible Civilian Firearms Industry," CalSTRS, November 14, 2018, http://www.firearmsprinciples.com/.

33. Aaron Blake, "Bloomberg Launches New $50 Million Gun Control Effort," *Washington Post*, April 16, 2014, sec. News, https://www .washingtonpost.com/news/post-politics/wp/2014/04/16/bloomberg -aims-to-spend-50-million-on-gun-control/.

34. Antonio Planas, "Cops Take Aim at Gun Trafficking in New England," *Boston Herald*, October 10, 2017, https://www.bostonherald.com/2017 /10/10/cops-take-aim-at-gun-trafficking-in-new-england/.

35. Rosabeth Moss Kanter, *Evolve: Succeeding in the Digital Culture of Tomorrow* (Boston: Harvard Business School Press, 2001), 42.

4. REVISITING THE PAST TO CREATE THE FUTURE: TELLING THE RIGHT STORY

1. For information on the relationship between the "identifiable victim effect" and charity, see Arvid Erlandsson et al., "Argument-Inconsistency in Charity Appeals: Statistical Information About the Scope of the Problem Decrease Helping Toward a Single Identified Victim but Not Helping Toward Many Non-Identified Victims in a Refugee Crisis Context," *Journal of Economic Psychology* 56 (October 1, 2016): 126–140; George Loewenstein and Paul Slovic, "Sympathy and Callousness: The Impact of Deliberative Thought on Donations to Identifiable and Statistical Victims," *Organizational Behavior and Human Decision Processes* 102, no. 2 (March 1, 2007): 143–153. For Martin's research about the power of stories, see Joanne Martin et al., "The Uniqueness Paradox in Organizational Stories," *Administrative Science Quarterly* 28, no. 3 (1983): 438–453.

2. David M. Boje, "The Storytelling Organization: A Study of Story Performance in an Office-Supply Firm," *Administrative Science Quarterly* 36, no. 1 (1991): 106–126; David M. Boje, "Consulting and Change in the Storytelling Organisation," *Journal of Organizational Change Management* 4, no. 3 (March 1, 1991): 7–17; David M. Boje, "Stories of the Storytelling Organization: A Postmodern Analysis of Disney as 'Tamara-Land,'" *Academy of Management Journal* 38, no. 4 (August 1, 1995): 997–1035; Stephen Denning, *The Leader's Guide to Storytelling: Mastering the Art and Discipline of Business Narrative*

(Hoboken, NJ: John Wiley & Sons, 2005), xx; Stephen Denning, *The Springboard* (Abingdon-on-Thames, UK: Routledge, 2012), xvii.

3. Landrieu told this story in speeches I attended and in his book: Mitch Landrieu, *In the Shadow of Statues: A White Southerner Confronts History* (New York: Penguin, 2018). He added information in an email dialogue.

4. Mitch Landrieu, *In the Shadow of Statues: A White Southerner Confronts History* (New York: Penguin, 2018), 164.

5. Mitch Landrieu, *In the Shadow of Statues: A White Southerner Confronts History* (New York: Penguin, 2018), 225–226.

6. Erving Goffman, *Frame Analysis: An Essay on the Organization of Experience* (New York: Harper and Row, 1974).

7. Rosabeth Moss Kanter and Ai-Ling Jamila Malone, "Hillary Clinton & Partners: Leading Global Social Change from the US State Department," Harvard Business Case 313-086, October 2012.

8. *50/50: Rethinking the Past, Present, and Future of Women in Power*, directed by Tiffany Shlain (San Francisco, CA: Refinery29/Let It Ripple, 2016), documentary, http://www.letitripple.org/films/50-50/.

9. Rosabeth Moss Kanter and Matthew Bird, "Milwaukee (A): Making of a World Water Hub," Harvard Business School Case 313-057, August 2012.

10. Rosabeth M. Kanter and Euvin Naidoo, "Nelson Mandela, Turnaround Leader," Harvard Business School Case 304-035, September 2003.

11. Rosabeth Moss Kanter and Grace Szu-Hua Chen, "Advanced Leadership Pathways: Tom Santel and a Community Based Approach to Early Childhood Health," Harvard Business Case 316-048, November 2015.

12. Rosabeth Moss Kanter, Penelope Rossno, and Peter Zimmerman, "Advanced Leadership Pathways: Doug Rauch and the Daily Table," Harvard Business Case 316-105, March 2016.

13. Marshall Ganz, "What Is Public Narrative: Self, Us & Now (Public Narrative Worksheet)," 2009; Marshall Ganz, "Leading Change Leadership, Organization, and Social Movements," in *Handbook of Leadership Theory and Practice*, eds. Nitin Nohria and Rakesh Khurana (Boston: Harvard Business Publishing, 2010); Marshall Ganz, "Public Narrative, Collective Action, and Power," in *Accountability Through Public Opinion: From Inertia to Public Action*, eds. Sina Odugbemi and Taeku Lee (Washington, DC: World Bank Publications, 2011), 273–289.

14. Gary Orren, "Persuasion: The Science and Art of Effective Influence" (PowerPoint presentation, 2005), http://www.atlas101.ca/pm/wp -content/uploads/2015/12/Orren_presentation.pdf.

15. Olga Khazan, "The Simple Trick to Getting People to Support Refugees, Immigrants, and Obamacare," *Atlantic*, February 1, 2017, https://www

.theatlantic.com/science/archive/2017/02/the-simple-psychological
-trick-to-political-persuasion/515181/.

16. Allan R. Cohen and David L. Bradford, *Influence Without Authority*,
3rd ed. (New York: John Wiley & Sons, 2017).

17. Peter Rogers and Susan Leal, *Running Out of Water: The Looming Crisis
and Solutions to Conserve Our Most Precious Resource* (New York: St.
Martin's Press, 2010).

18. Rosabeth Moss Kanter and James Weber, "City Year: The Journey,"
Harvard Business Case 311-080, April 2011.

19. Rosabeth Moss Kanter, Rakesh Khurana, and Daniel Penrice, "Raymond
Jetson's MetroMorphosis and the Effort to Transform Baton Rouge,"
Harvard Advanced Leadership Initiative Case No. 315-057 (Boston:
Harvard Business Publishing, December 2014).

20. Rosabeth Moss Kanter, Rakesh Khurana, and Daniel Penrice, "Advanced
Leadership Pathways: Raymond Jetson's MetroMorphosis and the
Effort to Transform Baton Rouge," Harvard Business Case 315-057,
December 2014.

21. Luis Hernandez, "Meet the Brains Behind South Florida's
#PublicTransitDay," *WLRN*, December 8, 2016, https://www.wlrn
.org/post/meet-brains-behind-south-floridas-publictransitday.

22. Rosabeth Moss Kanter and James Weber, "City Year: The Journey,"
Harvard Business Case 311-080, May 2012, 2.

23. PTI, "India Has 19 Health Workers for Every 10,000 People," *Hindu*,
March 13, 2015, sec. National, https://www.thehindu.com/news
/national/india-has-19-health-workers-for-every-10000-people
/article6990391.ece.

24. Rosabeth Moss Kanter and Matthew Bird, "Advanced Leadership Pathways:
Piramal E-Swasthya: Attempting Big Changes for Small Places—in India
and Beyond," Harvard Business Case 310-134, June 2010.

5. LIGHT A SPARK AND KEEP THEM FIRED UP: ACTIVATING ALLIES, CRAFTING COALITIONS

1. Rosabeth Moss Kanter, Penelope Rossno, and Peter Zimmerman,
"Advanced Leadership Pathways: Doug Rauch and the Daily Table,"
Harvard Business Case 316-105, March 2016.

2. Rosabeth Moss Kanter, Penelope Rossno, and Peter Zimmerman,
"Advanced Leadership Pathways: Doug Rauch and the Daily Table,"
Harvard Business Case 316-105, March 2016, 3.

3. Rosabeth Moss Kanter and Olivia Leskinen, "Advanced Leadership
Pathways: The Levees Repaired, a System Still Broken: Post Katrina

Turnaround at the New Orleans Public Defenders (A)," Harvard
Business Case 313-026, November 2012.

4. Rosabeth Moss Kanter and Olivia Leskinen, "Advanced Leadership
Pathways: Robert Whelan and the Student Loan Crisis (A)," Harvard
Business Case 313-009, July 2012, 10.

5. Rosabeth Moss Kanter and Anne Arlinghaus, "Advanced Leadership
Pathways: Shelly London and Ethics Education, 'Strengthening Our
Moral Compass,'" Harvard Business Case 313-028, September 2012, 4.

6. Rosabeth Moss Kanter and Pamela Yatsko, "Advanced Leadership
Pathways: Mahendra Bapna and Technology Education in India,"
Harvard Business Case 316-163, April 2016.

7. Rosabeth Moss Kanter and Olivia Leskinen, "Advanced Leadership
Pathways: Robert Whelan and the Student Loan Crisis (A)," Harvard
Business Case 313-009, July 2012, 11.

8. The communication networks laid out in this paragraph are drawn
from the following works: Arthur M. Cohen, "Changing Small Group
Communication Networks," *Journal of Communication* 11, no. 3
(September 1961): 116–124; Arthur M. Cohen, "Changing Small-
Group Communication Networks," *Administrative Science Quarterly*
6, no. 4 (March 1962): 443–462; Arthur M. Cohen and Warren G.
Bennis, "Continuity of Leadership in Communication Networks,"
Human Relations 14, no. 4 (November 1961): 351–367; Arthur M.
Cohen and Warren G. Bennis, "Predicting Organization in Changed
Communications Networks," *Journal of Psychology* 54, no. 2 (1962):
391–416; Arthur M. Cohen, Warren G. Bennis, and George H. Wolkon,
"The Effects of Changes in Communication Networks on the Behaviors
of Problem-Solving Groups," *Sociometry* 25, no. 2 (June 1962): 177–196;
Arthur M. Cohen, Warren G. Bennis, and George H. Wolkon, "The
Effects of Continued Practice on the Behaviors of Problem-Solving
Groups," *Sociometry* 24, no. 4 (December 1961): 416–431.

For further examples of communication networks, see Charles
H. Hubbell, "An Input-Output Approach to Clique Identification,"
Sociometry 28, no. 4 (December 1965): 377–399; Bruce W. Tuckman,
"Personality Structure, Group Composition, and Group Functioning,"
Sociometry 27, no. 4 (December 1964): 469–487; Wayne S. Marshall,
"Simulating Communication Network Experiments," *Management
Science* 13, no. 10 (June 1967): B656–665; Muriel Hammer, Sylvia
Polgar, and Kurt Salzinger, "Speech Predictability and Social Contact
Patterns in an Informal Group," *Human Organization* 28, no. 3
(Fall 1969): 235–242; Kenneth D. Mackenzie, "Structural Centrality

in Communication Networks," *Psychometrika* 31, no. 1 (March 1966): 17–25.

9. "Global Refugee Talent: Business Leaders Share Insights on the Skills and Potential of the Global Refugee Talent Pool" (Washington, DC: Talent Beyond Boundaries, September 2018), 6, accessed June 4, 2019, https://talentbeyondboundaries.org/s/TBB-BusinessPerspectivesReport -Sep2018.pdf.

10. "Fact Sheet Alcohol-Related Traffic Deaths," National Institutes of Health, October 2010, https://report.nih.gov/nihfactsheets/Pdfs /AlcoholRelatedTrafficDeaths(NIAAA).pdf.

11. Richard H. Thaler and Cass R. Sunstein, *Nudge: Improving Decisions About Health, Wealth, and Happiness* (New Haven, CT: Yale University Press, 2008).

12. Howard Koh and Pamela Yatsko, "Advanced Leadership Pathways: Jay Winsten and the Designated Driver Campaign," Harvard Business Case ALI-013, February 2017.

13. Howard Koh and Pamela Yatsko, "Advanced Leadership Pathways: Jay Winsten and the Designated Driver Campaign," Harvard Business Case ALI-013, February 2017, 11.

14. Hannah Riley Bowles, "Why Women Don't Negotiate Their Job Offers," *Harvard Business Review*, June 19, 2014, https://hbr.org/2014/06/why -women-dont-negotiate-their-job offers.

6. CROSSING THE DESERT TO THE NEXT OASIS: MASTERING THE MISERABLE MIDDLES

1. Rosabeth Moss Kanter, Juliane Caligo-Schwetz, and Patricia Bissett Higgins, "Advanced Leadership Pathways: Junko Yoda and Her Collaboration to Address Sex Trafficking in Asia," Harvard Business School Case 314-036, March 2016.

2. Rosabeth Moss Kanter, Grace Szu-Hua Chen, and Ai-Ling Jamila Malone, "Advanced Leadership Pathways: Tom Santel and a Community Based Approach to Early Childhood Health," Harvard Business School Case 316-048, November 2015.

3. Rosabeth Moss Kanter, Frank Jerome Lanasa, and Ai-Ling Jamila Malone, "Advanced Leadership Pathways: Paul Lee and Asian Americans Advancing Justice," Harvard Business School Case 316-040, November 2015.

4. Rosabeth Moss Kanter, Frank Jerome Lanasa, and Ai-Ling Jamila Malone, "Advanced Leadership Pathways: Paul Lee and Asian

Americans Advancing Justice," Harvard Business School Case 316-040, November 2015, 7.

5. Rosabeth Moss Kanter, Frank Jerome Lanasa, and Ai-Ling Jamila Malone, "Advanced Leadership Pathways: Paul Lee and Asian Americans Advancing Justice," Harvard Business School Case 316-040, November 2015, 8.

6. Rosabeth Moss Kanter and Kelsi Stine-Rowe, "Advanced Leadership Pathways: Vivian Lowery Derryck and African Governance," Harvard Business School Case ALI-002, November 2015, 8–9.

7. Rosabeth Moss Kanter and Renee Vuillaume, "Advanced Leadership Pathways: Robert Meaney and Technology for Agriculture in Sub-Saharan Africa," Harvard Business School Case 316-059, November 2015.

8. Rosabeth Moss Kanter and Patricia Bissett Higgins, "Advanced Leadership Pathways: Mike Critelli and Dossia Service Corporation," Harvard Business School Case 316-053, November 2015.

9. Rosabeth Moss Kanter, Oludamiloloa Aladesanmi, and Ai-Ling Jamila Malone, "Advanced Leadership Pathways: Inge Skjelfjord and the Cacao Supply Chain," Harvard Business School Case 316-051, November 2015.

10. Rosabeth Moss Kanter, Oludamiloloa Aladesanmi, and Ai-Ling Jamila Malone, "Advanced Leadership Pathways: Inge Skjelfjord and the Cacao Supply Chain," Harvard Business School Case 316-051, November 2015, 9.

11. Rosabeth Moss Kanter and Pamela Yatsko, "Advanced Leadership Pathways: Mahendra Bapna and Technology Education in India," Harvard Business School Case 316-163, April 2016.

12. Rosabeth Moss Kanter and Olivia Leskinen, "Advanced Leadership Pathways: Robert Whelan and the Student Loan Crisis (A)," Harvard Business School Case 316-009, September 2012, 12.

13. Rosabeth Moss Kanter and Olivia Leskinen, "Advanced Leadership Pathways: Robert Whelan and the Student Loan Crisis (A)," Harvard Business School Case 316-009, September 2012, 12.

14. Rosabeth Moss Kanter and Olivia Leskinen, "Advanced Leadership Pathways: Robert Whelan and the Student Loan Crisis (A)," Harvard Business School Case 316-009, September 2012, 12.

15. Rosabeth Moss Kanter and Renee Vuillame, "Advanced Leadership Pathways: Robert Meaney and Technology for Agriculture in Sub-Saharan Africa," Harvard Business School 316-059, November 2015.

16. Rosabeth Moss Kanter and Renee Vuillame, "Advanced Leadership Pathways: Robert Meaney and Technology for Agriculture in

Sub-Saharan Africa," Harvard Business School 316-059, November 2015, 7.

17. Rosabeth Moss Kanter, Grace Sza-Hua Chen, and Ai-Ling Jamila Malone, "Advanced Leadership Pathways: Robert Whelan and the Student Loan Crisis (B)," Harvard Business School Case 316-049, November 2015, 9.

18. Rosabeth Moss Kanter, Grace Sza-Hua Chen, and Ai-Ling Jamila Malone, "Advanced Leadership Pathways: Robert Whelan and the Student Loan Crisis (B)," Harvard Business School Case 316-049, November 2015, 10.

19. Rosabeth Moss Kanter and Daniel Lennox-Choate, "Advanced Leadership Pathways: Howard Fischer, Eric Jacobsen, and Gratitude Railroad's Impact Investing," Harvard Business School Case 316-047, November 2015, 9.

20. Donald M. Berwick, "What 'Patient-Centered' Should Mean: Confessions of an Extremist," *Health Affairs* 28, no. 4 (July/August 2009): 555–565.

21. Howard Koh and Pamela Yatsko, "Advanced Leadership Pathways: Jay Winsten and the Designated Driver Campaign," Harvard Business School Case ALI-013, March 2017.

22. Rosabeth Moss Kanter, "Change Is Hardest in the Middle," *Harvard Business Review*, August 2009, https://hbr.org/2009/08/change-is -hardest-in-the-middl.

7. GOOD TO GROW: THE ROAD TO IMPACT

1. Rosabeth Moss Kanter and Anne Arlinghaus, "Advanced Leadership Pathways: Richard Fahey and Robert Saudek—Lighting Liberia," Harvard Business Case 313-032, September 2012, 6.

2. Rosabeth Moss Kanter and Anne Arlinghaus, "Advanced Leadership Pathways: Richard Fahey and Robert Saudek—Lighting Liberia," Harvard Business Case 313-032, September 2012, 6.

3. Rosabeth Moss Kanter and Anne Arlinghaus, "Advanced Leadership Pathways: Richard Fahey and Robert Saudek—Lighting Liberia," Harvard Business Case 313-032, September 2012.

4. Jim Collins and Jerry I. Porras, *Built to Last: Successful Habits of Visionary Companies* (New York: HarperCollins, 1994); Rosabeth Moss Kanter, *SuperCorp: How Vanguard Companies Create Innovation, Profits, Growth, and Social Good* (New York: Crown Business, 2009).

5. Rosabeth M. Kanter, "Even Bigger Change: A Framework for Getting Started at Changing the World," Harvard Business School Background Note 305-099, March 2005.

6. Charles J. Ogletree, *All Deliberate Speed: Reflections on the First Half-Century of Brown v. Board of Education* (New York: W. W. Norton & Company, 2005).

7. Alice Gugelev and Andrew Stern, "What's Your Endgame?" *Stanford Social Innovation Review* 13, no. 1 (Winter 2015): 40–47; V. Kasturi Rangan and Tricia Gregg, "How Social Entrepreneurs Zig-Zag Their Way to Impact at Scale," *California Management Review* (forthcoming, fall 2019).

8. Peter Rogers and Susan Leal, *Running Out of Water: The Looming Crisis and Solutions to Conserve Our Most Precious Resource* (New York: St. Martin's Press, 2010).

9. The Hawthorne effect was developed in the following material: Elton Mayo, *The Human Problems of an Industrial Civilization* (New York: Macmillan, 1933); Elton Mayo, *The Social Problems of an Industrial Civilization with an Appendix on the Political Problem*, International Library of Sociology and Social Reconstruction (London: Routledge & Kegan Paul, 1949); F. J. Roethlisberger and William J. Dickson, *Management and the Worker: An Account of a Research Program Conducted by the Western Electric Company, Hawthorne Works, Chicago* (Cambridge, MA: Harvard University Press, 1939); H. A. Landsberger, *Hawthorne Revisited: Management and the Worker, Its Critics, and Developments in Human Relations in Industry* (Ithaca, NY: Cornell University Press, 1958).

10. Rosabeth Moss Kanter and Ai-Ling Jamila Malone, "IBM and the Reinvention of High School (A): Proving the P-TECH Concept," Harvard Business Case 314049, September 2013.

11. Rosabeth Moss Kanter and Ai-Ling Jamila Malone, "IBM and the Reinvention of High School (B): Replicating & Scaling P-TECH and Partners," Harvard Business Case 314049, September 2013.

12. Tara Garcia Mathewson, "More than 100 Career-Focused P-TECH High Schools Have Opened Since 2011," *Hechinger Report* (blog), August 30, 2018, https://hechingerreport.org/momentum-builds-for-career -focused-p-tech-schools/.

13. "Strengthening Career & Technical Education for 21st Century Act Signed," *Homeroom* (blog), August 2, 2018, https://blog.ed.gov/2018 /08/strengthening-career-technical-education-21st-century-act -signed-law/.

14. "Strengthening Career & Technical Education for 21st Century Act Signed," *Homeroom* (blog), August 2, 2018, https://blog.ed.gov/2018

/08/strengthening-career-technical-education-21st-century-act
-signed-law/.

15. Rosabeth Moss Kanter and James Weber, "City Year at 30: Toward Long-
Term Impact," Harvard Business Case 318-089, March 2018, 2; William
Foster, Gail Perreault, and Bradley Seeman, "Becoming Big Bettable,"
Stanford Social Innovation Review (Spring 2019), https://ssir.org/articles
/entry/becoming_big_bettable.

16. Jeffrey L. Bradach and Nicole Sackley, "City Year Expansion Strategy
(A)," Harvard Business Case 496-001, December 1995; Rosabeth Moss
Kanter and James Weber, "City Year: The Journey," Harvard Business
Case 311-080, April 2011; Rosabeth Moss Kanter and James Weber,
"City Year at 30: Toward Long-Term Impact," Harvard Business Case
318-089, March 2018.

17. Rosabeth Moss Kanter, *Confidence: How Winning Streaks and Losing
Streaks Begin and End* (New York: Crown, 2004).

18. Rosabeth Moss Kanter, Ryan Raffaelli, and Jonathan Cohen, "Advanced
Leadership Pathways: Jeffrey Dunn and Sesame Workshop: Bringing Big
Bird Back to Health," Harvard Business Case 317-086, January 2017.

19. "Sesame Workshop & International Rescue Committee Awarded $100
Million for Early Childhood Education of Syrian Refugees," MacArthur
Foundation, December 20, 2017, https://www.macfound.org/press
/press-releases/sesame-workshop-and-international-rescue-committee
-awarded-100-million-early-childhood-education-syrian-refugees/;
"The LEGO Foundation Awards $100 Million to Sesame Workshop to
Bring the Power of Learning through Play to Children Affected by the
Rohingya and Syrian Refugee Crises," Sesame Workshop, December 5,
2018, https://www.sesameworkshop.org/press-room/press-releases
/lego-foundation-awards-100-million-sesame-workshop-bring-power
-learning.

20. "Caribu Collects $1.3M in Financing," Caribu, October 3, 2018, https://
vcnewsdaily.com/caribu/venture-capital-funding/chjmczssjl.

CONCLUSION. AN ARMY FOR CHANGE: THE CALL TO LEAD

1. David Brooks, *The Second Mountain: The Quest for a Moral Life*
(New York: Random House, 2019).

INDEX

Credit: Peter Simon

ROSABETH MOSS KANTER is an influential and well-known professor at Harvard Business School (holding the Ernest L. Arbuckle
Professorship), specializing in strategy, innovation, and leadership
for change. She cofounded and, until recently, directed the Harvard
University Advanced Leadership Initiative, a Harvard-wide innovation
she coconceived in 2004 and launched in 2008, to build a growing
international model that helps successful leaders at the top of their
fields apply their skills to national and global challenges and build
a new leadership force for the world. She has received twenty-four
honorary doctoral degrees and numerous distinguished career awards
from prominent national and international organizations, including
the Academy of Management, American Sociological Association,
International Leadership Association, the World Teleport Association, and others. Dr. Kanter's most recent honor is the 2019 Lifetime
Achievement Award from Thinkers50, the global ranking of management experts. She has served as chief editor of *Harvard Business Review*
and on many boards and is a thought leader for numerous local and
national causes and for both major companies and start-up ventures.

PublicAffairs is a publishing house founded in 1997. It is a tribute to the standards, values, and flair of three persons who have served as mentors to countless reporters, writers, editors, and book people of all kinds, including me.

I. F. STONE, proprietor of *I. F. Stone's Weekly*, combined a commitment to the First Amendment with entrepreneurial zeal and reporting skill and became one of the great independent journalists in American history. At the age of eighty, Izzy published *The Trial of Socrates*, which was a national bestseller. He wrote the book after he taught himself ancient Greek.

BENJAMIN C. BRADLEE was for nearly thirty years the charismatic editorial leader of *The Washington Post*. It was Ben who gave the *Post* the range and courage to pursue such historic issues as Watergate. He supported his reporters with a tenacity that made them fearless and it is no accident that so many became authors of influential, best-selling books.

ROBERT L. BERNSTEIN, the chief executive of Random House for more than a quarter century, guided one of the nation's premier publishing houses. Bob was personally responsible for many books of political dissent and argument that challenged tyranny around the globe. He is also the founder and longtime chair of Human Rights Watch, one of the most respected human rights organizations in the world.

·   ·   ·

For fifty years, the banner of Public Affairs Press was carried by its owner Morris B. Schnapper, who published Gandhi, Nasser, Toynbee, Truman, and about 1,500 other authors. In 1983, Schnapper was described by *The Washington Post* as "a redoubtable gadfly." His legacy will endure in the books to come.

Peter Osnos, *Founder*